JOHN O'HARA

A Study of the Short Fiction

Also Available in Twayne's Studies in Short Fiction Series

Twayne publishes studies of all major short-story writers worldwide. For a complete list, contact the Publisher directly.

Twayne's Studies in Short Fiction

Gary Scharnhorst and Eric Haralson,
General Editors

JOHN O'HARA
Courtesy Wylie O'Hara Doughty.

JOHN O'HARA

A Study of the Short Fiction

Steven Goldleaf
Pace University

TWAYNE PUBLISHERS
New York

Twayne's Studies in Short Fiction, No. 76

Copyright © 1999 by Twayne Publishers

Twayne Publishers
1633 Broadway
New York, NY 10019

Library of Congress Cataloging-in-Publication Data

Goldleaf, Steven.
   John O'Hara : a study of the short fiction / Steven Goldleaf.
      p.   cm. — (Twayne's studies in short fiction ; 76)
   Includes bibliographical references and index.
   ISBN 0-8057-1680-7 (alk. paper)
   1. O'Hara, John, 1905–1970—Criticism and interpretation.
2. Short story.   I. Title.   II. Series.
PR3529.H29Z69   1999
813'.54—dc21   98-49014
                                                              CIP

This paper meets the requirements of ANSI/NISO Z3948-1992 (Permanence of Paper).

10 9 8 7 6 5 4 3 2 1

Printed in the United States of America

To Michael,
the only brother I have, and the best one I could have had

Contents

Preface

Often downright hostile to critics of his writing, John O'Hara has nevertheless graciously provided them with convenient divisions of his short-story output. Indeed, he even arranged to be born and to die in years, 1905 and 1970, that easily allow his work to be divided into distinct periods. During his first period of short-story production in the 1930s, O'Hara can be described as a writer evolving into a master of naturalistic technique. The 1940s O'Hara showed some signs of discontent with the rewarding, if sometimes facile, reproduction of society's quirks, and the 1950s version simply shut down: in the early autumn of 1949, O'Hara effectively stopped producing short stories. And in 1960, he promptly started up again, creating most of his finest short stories in that decade.

The eldest son of a prominent physician in Pottsville, Pennsylvania, O'Hara expected, despite a tempestuous relationship with his father, to be sent to some prestigious university where he could observe at close range the characteristics of America's elite. But when his father died suddenly in 1925 as O'Hara was preparing to begin college, his family quickly found itself several economic classes below that stratum. Deprived of the one formative experience that he would always feel would have helped him as a writer, he went to work as a newspaperman, a road traveled by such American short-story giants as Mark Twain, Ernest Hemingway, and Stephen Crane, acquiring the habits of efficiency, fluency, concision, and keen observation that would prove essential to his fiction.

This is not to say that the young O'Hara was a particularly gifted newspaperman: he changed jobs frequently, sometimes by his choice, more often at his bosses' insistence. It was far more typical of O'Hara to be fired because he had not done his reporting well enough—sometimes he would not do it at all—rather than for any principled disagreement with his employers. Drinking, acquainting himself with jazz, ardently falling in and out of love—all occupied the young O'Hara's time much more than any focused pursuit of a writing career.

Yet as little as he seemed to possess the makings of a literary career, O'Hara was gathering material for one. Soon after *The New Yorker* began publishing in the mid-1920s, he tried with increasing success to write for it; by the mid-1930s, he was one of its mainstays, at first contributing tiny vignettes about the vocal mannerisms, sartorial habits, and other quirks of his generation. Eventually, he described the whole of urban middle-class culture in *The New Yorker*'s characteristic voice. O'Hara began spending some of the fictional capital he had accrued in his youth, capital that he continued using during the course of his 40-year career. O'Hara's subject remained the Americans of Pottsville, New York City, and Hollywood during the 1920s and 1930s. In later decades, he would introduce stories with contemporary frames, but even his characters in the late 1960s, usually those in late middle age, would discuss at length some critical event that took place long before, during the period when O'Hara had been so attentively soaking up material.

Part 1 of this study is, by and large, organized chronologically and is arranged in five sections discussing O'Hara's stories of the 1930s, the 1940s, and (in the final three sections) the 1960s. His last decade is emphasized because of O'Hara's prolific story production in the 1960s and because of its literary excellence. Despite this emphasis, a lack of space prevented me from discussing most of O'Hara's stories from the 1960s or even mentioning many of them. Although taken up chronologically, the stories are also discussed geographically according to their settings: the early stories, mostly set in New York City, and then the later work, with its locales of Pottsville (which he re-created as Gibbsville) and Hollywood.

One significant setting that I barely touch on in Part 1 is suburbia; O'Hara devoted dozens of stories in the 1960s to the mores and various cultures of the contemporary suburbs, which he knew well because he lived in them, in Princeton, New Jersey, and Quogue, New York. Partly because of space constrictions and partly because O'Hara's suburbs are discussed thoroughly by Kathryn Riley in her essay "The Suburban Vision in John O'Hara's Short Stories," (included in Part 3) I chose to scant this setting, as I chose to emphasize and de-emphasize certain other elements in his varied and subtle stories.

I have also chosen not to discuss at any length O'Hara's stature as a writer of short stories, particularly in comparison with his contemporaries, other than to note here my belief that his mastery of the genre is very much underestimated. This general underestimation, paradoxically, is due to his own confidence in the quality of his work. He seems to have made difficult the republication of his stories (in textbooks and trade anthologies), perhaps because he felt in later life that the fees for reprinting them were too low for him to consider, perhaps because he felt his work might seem diminished alongside that of inferior writers, perhaps because of his general hostility to academic treatment of literature. Whatever the cause, the effect has been that several generations of students and general readers have been exposed to his stories far less often than their quality warrants. A succinct example of O'Hara's hyper sensitivity keeping him from advancing his reputation came when George Plimpton had wanted to conduct a prestigious *Paris Review* interview with him; for some unknown reason (Plimpton suspects his resentment of the *Paris Review* for interviewing Ernest Hemingway first), O'Hara would refuse to respond at all to his questions. "I'd call him up and I could hear him breathing at the other end of the line, but he would never say anything, either," Plimpton wrote in the *John O'Hara Journal* (Fall/Winter 1980), closing with the observation: "Certainly a difficult man."

His reputation, particularly as a writer of short stories, is now on the rise, due in part to the efforts of his family to seek actively all sorts of exposure for his short stories that they have not had for several decades. His publisher for the last half of his career, Random House, has begun reissuing his work in its revamped Modern Library series, and a new biography by Geoffrey Wolff is scheduled for publication in 1999.

Surprise is important in O'Hara's fiction, and I was pleasantly surprised to discover several sides of his short fiction I had not appreciated before beginning this study. One of these was his sense of humor that runs through his letters and, as the historian Shelby Foote pointed out to me, flavors such serious short stories as "The Skeletons" with a strange and riveting tension. O'Hara's major theme, as I see it, is the unpredictability of people, and he himself, his short stories, and his literary reputation may end up embodying the strongest proof of that endless capacity for surprise.

Acknowledgments

I would like to thank Douglas Berman for introducing me to O'Hara's work in 1970, starting with a discussion of "Graven Image," and for showing me how to read a text closely, and Lenny Hat for his part in that discussion and numerous others in the last 30 years.

Colleagues and friends David Castronovo, Walter Raubicheck, Johanna Ekberg, Tyler Orehek, Richard Fabrizio, Eugene Richie, Charles Grimes, and Charles Bassett were also helpful to me in the writing of this book. I wouldn't like to have done without Susan Ochshorn's support, care, and patience while I wrote this manuscript, most of it at her dining room table. I would also like to thank Amy Kahn and Peter Ochshorn for sharing their warm company and insights on some otherwise cold nights. I am grateful to the staffs of the Rare Books and Special Collections at the Pennsylvania State University Library, particularly its chief, the late Charles W. Mann, and the Seeley G. Mudd Manuscript Library and the Firestone Library of Princeton University, particularly the University Archivist at Seeley Mudd, Ben Primer, and Margaret M. Sherry, Reference Librarian and Archivist at Firestone Library, who were especially generous in helping a novice negotiate some intricate matters of permissions, ownership, and location. The staff of the Henry Birnbaum Library at Pace University was, as ever, inventive and diligent; the dean's office of Dyson College of Pace University, which arranged for me to take a sabbatical leave, the Scholarly Research committee, and the Kenan Committee, which partially funded my research, were also vital to this work. I owe special gratitude to Vince Balitas for his guidance and particularly to Wylie O'Hara Doughty for the graciousness, personal kindness, and thoughtfulness she showed to me. She remains John O'Hara's finest, and very much unpublished, creation.

A Note on Texts and Abbreviated Titles

Since there is no standard edition of O'Hara's writing, my citations refer to O'Hara's first American printings (listed fully in the bibliography). I have abbreviated (or, in the case of *Hellbox* and *Assembly,* not abbreviated) O'Hara's titles in Part 1 of the text as indicated here.

The Doctor's Son and Other Stories	*(DS)*
Files On Parade	*(FoP)*
Pal Joey	*(PJ)*
Pipe Night	*(PN)*
Hellbox	
Sermons and Soda-Water	*(S&S)*
Assembly	
The Cape Cod Lighter	*(CCL)*
The Hat on the Bed	*(HB)*
The Horse Knows the Way	*(HKW)*
Waiting For Winter	*(WFW)*
And Other Stories	*(AOS)*
The Time Element and Other Stories	*(TE)*
Good Samaritan and Other Stories	*(GS)*

The following are other works by O'Hara and some frequently used secondary sources cited in Part 1.

Appointment in Samarra	*(AIS)*
"An Artist is His Own Fault"	*(Artist)*
Selected Letters of John O'Hara	*(Letters)*
The O'Hara Concern (Matthew J. Bruccoli)	*(OHC)*
O'Hara (Finis Farr)	*(Farr)*
The Life of John O'Hara (Frank MacShane)	*(MacShane)*

I have dispensed with page references wherever the context makes clear that the quotation comes from the very beginning or ending of a story, and in O'Hara's earliest stories generally, which are often not much more than a page long. Readers who would like page references to the early uncollected *New Yorker* stories should refer to Matthew Bruccoli's *John O'Hara: A Descriptive Bibliography*, his *John O'Hara: A Checklist*, or his *O'Hara Concern*, all of which contain detailed bibliographical listings of O'Hara's short stories in periodicals.

Part 1

THE SHORT FICTION

A Long Apprenticeship

By the end of 1940, John O'Hara had lived more than half his life and was regarded as a masterful writer of short stories, having published over a hundred of them in *The New Yorker*, most recently the Pal Joey series that he had just transformed into a lucrative and popular musical still being revived today. But his short fiction up to that point, and arguably up to as late as 1960, was in a very real sense mere apprentice work, derivative of O'Hara's acknowledged masters—Ring Lardner, Dorothy Parker, Sinclair Lewis—and derivative in spots of writers as diverse as Damon Runyon, whose work O'Hara regarded as "fundamentally dishonest," and F. Scott Fitzgerald, whose work he revered (*Artist*, 107).[1] O'Hara truly became a master of the short story only in his final decade, when most of his 4,000 pages of short fiction were published, with their quality surpassing even their astounding quantity.

Had O'Hara died in early 1960, instead of 10 years later, he would still hold a lofty place among American short-story writers, although his surviving reputation would most likely be as a quirky, prolific recorder of the mores of his time and as a founder of the *New Yorker* story still with us: an elliptical, inexplicitly resolved, socially allusive observation of contemporary urban life. O'Hara's influence, visible in *New Yorker* stories by J. D. Salinger, John Cheever, and John Updike, would still have extended as far as Donald Barthelme's work, in that O'Hara's pre-1960s stories were so spare and often so mysterious as to provide a segue to Barthelme's experiments in minimalism.

But in his final decade, one so bountiful it should be regarded as O'Hara's golden period of short-story writing, having assimilated all the techniques he could from those writers who had influenced him earlier, he created his own fictional world and emerged as a truly original stylist. The final three sections of Part 1 of this study will examine O'Hara's work in the 1960s, while the first two sections will examine O'Hara's long apprenticeship, covering *The Doctor's Son and Other Stories* and *Files on Parade*, and then his troubled middle period, in which he doggedly tested the limitations of his naturalistic style and finally abandoned story writing entirely for more than 10 years.

Some critics believe O'Hara's early work to be his best and his late work to be a diffuse rambling from that early promise. Brendan Gill believed passionately that O'Hara's later "stories were rarely improved by their greater length."[2] The later stories, according to Gill, "were longer and looser, to the point of being flaccid; one no longer believed at once in the authority of the dialogue and the description" (Gill, 279). Morris Freedman thinks that O'Hara's early "minimalist short stories [represent him most favorably and characteristically] since they compel an uninterrupted, concentrated reading, making it awkward to be diverted by shortcomings."[3] And Charles W. Bassett, whose essay on the 1931 story "Alone" is excerpted with Freedman's in this volume, also agrees: "[C]ritical consensus would seem to point to the earlier stories as more aesthetically balanced and more psychologically acute—indeed, as more characteristic of John O'Hara."[4]

The stories most admired by these O'Hara scholars, however, bear strong compositional, thematic, and technical resemblance to O'Hara's very earliest stories, which immediately precede them and which he quite wisely never published in book form. These stories, written in the late 1920s and early 1930s, are barely stories at all. Character sketches, vignettes, anecdotes, dramatic monologues, snippets of dialogue, and scene paintings all describe O'Hara's earliest fiction more accurately than does the generic term short stories, because these works tell no stories and rarely even imply the existence of a plot. O'Hara's first few story collections, extending as late as *Hellbox* (1947), feature the understandable excesses of O'Hara's very earliest writing: the occasional affectation, technical overreaching, failed experiment, overly broad parody, and most of all his early reluctance to engage his characters fully in explicit conflict. Still, O'Hara's first successful stories—"On His Hands" (1930), "Alone" (1931), "Frankie" (1932)—are built on the foundation of his raw talent, which comes across even in the earliest sketches, making them worth examining briefly.

O'Hara arrived in New York City in the early spring of 1928. By April 9th he had sold his first piece of fiction to the three-year-old *New Yorker,* whose editor, Harold Ross, referred to all sections of the magazine that did not belong to a specific department as "casuals," a particularly apt description of O'Hara's early work (*OHC*, 58, 296). Barely 23 years old and fresh from working as a reporter on extremely unliterary newspapers in small-town Pennsylvania, O'Hara had some training, and a good deal of talent, as an observer. But mostly what he had was a great ambition to write; what he lacked was a subject to write about. *The New Yorker,* recognizing his gift for writing casuals, bought several dozen of them over the next half decade.

The writers he admired, such as Sinclair Lewis, were satirists, and his first published pieces lampooned common upper-crust types, particularly those who had recently attended Yale. That university held a continuous fascination for O'Hara, who perhaps would have graduated from Yale around this time had his father lived to send him there. Fortunately, the fledgling *New Yorker* was eager for material appealing to barely post-undergraduate readers just before it took off as the most successful popular literary magazine of the twentieth century.

The editor who bought O'Hara's first piece for *The New Yorker* called these sketches "elliptical," a word that stung O'Hara, who remembered it 30 years later in a letter complaining to Ross's successor, William Shawn, about the shabby treatment he felt he had received from the magazine. Had it not been for other magazines valuing his work more highly, O'Hara pointed out to Shawn in 1961, he would "still be writing those dreadful little potboilers in the back of the book" (*Letters*, 383). Resentment of his editors' insufficient appreciation could not change the fact that his early casuals *were* elliptical or that they ran in the magazine's back pages because they were only a step above the level of filler. While O'Hara taught himself tonal control and mastery of technique, *The New Yorker* nurtured his talents until he could create stories with some tangible plot elements.

For a long time, O'Hara relied on the techniques and the bareness of plot seen in such master satirists as Sinclair Lewis, Dorothy Parker, and Ring Lardner. In a 1933 letter to F. Scott Fitzgerald, he described himself as "a frank imitator of Lardner"; this was five years before he wrote his first Pal Joey story, the clearest derivative of Lardner's work (*Letters*, 79). Around this time, he had been evaluating his own work as trivial: "I know so much better than anyone else that I have an inferior talent," he confessed in August of 1933, explaining that

> when I write I can't sustain an emotion. It isn't that I don't feel things, but when I begin to write out of hate I find myself being diverted into tolerance; and when I write about love, or from love, I get critical and nasty. Only once in a while can I sustain either of the two, and the pieces in the *New Yorker* are the ones that start from hate. . . . (*Letters*, 77)

This inability to maintain tonal control for extended periods prevented him from writing real stories and, to a large degree, made even his satir-

5

ical work fall short of achieving its goals. His failure to manipulate his reader completely was exactly the reason his editors called his work elliptical. Sustaining a consistent point of view came hard for O'Hara: he originally conceived his first novel, *Appointment in Samarra* (1934), as a pastiche of linked stories, adding coherence and eliminating diffusiveness as he progressed.[5] The uncollected dramatic monologues of 1928–1929 showcased a variety of speakers unwittingly revealing their character flaws, an irony that he continued using throughout his career, though it did not dominate his later stories as it did his first five short-story collections.

The very first fiction published by "John H. O'Hara" (as he signed his first two stories), entitled "The Alumnae Bulletin," is a single paragraph in which a woman reacts out loud to her college alumnae magazine notes. (Her audience is her spouse, presumably only half-listening to her rattling on.) She criticizes the men her classmates have married, the number of babies her classmates have had, and their lives in general. O'Hara takes care to transcribe carefully, and thus mock, her speech patterns ("Lord and TAY-lor! Look at this! . . ."), concluding with an ironic sentence ("I wonder what anybody reads this stuff in the *Bulletin* for, anyway") that splashes her lack of self-awareness across the page. O'Hara's first published piece, unsurprisingly, takes its theme from the obtuseness of college grads from a certain type and class (the names of the various alumnae are all Anglo-Saxon or German). Lampooning is especially characteristic of O'Hara's early work, written at a time when he most keenly resented the upper classes.

The pleasure in reading such monologues is in deciphering their tone. The next published piece, "OVERHEARD in a Telephone Booth," consists of five paragraphs of a young man's reaction to his girlfriend's announcement that she wants to date someone new, his friend Bill. "Oh, it would be Bill," he says. "You've never quite gotten over *that* interlude, have you? Oh, have you? Oh, *what* have you? My God! What a thing to say at a time like this." The "thing" she actually said "at a time like this" can be only imagined, probably more usefully than any "thing" O'Hara could have supplied; by omitting it, he forces the reader to pick up a racquet and return his serve, which is the whole point of O'Hara's game here. In addition to forcing the reader to supply the missing half of the dialogue, this snippet of "OVERHEARD" illustrates several other standard practices of monologue form: overpunctuation, heavy reliance on italics, and repetition (all to emphasize the speaker's tone of voice).

The slightly misused diction also characterizes the speaker's pretensions (e.g. the use of "interlude" for "episode" or "incident").

The first story bylined "John O'Hara" is another monologue, "Tennis," in which a young man expresses a preference for that sport over golf. The monologue's one objectionably racy line is supplied off the page, so to speak, by the unheard interlocutor (but understood by O'Hara's reader) after the speaker tells of his pleasure in taking a post-exercise shower: "Boy! there's nothing in the world like it. . . . No, not even that" (ellipsis O'Hara's).

O'Hara's next three *New Yorker* stories, dialogues rather than monologues, continue to record, briefly and accurately, the speech of various New Yorkers: "The Follow-up," a phone conversation about a college fund-raising dinner; "Do You Know—?" in which two Yalies shuffle their memory decks searching for a common acquaintance, a conversation freely peppered with undergraduate jargon ("Charlie Weeks. Was he Sheff or Ac?"); and "Spring 3100," a heavy-handed attempt at dialect in which a gentleman calling the New York City police commissioner cannot penetrate the Manhattan accent and attitude of the cop answering the telephone (the piece begins "Tweennyfustreet stationhaw. Looten Bgrm sping").[6] His use of nearly impenetrable dialect in these stories anticipates O'Hara's interest in showing his readers the language that men really use, some of it elitist ("Sheff or Ac?"), some of it street lingo. In a few years, O'Hara would incorporate out-and-out double-talk into his fiction; this early use of a deliberately confusing English is the start of a long experiment testing his readers' energies. Not nearly as rigorous an experimenter as William Faulkner, whom he thought the most gifted writer of his generation, O'Hara sought to modify his stylistic demands on his readers by choosing accessible subject matter.

These uncollected early stories are mostly vocal renditions: either snatches of conversation (monologues or dialogues) or speeches. In one series of speeches, the chairwoman of the Orange County Afternoon Delphian Society addresses her group, and in another an employee of the Hagedorn and Brownmiller Paint and Varnish Company addresses his fellow workers. The Delphian series has a sharper edge to it than the Hagedorn and Brownmiller stories. Its ladies extend noblesse oblige to their upstate New York community, and the self-important chairwoman bullies her audience into supporting her unenlightened positions.

The main narrator of the 14 Hagedorn and Brownmiller stories speaks less imperiously (and less grammatically) than the Delphian chairwoman, though he too relies on bullying and not-so-subtle peer pressure to ensure that his wishes are followed. In "The Boss's Present," when the speaker cajoles the rest of the small staff into chipping in five dollars to buy the boss a Christmas gift, he makes a point of publicly asking the newer employees to go along with the tradition, instead of seeking them out before the meeting, when they can demur with less embarrassment. "I don't want you to think we're making up your minds for you," he says, though that is exactly what he is doing, "but I think you'll agree that since the five-dollar arrangement has been so satisfactory in the past it would be a good idea to just continue it without any change one way or the other." But in fact the price is not fixed, at least not at the upward limit. The speaker pushes his advantage at the meeting's end when he further announces that "if it came to a pinch why none of us would seriously object to handing out a half a dollar apiece in addition to the original prorata share of five dollars, eh?"

The Delphian Society speaker also engages in this kind of sandbagging, although her version is more high-toned and much more sententious. In seeming to discuss the issue of the Society's traveling soup kitchen, which the local community seems to need far less than surrounding ones, the speaker directs the Society's conclusion. Instead of lending it to the other communities, as they have asked, she would rather let it sit idle: "I don't want to intrude my own personal feeling into this matter," she piously claims. "But I am sure that if we discuss it and have a vote, there will be no two ways about what we should do with the Afternoon Delphian travelling soup kitchen."

Her insensitivity precedes the Great Depression. Although the matter of the soup kitchen comes up in a piece appearing in the 7 November 1931 issue of *The New Yorker*, in "The Coal Fields" (21 October 1928) the same speaker, a Mrs. Uhlein, reports on her visit to the Pennsylvania coal fields and the conditions there with no more enlightenment. Traveling to the wrong coal region, Mrs. Uhlein spends two weeks in Scranton instead of Pittsburgh, a difference of several hundred miles, but she profits from her mistake, staying in hotels, attending parties, and making friends during "a perfectly marvelous . . . stay in Scranton." Dispensing gossip and chitchat about the decor of the hotel suites and guest rooms in which she stayed, Mrs. Uhlein notes in passing the "arrogance of some of the coal miners in refusing to leave their homes when they were evicted and their strikes and so on. Really, dear friends, it is astounding. And most of them were so dirty." She has drawn these conclusions, no doubt, because she was introduced around the area by a coal company executive. Her skewed perspective and O'Hara's satirical intent inform her pompous final sentence: "If I have in any way given you an idea of how things really are" which she, of course, has not, "then my trip was not in vain," which of course it is.

Her role as spokesperson for the community is ridiculed throughout the series. Clearly, she has no authority either to form the Delphian Society's views or to represent accurately the role the larger community would like it to play. She, like most do-gooders, is clueless as to her own uselessness and that of the group she claims to represent.

A late variant on the Delphian Society series came as Franklin D. Roosevelt's first presidential campaign gathered steam. A member of the Society calls a meeting for the Orange County Liberal Woman's Society, announcing that, though she is a member in good standing of the Delphian Society and the State Women's Republican Society, her new organization is being assembled to support "Franklin D. Roosa-velt . . . and John M. [sic] Garner . . . for President of the United States and Vice President." She denounces President Hoover at length, delivering some lofty oratory about Roosevelt's divine mission. The comical part of the piece, entitled "It Is Easy Enough to Blame Russia," comes in the last line, when the first person she calls on for discussion, who has presumably been waving a furious hand for recognition, is none other than Mrs. Uhlein, whose loyal Republican response O'Hara's well-trained reader can easily imagine.

The Hagedorn and Brownmiller series portrays noblesse oblige from the point of view of its beneficiaries, the workers discussing their boss's attempts to boost their morale. These attempts are intrusive and demanding, in addition to being demeaning. The boss accepts the workers' annual tribute of an expensive Christmas gift and presumes that after putting in time at the office, his workers would want to spend their leisure at various time-consuming (and sometimes dangerous) evening or weekend rituals: the Halloween party (at which one office worker, we learn, had drowned two years before), or the evening dance, to which no male worker will be permitted to escort a female coworker. Inevitably described as rewards, these social obligations appear far more a duty than an unadulterated pleasure.

O'Hara's important themes emerge in each series. Scapegoating appears in the Hagedorn and Brownmiller series, in which Mr. Cleary is often mentioned, usually for having violated some petty company policy: arriving late at a meeting, leaving a door ajar, asking the wrong person to be placed in a certain office. "Mr. Cleary Misses a Party" concerns the violation of the unspoken company policy that every employee attend every function or risk public embarrassment. The entire story is narrated for Mr. Cleary's benefit, outlining the wonderful time he missed, although every detail of the party supports the young man's wisdom in skipping the affair. Mr. Cleary feels able to flout Hagedorn and Brownmiller codes of behavior because of his position: the son of one of the company's top executives, Mr. Cleary exempts himself from conventions that his peers are cowed into following slavishly. His superiors resent his independence but are restrained from rebuking him too openly because of his father's influence with their superiors. Young Mr. Cleary's position in the company is a source of ongoing tension in the series, tying several episodes together and embodying O'Hara's themes of privilege and victimization.

Although O'Hara omitted the Hagedorn and Brownmiller series (and another series set at the Idlewild Country Club) from his first collection, he did think enough of the Delphian series to include one of the pieces in *The Doctor's Son*, "Ten Eyck or Pershing? Pershing or Ten Eyck?," a Sinclair Lewis–style satire, deals with the short-lived patriotic impulse to rename a street in honor of World War I's General Pershing and the rationalizations of small-town leaders in doing so. But O'Hara did not abandon the monologue or dialogue form for many years to come.

O'Hara had published over a hundred stories in *The New Yorker* between 1928 and 1935 when he assembled his first collection, *The Doctor's Son*. He chose no stories from 1928 or 1929 and only 5 from 1930, despite having a total of 58 *New Yorker* bylines in those three years. The earliest *New Yorker* story collected in *The Doctor's Son* takes the form of a monologue (fleshed out slightly by some introductory narrative and a few truncated interjections by the story's listener) told by a snobbish Princeton undergraduate complaining about the young women he has on his hands (hence the story's title) and the pains he takes to learn whether they come from old-moneyed families or the nouveau riche.

Brand names (Wetzel, a prominent men's clothier of the time; the Pierce-Arrow limousine) and proper names (Gauss, the surname of the Princeton dean) are dropped into "On His Hands" with little or no explanation. Throughout his career O'Hara would suffer much criticism for using brand names to convey shades of meaning, a practice he defended with the claim that the brand names connoted precise levels of social knowledge. Far from tossing them around indiscriminately, he deliberately used them to convey shades of social realism that could not be conveyed otherwise. Moreover, in dialogue, it is O'Hara's speaker who uses the brand names to distinguish levels of wealth. (He dresses in Wetzel's suits even though he is short on cash. It is better to owe Wetzel money, presumably, than to buy a cheaper suit.) It is O'Hara's speaker, too, who judges his potential girlfriend's family by its car, thus revealing his own acute consciousness of class: "Well, she met me at the station, in a 1921 Pierce limousine. That was a pretty good start, because no damn *nouveau-riche* family has a 1921 Pierce limousine. They'd have a brand-new shiny wagon, all brass. So that old Pierce was a good sign" (*DS*, 115).

Other monologues in *The Doctor's Son* show off O'Hara's versatility, revealing the limited insights of working-class Americans as well as their wealthier counterparts. "I Never Seen Anything Like It" tells in juicy Brooklynese of a robbery that leaves its victim (and narrator) awestruck by the robbers' ingenuity (the story ends with the dim narrator's dawning realization that the robbers had inside help: "But the thing I don't unnastand is how they ever knew my name was Paul"). In "Back in New Haven," equally deft is the lampooning of an undergraduate who is thinking about his older lover and her even older husband (also a Yale man, some 20 years his senior). His affected diction mocks the grandiose thoughts late adolescents devote to analyzing their love lives. "Back in New Haven" might be labeled "fiction to wince by," at least for O'Hara's post-undergraduate readership.

Back at the lower end of society, O'Hara tries another experiment in Brooklynese, this one a dialogue entitled "Coffee Pot." O'Hara's rendition of Brooklyn speech patterns is nothing special; nonnative writers from Thomas Wolfe to Tom Wolfe, and native New York writers from Mailer to McBain, have used the stock orthographic tricks O'Hara applies here: the "verce" over the phone, the speaker who "dowanna petrude" his own ideas too much.[7] The genuine innovation here is technical: the entire story—the resolution of a conflict between two coffeeshop owners over what to call their new low-class "restrunt"—is told exclusively in dialogue, without so much as a single "he said." Telling the whole story within quotation marks, a real tour de force, showed O'Hara he could write a successful story without a single word of narrative.

Even as O'Hara went on to write much longer, more plot-filled, and more varied stories, he—alone of all the American naturalist writers—would never abide the use of much descriptive writing in his work. If he does describe something, it might be a landscape, a car, or a man's suit, but is very rarely a person. "O'Hara almost never gives a physical description of his characters," says Gore Vidal, who generally finds O'Hara lacking in commendable traits, particularly that of restraint, "a startling continence for a naturalistic writer, and more to be admired than not."[8]

Another story set in a coffeeshop, "Pleasure" is a two-page sketch of a young woman's attempt to dignify her menial job (she prefers to think of herself as a hostess who makes customers comfortable, rather than as just someone busing tables and refilling water glasses) and to save money for something better. The sketch ends as she berates herself for not having saved more, then, feeling the need for a little pleasure, she allows herself to light "a whole cigarette." This understated story rests on the single adjective "whole," forcing O'Hara's middle-class readers to draw a tangible distinction they may never have drawn before. The adjective "whole" implies its absence and implies that O'Hara's character routinely rations her pleasure, be it cigarette portions or more profound indulgences. A more directive writer would have provided her salary in dollars and cents, or described her wearing a shabby article of clothing, or supplied a plot element that pointedly stressed her poverty. But those easy options would have cheated O'Hara's readers out of the conclusion they could more satisfyingly earn.

O'Hara was quite consciously experimenting with minimalism in these vignettes and sketches, seeking to learn how to direct the reader's attention to a few well-placed details to summon the desired effect. Perhaps his oddest experiment concerned "a short story in which no human being appeared." O'Hara described this never-published experiment: "When you finish reading the story you know that the man who had been occupying the room had been on the town the night before, that he had quarreled with his girl, and that he had committed suicide by jumping out the window" (*Artist*, 12). To convey such subtle effects, O'Hara dropped crucial details into his stories at key points where his reader was least likely to be lost or distracted—such as the title, the first line, or the last line. O'Hara would seize upon even such seemingly insignificant points as the first line of dialogue following a long, intricate narrative passage, and pack those points with meaning, knowing that the reader would be paying peak attention there.

The title "Pleasure" creates a tension that is relieved only by the story's final line: the reader wonders what earthly pleasure this story of hardship can yield, and the ending gives the answer. Embedding that information in the story's two most prominent points—its title and its last line—allows O'Hara to understate. His less successful early stories would disguise his point more subtly, creating that overly tricky elliptical effect his editors complained about. "[T]he ending was too subtle," he advised a would-be *New Yorker* writer in 1932. "That's something to bear in mind when writing for that magazine. You must be subtly obvious, but not subtle and not obvious" (*Letters*, 63). In other stories, the point he was attempting to make would be less deserving of O'Hara's attention. But in "Pleasure," the understatement is effective and the point is worth making.

O'Hara's method, especially in these early stories, is to risk supplying too little information or too little story, rather than too much. His readers, he felt, were clever enough to figure out his implications. "I don't give a damn for the hasty reader," he explained (*Artist*, 13). Moreover, readers trained to think O'Hara's way would enjoy deciphering his meaning much more than they would lose by the occasional puzzling passage.

"New Day" is a somewhat less effective story narrated with seeming objectivity. Like "Pleasure," its title is ironic: the morning described in it, that of the comfortably middle-class wife of a stockbroker, is a new day literally, but the events of that new day are by implication similar to every other day of her uneventful life. The woman leaves her apartment building, has breakfast in a nearby restaurant, and decides to take a swim, informing her husband of this decision in a bland unsigned telegram. The last line of the story—"The telegram was unsigned"— might seem meaningless or it might seem indicative of some quality in the woman, in her marriage, or in her society. Matthew J. Bruccoli thinks it signifies that "she is as isolated from him as she is from everyone else," but it could as easily be argued that it signifies her self-centeredness, presuming that her husband receives telegrams at work only from her, or her egotism, thinking that the message she conveys and the manner in which she conveys it are so unique that a signature is redundant (*OHC*, 73). Of course, she could be *both* lonely and narcissistic, and probably is, but O'Hara refuses to emphasize one characteristic over the other. He wants his reader to characterize her by his sparse details. In this story, however, his details do not communicate quite what he wants them to. The effect can be haunting, leaving O'Hara's readers shaking with apprehension; or it can be merely puzzling, leaving them shaking their heads.

The early sketches, from before *The Doctor's Son* and extending as late as *Hellbox* in 1947, are largely finger exercises in naturalistic technique.[9]

Amazingly, even though he was a fan and friend of the sensitive O'Hara, Wolcott Gibbs devotes much of his preface to *Pipe Night* (1945) to the limitations of O'Hara's early work (meaning all his work up to that time) and does so by using the finger exercise metaphor:

> Nothing much ever *happened* to the clubladies and paint salesmen, and while it was easy to admire them as examples of fine stenography, it was also possible to find them rather tough reading.
>
> I think Mr. O'Hara knew that all himself, regarding these pieces largely as finger exercises, enabling him to eat, more or less sporadically, while he got his bearings.

The purpose of finger exercises is to improve the artist's technical abilities, of course, not to improve the audience's mind, so it is impressive that O'Hara was able to sell so many of these plotless sketches. *The New Yorker* bought many of them for their value as literary puzzles almost as much as for their worth as literature. Harold Ross, the magazine's editor until his death in 1951, angrily vowed "never [to] print another O'Hara story I don't understand," though his fiction editors persuaded him that understanding the stories wasn't exactly the point of them.[10]

O'Hara would create a character trait, sometimes complex or subtle, and attempt to make his reader identify and recognize that trait while never once isolating or discussing it explicitly. Instead, O'Hara felt himself honor-bound by certain unwritten rules of contemporary short-story construction, which he was sometimes devising and other times obeying, to tell nothing and to show everything. If a character were, for example, miserly, it would not do to write "Harrison hated to part with a dollar." Such a description might have been appropriate for older writers who needed to characterize quickly in order to move on to crucial issues of plot, but writers of O'Hara's generation, much more than their elders, wanted to write stories that required some interpretative interaction between reader and text. Ernest Hemingway's terse prose was the model for readers and writers who believed that less is more, but his themes ran close below the surface of his prose. An O'Hara reader could negotiate the sentences, deduce which unspoken or undescribed matters were important, and still come away with no profound understandings. Characterizing a bitter, mixed-up, and inarticulate person, as he did in "New Day," was difficult to achieve within the constraints O'Hara set for himself, but even if a writer did it successfully, all that he or she would have communicated was a small satiric portrait of an otherwise undistinguished individual. For some readers, that was not enough. For O'Hara's early readers, it was all.

Many of the pieces in *The Doctor's Son* are narrated objectively. All the monologue speakers are presented without authorial comment, as are nearly all the dialogue speakers ("Coffee Pot" containing the least authorial intrusion possible in a dialogue). The character sketches, too, lack an overt narrator. O'Hara can sometimes be seen trying to create a narrative voice he feels comfortable with. After 30 more years of experimenting, O'Hara would achieve that goal with the creation of Jim Malloy in *Sermons and Soda-Water* (1960), but only after O'Hara decided to merge Malloy's consciousness with his own. Before that point, O'Hara would test different names and characteristics for his alter-ego first-person narrator.

For many years O'Hara was ambivalent about employing any narrator. Aware of himself as an outlander in Manhattan, as a Catholic in a country run by Protestants, as a prep school graduate among college degree holders, O'Hara tried to blend in with the crowd; in terms of his fiction, this meant writing stories that, for all their perceptions of urban, educated society, seemed as if they came from nowhere in particular and were written by no individual. In terms of his career, this effort to conform meant knowing what *The New Yorker* wanted.

In a telling letter about the kinds of stories he felt *The New Yorker* was seeking to publish, O'Hara explained to his teenaged brother, Thomas, that *New Yorker* editors "don't like to accept pieces that are not New Yorkish. By that I mean the piece must either be laid in New York, or in a place that would be familiar to the smart New Yorker" (*Letters*, 64). Only four years into his long relationship with the magazine, O'Hara could not anticipate that many of his best *New Yorker* stories would be set in the Pennsylvania town where he and Tom O'Hara grew up. Those stories would not be published, of course, for several decades, during which time the magazine, as well as O'Hara's stories, would change; but the narrowness of this formula for setting stories in New York City was far more indicative of the young writer than it was of the young magazine.

By 1932, O'Hara, already a prolific contributor to *The New Yorker*, was fully qualified to give advice, but he was still years from earning a living as a writer and still writing eager query letters to *New Yorker* editors, trying to impress them with his intimate knowledge of metropolitan ways.[11] This young man's eagerness to please and to entertain but, above all, to get work is almost as charming as he wishes it to be, and these query letters continued for several years, not fully calming down until O'Hara achieved financial independence around 1940. At the beginning of his career, his few first-person stories were narrated in the anonymous voice of a would-be cosmopolitan still entranced by Manhattan life.

This voice narrates "The Man Who Had to Talk to Somebody," a compassionate portrait of Williams, a desperately lonely middle-aged clerk who forges unwanted friendships with his coworkers, including the narrator. Over lunch at a "terrible" hash house, the creepy, slightly deranged Williams reveals that his rich friends from Yale have helped him with "his trouble," the bouncing of some checks, for which he went to jail and for which his wife and young daughter have left him. This is a character sketch of a man so severely traumatized by a serious mistake that he can never rejoin society. His derangement is progressive: by the story's end, after he inappropriately asks a teenaged girl in the office to a movie, he gets fired from his miserable job. He leaves the office laughing, his isolation from humanity so great that no further separation seems possible.

Similar to character sketches of lonely people such as "Pleasure" or "New Day," this story introduces the potential for conflict, at least in the mind of the sympathetic young narrator. This dramatic tension never materializes, however, since the narrator stays in a strictly narrative role. At one point, Williams assumes that the narrator also attended Yale, suggesting all sorts of potential interactions: the narrator might realize that a Yale degree cannot assure him that he will not end up like Williams, for example, or it could form a bond that makes Williams much more sympathetic. These possibilities do not occur, however. The narrator just says, "No. Nowhere."[12] Because so little happens in these early sketches—and because, as here, there is so much potential for a plot to develop—they serve chiefly to let O'Hara teach himself control of the techniques he would soon use to set his characters into action and interaction.

"Hotel Kid" is narrated by Kelly, a New Yorker who meets a boy while living in a hotel in an unnamed "strange city" resembling Pittsburgh.[13] Again, Kelly could develop some sort of relationship with the hotel kid, or examine his life in detail, or incorporate him into a larger work. Instead, Kelly merely describes what little he sees of him, presenting a few of the boy's pranks (he tricks Kelly into flirting unsuspectingly with a female room clerk at the hotel and vexes the elevator operators by summoning them incessantly). Kelly suggests but does not state the pain of growing up in such lonely surroundings. He sensitively hints at the kid's isolation, but neither O'Hara's accurate and evocative narration nor his narrator get very caught up in his life.

Kelly is almost, but not quite, Jim Malloy. O'Hara was not yet comfortable with a narrator who would speak for him and still searched for a way he could tell his stories through a narrator who would remain a wholly fictional creation.

The title character in "Mary" is a beautiful girl living in Pennsylvania, where the first-person narrator grows up and falls in love with her. Nothing comes of his infatuation, and they separately escape the mining town for New York City, where he continues to monitor her flirtation with society and with various men. This mystifying but detailed picture of a small-town girl laying siege to the big city is exceptional only for O'Hara's overlapping with his otherwise unidentifiable narrator: Mary addresses him as "Doc," O'Hara's boyhood nickname (*OHC* 23, 25). At the time O'Hara wrote "Mary," of course, his readers would have no reason to connect the author to the young narrator and would have every reason to think that Doc was a purely fictional character.

"I do not keep a diary now," O'Hara wrote in a letter around this time. "I could use one, but these days I write pieces instead of a diary" (*Letters*, 86). "Mary" appears to be one of these pseudodiary entries, both because of the Doc reference and because the character of Mary appears elsewhere—in *Appointment in Samarra* and the play *The Way It Is*—in a manner consistent with her depiction here (*OHC*, 81). The play concerns an extended, sporadic love affair between Mary and Johnny, similar to tragic affairs O'Hara describes in later stories such as "Andrea" and "A Few Trips and Some Poetry."[14]

O'Hara narrated three early first-person Gibbsville stories in the voice of Jim Malloy, including the superb autobiographical title story of O'Hara's first collection, *The Doctor's Son*, making his sparing use of this successful voice seem peculiar, if not almost perverse. Why did O'Hara fail to exploit this narrator further? Critics, after all, admired "The Doctor's Son" almost unanimously for its sensitive rendering of young Malloy's emotions.[15]

The positive reaction to the sensitivity of "The Doctor's Son" might have encouraged O'Hara to mine that vein (to say nothing of his own aesthetic judgment, since he chose "The Doctor's Son" as the first and title story of the collection), but, for one reason or another, for many years he explored avenues other than Gibbsville as seen by Malloy. Further encouraging O'Hara to take that path, several reviewers compared

Malloy to Hemingway's Nick Adams, particularly comparing "The Doctor's Son" to "Indian Camp" in which Nick, like Jim, witnesses his father's surgical skills under trying field conditions. Given O'Hara's all-but-idolatrous regard for Hemingway, he must have rejected the path recommended by critics out of a mistrust for his youthful memories as a source of fiction. Edmund Wilson, comparing Hemingway's poetic writing to O'Hara's social commentary, presciently observed in 1940 that O'Hara's work would improve if he would rediscover Gibbsville, the setting, in Wilson's view, of his two best pieces, *Appointment in Samarra* and "The Doctor's Son."

Malloy actually appears in all three novels O'Hara wrote in the 1930s: he is mentioned briefly in the first chapter of *Appointment in Samarra*, he plays a small but active part in *Butterfield-8*, and is the main character and narrator of *Hope of Heaven*. The dozen novels written after *Hope of Heaven* omit Malloy entirely, but he appears more and more frequently in the short stories and, in the 1960s, becomes O'Hara's all-purpose narrator of short stories.

In the 1940s O'Hara went through a crisis that made him reconsider his ambitions in the novel, in the short story, in other genres (particularly drama), and in his own life. Malloy appears in the third person in several stories in the 1940s, when O'Hara still required some objective perspective between his own life and Jim Malloy's. O'Hara had sound pragmatic reasons, outlined in his letters to his brother, for keeping Malloy at a distance: the nonironic first-person story was a hard sell to *The New Yorker* editors.[16]

With the exception of "The Doctor's Son," O'Hara resisted the impulse to develop a complex, long, nonironic story. "The Doctor's Son," by appearing first in book form, astonished some readers. Out of nowhere, this writer who seemed to have a movie camera's ability to record nuance (but also a movie camera's objective distance from its subjects) was writing a warm, intensely subjective story. This obviously autobiographical story, furthermore, did not remain focused on one or two characters' carefully selected traits but painted a panoramic view of a small town with many intermeshing, complicated characters, including the testy, much admired doctor of the title; his teenaged son narrating a tale of both loyalty to his father and of fierce independence from him; and the son's girlfriend, who notices the strange, furtive behavior of her mother and the medical student who temporarily takes over the duties of the ailing doctor.

Most of the tales beginning with those in *The Doctor's Son* and continuing through the *Hellbox* stories lack a first-person narrator and certainly lack the narrator named Jim Malloy, whose voice gives the later stories their synoptic moral stance. These earlier stories are, instead, further experiments, full of developing techniques devised in the first uncollected stories: overheard snatches of dialogue, detailed characteristics of people O'Hara has observed, vignettes of interesting incidents he has seen or imagined. The best of these are very good indeed, but their technique, coupled with O'Hara's principle that their interpretation remain open, often lets their intended points go astray.

The technique in "Sportsmanship," however, represents a true advance: either of two separate interpretations of its ambiguous ending is satisfying and plausible. Like O'Hara's other early fiction, the story is brief, both in its actual length and its scope of action, but it delves much deeper because of its deliberate and controlled ambiguity. In "Sportsmanship" O'Hara uses the same spareness of detail of his simpler character sketches to tell a delicately shaded story with a clear plot.

Set in a Bronx pool hall, the story promises to be confusing only to outsiders: the Subway Arcade sign outside the pool hall is "misleading only to strangers to that neighborhood; there was no subway anywhere near, and it was no arcade" (*DS*, 260). The readers are the strangers, trying to understand the special language and mores of this place. Frank, who owns the pool hall, is initially annoyed by the sudden appearance of Jerry, a pool shark who has just served time for stealing money from Frank. After pretending not to recognize him, referring to him as "stranger" and telling him of his resemblance to a "rat" and a "heel" named Jerry, Frank surprisingly accepts Jerry's offer to work off the stolen money. Frank promises to play him in a game of pool after Jerry has worked two weeks for free, while polishing his pool shooting in his spare time. If Jerry wins the game, Frank will hire him, but if he loses, he must leave. When the two weeks are up, Jerry is easily winning until the referee, hired by Frank, declares Frank the game's winner. "What a sap I been," Jerry says, realizing that Frank's plan has been all along to add these two weeks to his jail term. But Frank's revenge is far from complete. Observing how poorly Jerry is taking his loss, Frank suggests to the referee that he be taught a little sportsmanship. The referee then cracks a pool cue over Jerry's hands. Jerry cries out, "You broke me hands, you broke me hands," giving Frank the story's tag line: " 'Keep them out of other people's pockets,' said Frank. 'Beat it.' "

Part 1

"Sportsmanship" is a morality tale whose moral is open to interpretation: its plot is as simple as its theme is complex. Frank's punishment of Jerry is unquestionably harsh, but O'Hara leaves to his reader to decide if it is merely cruel or also just. Was Jerry's offer to repay the stolen money a brave and honest attempt to rectify his misdeed, or was it a brazen attempt to compound the offense? Because O'Hara hides Frank's plan and his hatred of Jerry until the story's end, he forces readerly sympathies on Jerry, but his ending shows that those sympathies may be misplaced. There is a certain cruel justice to Frank's revenge, yet Jerry's proposal to work for him can be argued as either self-serving or courageous.

The other tightly controlled story in the first collection is the final one, "Over The River and through the Wood," about a series of humiliations suffered by an elderly man traveling with his granddaughter and her friends to his daughter's house for Thanksgiving dinner. The former owner of the house, he sold it to his son-in-law at a time when he "certainly needed the money" (*DS*, 290). Having relinquished authority, he is reminded of his powerlessness by his thoughtless granddaughter all through the long trip. She makes him sit in the least comfortable seat in the car, in a terrible draft, and excludes him from the teenagers' conversation. She notices him only to recommend that he stop at a rest room along the way, pointedly at the request of her mother. When they arrive, the mother is not much more considerate of his feelings, offering him hot cocoa as a reminder that he has given up drinking alcohol. He decides to offer some cocoa to one of the teenaged girls "as a former master of this house," but at her bedroom door he mistakes her comment "in a minute" for "come in," and so he barges in, finding her "standing in the middle of the room, standing there all but nude." Given his family's clear contempt for his powerlessness, he understands that his version of this event will be stifled by her outrage. This, he realizes, will be "the end of any worthwhile life he had left" (*DS*, 293).

Before the story opens, old Mr. Winfield had, like Jerry in "Sportsmanship," behaved badly. His daughter's contempt stems from her perception that he had mistreated his ex-wife, her mother. As in "Sportsmanship," the question is whether the protagonist's punishment is too severe. Because O'Hara supplies access to the old man's mind, we can judge him more surely by his intents and not his deeds, and conclude that the punishment is harsh. But his family, who can see only his actions, is disposed to think his punishment long overdue.

Because this story shows Mr. Winfield's thoughts, O'Hara can afford to dispense with the explicit ending that was so strong in "Sportsmanship." Here its omission is equally strong. These endings illustrate the quandary of Wallace Stevens's "Thirteen Ways of Looking at a Black-bird," whose speaker cannot choose between "the beauty of implications / Or the beauty of innuendoes, / The blackbird whistling / Or just after." Classicists, preferring their violence offstage, will prefer "Over the River . . ." to "Sportsmanship," but it is not clearly the better story. Both protagonists' fates are inevitable—Jerry's just takes place before our eyes.

Every O'Hara short-story collection pays some attention to the Hollywood movie industry, which he found fascinating, particularly the economic structure that paid astronomical salaries to actors, directors, and writers, many of whom, until their big break, had been poor and lower-class.[17] "Sidney Gainsborough, Quality Pictures" provides an occasion for Mr. Frank, a movie publicist (a job O'Hara held in the early 1930s), to get off a wisecrack about the predictable backgrounds that studios invent for their actresses. The self-important title character, a studio executive, asks Frank to research an actress's hometown, and Frank flippantly answers, "New Orleans. They all come from New Orleans," getting himself in trouble with the offended movie executive. O'Hara had been fired from many similar jobs because he could not take seriously Hollywood pretensions. O'Hara's Hollywood stories indicate that he found the chasm between the sexual liberties practiced within the film industry and the pious morality seen in the films themselves especially ludicrous. The movie Frank is publicizing and failing to take seriously is entitled "Strange Virgin," a title that recurs in several of O'Hara's stories during the 1930s and 1940s; the title is absurd mainly because the word *virgin* could not be mentioned in a movie, much less in a movie title, until director Otto Preminger broke the taboo in *The Moon is Blue* in 1953.

"Strange Virgin" next appears in "Salute a Thoroughbred," a bitter monologue spoken by a screen actress whose producer-boyfriend throws her over. The unnamed actress is probably Patsy Vane of "Sidney Gainsborough, Quality Pictures" whose hometown Mr. Frank is told to look up, because her monologue reveals she starred in "Strange Virgin," which, she says, is "the picture they released under the title 'Adorable Girl' when the Catholic Church made all that stink." The title of the story is taken from the movie's silly dialogue, which O'Hara uses in two opposed contexts. In the film, a male character tries to woo a desirable woman with the line "My love, I salute a thoroughbred," but in the story, the film's producer recites that line to the same woman, the actress who played the part, as he breaks up with her. The early Hollywood stories mainly show film stars struggling to maintain their classy screen personas.

"Screen Test" contrasts outward and inward values or, in O'Hara's terms, deep surface values with shallow ones. On a street corner, a young and beautiful actress about to take a screen test runs into a young musician who had lent her money some months back. Seeming to care deeply about the money and to be annoyed by her brief pretense of forgetting his name, the musician berates her, finally cajoling her to promise to repay him immediately. What he really cares about, though, is being seen talking to her. As the ending reveals, he gets his money's worth without a penny changing hands: When he returns to his friends loitering nearby, he responds to their questions only with a mysterious, "Nice, huh?"

As in *The Doctor's Son*, O'Hara's Hollywood stories in *Files on Parade* satirize the personae of screen stars (as in the self-centered performers of "Most Gorgeous Thing") or give O'Hara chances to display his special knowledge (of music cribbing, in "Richard Wagner, Public Domain") or his technical skills ("Brother," dealing with movie-business types teasing a young starlet's brother, is told nearly entirely in dialogue with few identifying tags to distinguish the speakers). "Saffercisco" in *Files on Parade*, however, ventures past the merely satirical. Instead of sending up the pretensions of a very successful movie star named Jack Grant, the story exposes his rather touching naiveté. Having fallen in love with a married actress, Jack decides to confront her and her husband at their home to announce his intent to marry her. To his surprise, she is not there when he arrives for dinner, so Jack and her husband have a few drinks, after which the husband confides that his wife is up in "Saffercisco" having an affair with her director. Having an unfaithful wife was at first very hard to accept, the husband concedes, but "Jack, old boy, you had better get used to it, too," showing not only his awareness of Jack's dalliance with his wife but his more accurate assessment of her faithlessness. The tale of the biter bit is, in O'Hara's version, that of the sophisticate outsophisticated. Jack wears his best set of formal tails to this dinner, determined to be "open and aboveboard" in discussing his unconventional intent to marry a married woman, but he has his sophisticated notion of marriage thrown in his face by a woman who has no use for marriage, conventional or otherwise.

"Saffercisco," which O'Hara properly labels a dressed-up anecdote, uses its modicum of plot efficiently. The period's general reaction against plot, as evidenced by the basically plotless *New Yorker* story that O'Hara specialized in, was a reaction to the previous generation's over-reliance on plot, as exemplified in the trick endings of O. Henry's popular stories, which scanted character and individuated dialogue and all the rest of O'Hara's mainstays. But by the end of the 1930s, O'Hara came to think better of the trick ending, which shows that characters are always capable of astonishing us—no matter how late in their stories or in their lives we might meet them.

It might seem strange then that O'Hara's other major theme would be that of inevitability. Closing one early letter to *The New Yorker*, O'Hara confided that his "favorite word" was "*inevitable.*" Nearly four decades later, he consoled a friend whose son had killed himself, with a sensitive letter ending with the same word: "[N]o one who committed suicide could have done anything else. . . . We are sorry for the sadness to you . . . but who can argue with the power of the inevitable?" (*Letters*, 41, 480).

The conjoining of these two seemingly paradoxical principles—inevitability and the capacity for surprise—is at the root of O'Hara's essentially tragic vision. Mere inevitability in literature leads to mechanical determinism, while mere surprise leads to unearned endings that are equally mechanical. O'Hara stood accused of committing both faults, yet his first novel, *Appointment in Samarra*, fuses the two modes perfectly: the death of Julian English is both shocking and, in hindsight, perfectly inevitable. The inevitability derives from our individual characters, each ingrained at birth, O'Hara seems to say, while a random universe—filled with millions of other equally powerful individual characters, plus natural and seemingly accidental occurrences such as disease and weather and economic upheavals—creates endless surprise. These two forces work at cross-purposes but often join forces and, as often, diverge again, creating a limitless supply of plots and patterns for O'Hara to exploit in his fiction.

Sometimes O'Hara is forthright about his admiration for one of his characters, though such admiration rarely augurs well for that character. His characters' occasional good deeds prove the axiom "No good deed goes unpunished." Even careful readers, however, sometimes miss the good deeds' dire implications. "The cruel side of social snobbery," claims Edmund Wilson, "is really Mr. O'Hara's main theme. Only rarely, as in the excellent story 'Price's Always Open,' do the forces of democracy strike back."[18] But in "Price's Always Open," the cost of striking back is, in the end, ruinous to the forces of democracy. In the story

O'Hara does not list Price's abstract virtues—loyalty, discipline, reliability, courage, modesty, and endurance—or even allude to them, but simply cites factual evidence: he was "always there"; he "had one leg, having left the other . . . back of Chateau-Thierry" in World War I; "he did not need much sleep"; and so on (*FoP*, 4). In the end, when Price displays his loyalty and courage at great personal cost, he seems not to be making a choice but, inevitably, to be doing what his character demands.

"Price's Always Open" seems at first to tell the story not of Price but of Jackie Girard, a native of Cape Cod, where Price's eatery is the local late-night hangout for well-off preppies. Jackie is no preppy: he is a French-Canadian carpenter's son who attends Holy Cross College, but he blends in on summer nights with the vacationing Harvard and Smith students and—as Price wisely perceives—is falling for one of the Smith girls. He is also Price's personal favorite, which is O'Hara's tip-off that the gods like Jackie as well.

One night, in front of the girl Jackie is attracted to, a Harvard snob cruelly puts Jackie in his place. The girl pretends not even to know that Holy Cross is the name of a college. When the Harvard fellow takes a punch at Jackie, to the Smithie's breathless admiration, the one-legged Price suddenly intervenes and saves Jackie from a severe beating.

This deus ex machina rescue saves Jackie's hide but antagonizes the crowd Price's small diner relies on. O'Hara noted that neither he nor *The New Yorker* had much use for the deus ex machina ending, but he concluded that certain stories can compensate for such an ending by it being set up properly (*Letters*, 190). In this story, the information that sets up the ending is Price's previous war heroism coupled with his unexplained liking for Jackie, which combine to make plausible his somewhat improbable, self-destructive rescue.

The title "Price's Always Open" is obviously ironic because the ending demonstrates that the hard-working Price will have to close his pleasant and useful 24-hour diner. The title also implies an emblematic reading that is ironic. In addition to the literal meaning of "Price's Always Open," the title also connotes that dollars and cents are flexible but, in Price's situation, they are not. His inflexible need to keep money coming in, his dependence on his clientele's continued spending, dooms his diner. But his heroism derives from his choosing to antagonize the source of his income.

O'Hara's story titles show increasing depth in the late 1930s and early 1940s. In *The Doctor's Son* he titled his sketches with the name or description of the main characters ("Frankie," "Mary," "Ella and the

Chinee," "Mrs. Galt and Edwin," "Hotel Kid," "Master of Ceremonies," "Mort and Mary," "Mr. Cass and the Ten Thousand Dollars," and several others including the title story). In addition,, the titles of other stories in *The Doctor's Son* come from a key phrase in the story itself, either spoken ("It Wouldn't Break Your Arm," "Except in My Memory," and "I Never Seen Anything Like It") or narrative ("On His Hands," "Pleasure," and "New Day"). In choosing his titles from one of these three sources, O'Hara could pretend to be objective: the title would seem to come not from him but from the story itself. On the rare occasions he imposed a title deriving from a place outside the story itself (as in "Of Thee I Sing, Baby" and "Over the River and through the Wood"); the title would invite interpretation because it had been deliberately selected for its thematic value rather than for its value as a generic label.[19] Titles containing the names of main characters would never again appear as often as they did in *The Doctor's Son*.

The title "Trouble in 1949" is significant for several reasons, one of which may not be obvious. Written in the summer of 1938, when the story takes place, the year of the title was intended to conjure up the distant future rather than the vanished past. As such, it was a somewhat disturbing title, as can easily be imagined by adding 11 to one's present year and then imagining a perfectly realistic present-day story entitled "Trouble in [that future year]." Only at the story's end does O'Hara's meaning become clear: in 1938, two lovers separated for 11 years spend an afternoon together, at the end of which the protagonist imagines another meeting 11 years in the future, but he finally rejects that vision because it will be "too damn much trouble" to meet in 1949.

Coincidentally, within a few months of O'Hara's writing the story, his friend and mentor F. Scott Fitzgerald wrote a story with an almost identical plot, "Three Hours between Planes."[20] Both stories feature a traveling businessman from New York City with some time to kill on a warm summer's day in a small Midwestern city. Both decide to telephone an old girlfriend living in that city. Being now married, both men are pleased to arrange to spend a little time with their former girlfriends, now married to other men. The actual meetings, however, turn out to be somewhat chastening, and each leaves town disheartened.

O'Hara's handling of this plot is, in a word, far less romantic than Fitzgerald's version. O'Hara's story, past and present, contains sexually mature characters: Jock Barry and Judy Hayes, now in their early thirties, had broken up 11 years earlier, when they were young adults. Fitzgerald's reunited lovers, on the other hand, had last seen each other shortly before adolescence. Fitzgerald recounts in detail the childish events of that breakup; O'Hara withholds his details, suggesting only in the somewhat Catholic name J. J. Barry and the somewhat Waspy name Judy Hayes the possibility that their ethnicities might have wedged them apart. Fitzgerald usually chose character names that had emblematic value, and in his story the bland and generic surname of his protagonist, Donald Plant, contrasts clearly and sharply with the surname of Donald Bowers, the romantic boy for whom he has been mistaken. (Fitzgerald's plot hinges on the old girlfriend mistaking the name of one Donald for the other; when she catches her mistake, she quickly dismisses the would-be suitor.) O'Hara's names, however, are rarely emblematic.[21] The characters' vaguely ethnic names and their ages at the time of their breakup are the story's only hints as to the causes of the past events. Unlike Fitzgerald, O'Hara assumes that his readers can supply their own reasons and that such imagined reasons will seem far more real than any he might supply.

Where Fitzgerald's story is a characteristically dreamy fable, O'Hara's bursts with his characteristic weight of detail: "Trouble in 1949" opens by describing Barry's deliberate evasion of his business associate's social invitations. O'Hara goes on to describe all sorts of mundane but significant details, including the temperature of the shower in Barry's hotel, the size and type of cocktail he orders from room service, the material his dressing gown is made of, and so on. O'Hara referred to such fine points as "characterizers" and in fact had praised Fitzgerald for peppering his work with just such accurate details, albeit on a smaller scale (*Artist*, 147). But Fitzgerald, as O'Hara knew well, observed such surface features primarily in order to describe his characters' inner natures. Having less faith that people's inner natures are knowable or explicitly describable, O'Hara used these details to describe his characters' social behavior and social contexts. As a result, there would be—and in these stories, there is—a sharp distinction in what these authors describe and how they choose to describe it.

In "Three Hours between Planes" Fitzgerald recounts small emotional episodes in his characters' pasts—remembered details about parties and picnics and sleigh rides comprise most of the conversation— and he avoids the use of everyday dialogue that O'Hara finds telling. O'Hara lingers over juicy oddities of everyday speech ("innaresting" as opposed to "inchresting," the delayed caesura in "Notta tall") with little or no plot advancement, while Fitzgerald spares his reader these quotidian details.

Although Fitzgerald's story closes promptly with an improbable plot twist, much as a literal dream sometimes ends at its most climactic point, O'Hara continues beyond the reunited couple's sudden breakup. Despite his racy reputation, there are only two kisses in "Trouble in 1949," both rather chaste, the second of which parts the would-be lovers; they have realized that their lives have changed and that at least Judy's life has grown complicated with new emotional entanglements that do not involve Jock. Whereas Fitzgerald closes off all possible communication between his lovers by ending abruptly, O'Hara's denouement has his lovers realize how little their past touches their present. They reject the romantic yearnings that Fitzgerald's couple still nurture. In O'Hara's last scene, Jock accepts the complex truth of what he sees, not what he wants to see:

> He looked at her, and there was something besides tears in her eyes. It wasn't one thing; it was a lot of things. There was something he had seen a long time ago, when he had said he would be good to her. But now there was something else, and he thought he knew what it was; it was the need of someone to tell, someone to tell. (*FoP,* 29–30)

Having hoped she would become his lover again, Jock comes to accept the idea that if she needs him at all, it would be as a confidant. He accepts in the story's final line the foolishness of having tried to recapture the past and resolves not to attempt this Gatsbyian miracle again in the future.

When in 1936 O'Hara described to Fitzgerald the stories he "wrote for the New Yorker, some of them so vague that when I send them away I almost include a plea to the editors that if they can understand them, please to let me in on the secret," he was being facetious, but not very (*Letters,* 115). That is almost how resistant his stories were to interpretation. The 1939 story "Do You Like It Here?" is wide open to interpretation yet intensely focused on a dynamic confrontation. Though it is one of the very few stories O'Hara interpreted himself, his interpretation runs contrary to that of most of his readers, and is finally—if improbably—wrong.

"Do You Like It Here?" tells, in O'Hara's words, "about a boy that came to a new school and stole a watch. At least we think he stole the watch. Maybe that isn't what the author intended. The author is very vague" (*Letters,* 145). This "interpretation" accompanied the story when O'Hara mailed it in to *The New Yorker,* so its vagueness was obviously acceptable to both author and editor.

The ending of "Do You Like It Here?" in fact shows the author's bias more clearly than most O'Hara stories did up to this time: "Over and over again, first violently, then weakly, he [the accused boy] said it, 'The bastard, the dirty bastard.' " As with old Mr. Winfield, O'Hara has already given us crucial access to the character's mind. The accused boy denies ever having seen the watch, and O'Hara adds, "He was glad to be able to say it truthfully," making unclear his reason for thinking the reader would "think he stole the watch." Further complicating this interpretation is an anecdote Frank MacShane tells of the story's origin. As a teenager, O'Hara was several times

> thrown out of the Schuylkill Country Club. Once, in what was plainly an effort to discredit him, O'Hara was accused of having stolen a watch at the country club. His friend Jack Bergen asked him whether he stole it, and O'Hara answered "What do you think?" In a column years later, he wrote of being "brought up to tell the truth. The word honor meant a lot in my family and still does." . . . O'Hara never forgot the false charge at the country club. In a story derived from it, he spoke of the accuser as the "bastard, the dirty bastard." (MacShane, 30)

Even further complicating the interpretations of "Do You Like It Here?" is Sheldon Norman Grebstein's reading. Praising O'Hara's "extraordinary insights," Grebstein asserts that "the story suggests . . . that there has been no theft at all and that a sadistic instructor torments his chosen victim for his own pleasure."[22] So the facts are as clear as mud: a boy steals a watch (O'Hara's letter) and "truthfully" denies stealing it (O'Hara's story) in a story suggesting that the watch was never stolen (Grebstein), a story based on an real incident in which a watch was stolen (MacShane). Add to this interpretative welter Joseph McElroy's reading (excerpted in Part 3 of this book), which claims the story's attraction lies, at least potentially, not in the tortured psyche of the boy but in the twisted psyche of his accuser.

That the story sets readers (and writer) off in so many different directions suggests that it fails to cohere. But O'Hara's readers agree with his assessment of "Do You Like It Here?" (The year before he died, he picked it for inclusion in *The O'Hara Generation*, which collected 22 of his best stories. In 1956, he chose it to appear in *Selected Short Stories of John O'Hara*, one of only five stories chosen for both collections.) These readers differ over the events of the plot, namely, whether the watch was stolen and, if so, who stole it. But O'Hara has always held plot issues in low regard. The wonderfully controlled ambiguity stems from the Kafkaesque position the accused boy is in, that of being forced to prove a negative proposition—that he did not steal the watch.[23] Whether he stole the watch or not, his helplessness makes him cry out "violently, then weakly" at the end. A new arrival at school, friendless, a product of a broken home with no sense of security, peripatetic (as the headmaster says in his educational summary), utterly reliant on the goodwill of his masters, the boy has no power over his life. The headmaster, whose power is complete, seeks to demoralize the boy and, in the closed world these two inhabit, he can do that and he will. All that these dissenting readers are arguing about, ultimately, is: Why would he want to?

The misdirection provided by O'Hara's letter accompanying the story is intriguing. While it is possible that the version he submitted was changed from a story about a boy who clearly stole a watch to one about a boy who almost certainly did not, no record exists of any changes in "Do You Like It Here?" (and there is an extensive record of correspondence between him and *The New Yorker*). Another possibility is that O'Hara was deliberately misstating the plot to prove that his stories did not depend on plot events to be successful.

In George Monteiro's ingenious reading, the 1956 novella *A Family Party*—a moderately long short story, at 12,000 words—provides an even better example of O'Hara concealing a complex theme behind a seemingly simple plot. *A Family Party* seems to tell an old-fashioned and sentimental tale about a dedicated and self-effacing country doctor, not unlike O'Hara's own father. It had a widespread readership, having been first published by *Collier's* magazine, then by the *Reader's Digest,* which condensed it for its irony-impaired readership. Despite its appearance in publications directed mainly at middlebrow readers, Monteiro maintains that the story itself is highly ambiguous and charged with irony throughout:

> *A Family Party* is not the heart-warming story about a doctor's dedication to his patients and their expression of gratitude for his forty years of service that *Collier's* paid for and published. Rather it is the story of the American small town that invariably "uses" its benefactors, scraping up its thankfulness at the last in one showy gesture. . . . They have chosen their spokesman . . . because, as O'Hara makes deftly clear, he is the self-satisfied, self-congratulatory, self-deceiving voice of the suggestively named town of Lyons. What should be recognized is the subtlety of O'Hara's execution of his decision to tell his "small town" story as a poker-faced parody, drawing upon the familiar form of the honor-

ing speech at a retirement dinner. Entirely in the hands of a "heart-warming," not entirely reliable narrator, *A Family Party* offers his readers a special instance of O'Hara's narrative virtuosity and, perhaps, his feelings as a doctor's son.[24]

In other words, the story is an ironic monologue, consistent not only with the attention paid to the speech patterns and limited self-awareness of the speakers of the Hagedorn and Brownmiller, Delphian, and Pal Joey series but also with their vicious lampooning as well. If any author were to write a tribute to his hardworking, underappreciated, honorable father—and every reader from the most naive through George Monteiro agrees O'Hara has done that in *A Family Party*—would he not be likely to attack those who failed to appreciate or honor him properly? Given O'Hara's combative and defensive disposition, would he not be the likeliest of all authors to do so? It is as hard to imagine O'Hara penning a sweet and gentle encomium to a subject as it is easy to imagine him taking a nasty, even deliberately excessive swipe at his target.

The main plot element in *A Family Party* concerns the attempts of self-sacrificing Dr. Merritt (who, as Monteiro points out, is emblematically named) to start a community hospital. He raises thousands of dollars, including his own life savings, only to see the money contributed to a nearby community's hospital, with Merritt getting neither the glory, the thanks, nor the hospital his effort deserves.

Although Frank MacShane does not draw any connection with *A Family Party*, which he regards elsewhere as a "sentimental portrait," he tells of a "quarrel" Dr. O'Hara was involved in at the time of his death. In 1924, he "was forced with some of the other Roman Catholic doctors to leave the [Pottsville] hospital and set up a new one," adding hours of grueling work to his already brutal schedule. John was already "so angry he wanted to beat up the Protestant doctors physically." When his father died soon afterwards, his rage can only be imagined. His fury at the whole town for hastening the death of his father boils over in *A Family Party* but in such a subtle form that those he attacks most fiercely are precisely those who think he is writing an affectionate memoir of them. This must have been the most satisfying irony of O'Hara's career. Everyone agrees that O'Hara's ambition to prove himself as a writer stems from his thwarted relationship with his father in this first great crisis of his life. His father's death caused him not only to be sent to work instead of to Yale but it also created numerous other daily hardships that he had never faced before; and it engendered O'Hara's sympathy with the victimized, as is displayed in "Do You Like It Here?" and dozens of O'Hara's other stories.

"Price's Always Open," "Trouble in 1949," "Do You Like it Here?" and a few other well-developed stories aside, O'Hara still had not found consistently compelling subject matter in the *Files on Parade* stories until 1938, when he got the idea for a character named Pal Joey. Joey would write a series of comic letters to "friend Ted" containing malapropisms, boasts, exaggerations of his successes, and the like. This was not a bold advance in O'Hara's career. The boastful letter, as a subgenre, plainly derived from Ring Lardner's *You Know Me Al*, a series of letters from an obnoxious, ambitious ballplayer to his friend. Furthermore, Joey's letters were derivative of O'Hara himself. One of the minor pieces in *The Doctor's Son* is a monologue entitled "Master of Ceremonies," aping the patter that a flip and shallow nightclub M.C. might employ between the acts he introduced. But on this run through O'Hara's typewriter, the idea caught on.

It had help. Harold Ross, usually reluctant to see the virtues in O'Hara's fiction, liked the Pal Joey stories and ordered more of them, which O'Hara was easily able to supply. O'Hara also grew to like the character of Pal Joey as he developed, admiring the cheek of this self-serving scamp who chiseled and conned his way to success. O'Hara got some mileage out of the stories, including 6 of them in *Files on Parade*, then publishing all 14 of them in a separate collection called *Pal Joey*.[25] But the greatest help the series would get came after the stories were collected.

A friend suggested to O'Hara that these stories had the potential to be a hit musical. O'Hara contacted Richard Rodgers and Lorenz Hart, and within a year *Pal Joey* was a hit on Broadway, bringing to O'Hara his first real success, if success be measured in terms of fame and money. For the first time, John O'Hara had both in quantity, and he had Pal Joey to thank for it.

Just before the War with *The New Yorker*

The musical version of *Pal Joey* brought O'Hara popular acclaim and a critical reception that have caused the play to become an often-revived Broadway classic. Its lucrative run allowed him, for the first time in his life, to live comfortably while he did his other writing. It let him consider for the first time how to shape his career. Furthermore, the play's success gave him a taste of true celebrity, enabling him, for example, to appear as a frequent guest on popular radio programs (*OHC*, 169). For the rest of his life, when he entered any room where a band was playing, he could expect to hear one of *Pal Joey*'s hit songs played in his honor. But critical praise, money, and fame nearly derailed O'Hara's career as a serious writer.

Before writing the first Pal Joey story in the fall of 1938, O'Hara was producing an impressive quantity of stories, though he knew that many of them were more facile than profound. He could do the police in different voices, but he wanted to be more than the world's most up-to-date police transmitter. He wanted his career to go somewhere but he had no idea where. In the middle of this crisis, he invented Joey and was besieged with unprecedented encouragement to give his readers more of him.

O'Hara noted later how Harold "Ross wanted me to make a career of the Pal Joey pieces" in 1938 (*Letters*, 383).[26] Then, when *Pal Joey*'s Broadway run ended in 1942, Ross "thought it would be a swell idea to have Joey join the Navy and write a modern version of [the successful World War I epistolary series] *Dere Mable*" (*Letters*, 383). Ross, who pestered O'Hara with his constant queries about minute details in O'Hara's fiction submissions, was wholly supportive of the Pal Joey series, giving O'Hara more freedom than he had ever had at *The New Yorker*.[27] Since it was *New Yorker* policy (and Ross's policy in particular) to pay for pieces on acceptance, not on assignment, Ross's enthusiasm, though falling short of actual payment, amounted to commissioning future stories. O'Hara took great pleasure in this breakthrough.

For all of O'Hara's writerly pride, however, his perception of the Pal Joey character and series was that they were the work of his left hand.

"[T]hese damn things," O'Hara wrote in 1940, "are the most successful things I've ever done for the NYer. I beat my brains out writing fine, sensitive prose, careful streams of consciousness, lean spare sharp exposition, accurate shot of dialog [in his non-Joey stories], and what do I get yet?" (*Letters*, 156). For his "sensitive" work, the answer was "Not much," but the Pal Joey stories—after the book, play, and movie had been adapted from them—yielded more than a million dollars, and a lot of encouraging if misdirecting praise (*OHC*, 151).

Some of the misdirection was to encourage him to think of his talent primarily as a gift for writing plays.[28] It is natural but unfortunate that O'Hara interpreted the success of the musical version of *Pal Joey*, for which he wrote the spoken dialogue, as a sign that he should pursue a career as a playwright. In the 30 years he lived after *Pal Joey*'s staging, he sunk time and energy into the crafting of plays but never came close to another Broadway show, much less a hit. His talent was for writing dialogue for the page, not for the stage, though it is difficult, given *Pal Joey*'s critical and financial success, to blame him much for testing those waters.

O'Hara expressed the difference between writing dialogue for the stage and the page:

> I *do* tend to overburden my dialog with matters that rightly belong in the unspoken part of a script. . . . One of my troubles may be that I *like* to hear my people talk, especially because everything everybody says contributes to a fuller knowledge, and therefore, better understanding of character. . . . I stubbornly believe that plot is diminishingly important and that a little bit of action goes a long way, but the one thing that makes you remember a picture or a book or a play is the people. (*Letters*, 261–62)

O'Hara initially created Pal Joey in order to develop Joey's devious character, with whom, O'Hara admitted, he had a lot in common. He even described his original impulse to create Joey's character as autobiographical, which is much too harsh a self-assessment (*OHC*, 150; *Letters*, 156).

When he was creating Joey, O'Hara wrote a letter to a British friend in which he lapsed suddenly into Joey's argot:

> At least our mob knows that the fixeroo is in, and if we want to copper our dime we can still do it before the flag is up. The mouse and me give one another the office, and I give you the tiperoo: lay it off from

here to Chi, if you are on that dog the Admiral. Admiral aint got a play.
I give it to you once again, Kiddie: you're on the Admiral and the bruise
will be but terrific. But terrific. (*Letters*, 140)

It amused O'Hara to show off his mastery of this hepster-mobster lingo,
which was practically unintelligible to outsiders. (A "mouse," as *Pal
Joey*'s context makes clear, is a young woman, a "bruise" is a bill, "Chi"
is Chicago, and so on.) O'Hara must have especially enjoyed showing off
this language to his British correspondent, a "distinguished bibliogra-
pher" (*OHC*, 149). O'Hara developed this lingo with his night-clubbing
friends and had fun using it in his fiction, at least until producing the
Pal Joey stories became primarily a commercial enterprise.

About halfway through the series, O'Hara "got pretty fucking bored"
with Pal Joey but kept writing the stories because they were "as easy
money as you can get without actually inheriting it." He compared the
stories to watered-down jazz, as typified by the cloying music of Guy
Lombardo, which O'Hara claimed he liked the first time he heard it,
but the

> second record of his made me want to smash the phonograph. But not
> the dear readers of the Joey series, any more than the listeners to Lom-
> bardo, who I am afraid may be pretty much the same people. Not alto-
> gether, but pretty much. Well, the Joey stuff got readers and I got
> applause and money. . . . (*Letters*, 153–54)

Applause and money, however, were not his only goals. As he stated in a
talk near the end of his life, a writer's "distractions and diversions . . .
can be anything from . . . greed to too much praise," and at this stage of
his career O'Hara certainly felt the tug of money and the acclaim of
strangers who misunderstood what he was about (*Artist*, 113). Resisting
that tug, O'Hara understood himself to be an artist. In 1939, O'Hara
expressed pride in his "use of the vernacular. Even if people don't get it
at first, they will." He plainly felt great pride in introducing his readers
to new language, not in simply reporting the language they felt most
comfortable reading, even at the risk of puzzling them. "I was the first
person ever to do a piece about double talk," he wrote, ". . . and several
things in that piece have become established slang. It is a point of
artistry with me" (*Letters*, 144).

He went on to use double-talk in several other pieces, including the
title of one of the best Pal Joey stories, "The Erloff." (Double-talk

introduces deliberately nonsensical but plausible-sounding syllables into otherwise intelligible sentences, as distinct from the specialized but still meaningful jargon that Joey's letters consist of.) The piece about double-talk that O'Hara took such pride in, "Portistan on the Portis," is limited in scope and length, like many of his early stories. It is an anecdote about a prizefight manager who bedevils waiters with double-talk, demanding to be served "portis on the portistan on the *veal* portis and the veal—call the head waiter!"; and the head waiter gets the same routine, all for the amusement of the narrator and his friends.[29] They drive to Newark, asking strangers along the way—cops, young hoodlums, tollbooth attendants—"What do you hippum the mob?" puzzling and sometimes upsetting the strangers, which is the idea behind double-talk. It is a means of distinguishing those who know the in-talk from those who do not. Since "doubletalk isn't Pig Latin [and] isn't anything," as O'Hara avers in "Portistan on the Portis," it hardly matters that double-talk is a content-free language in which meaning is nothing and nuance is everything. For O'Hara, double-talk sums up one of the most prominent uses of language: to keep the ins in and the outs out.

In "The Erloff" Joey slowly gets wise to it. On his late-night rounds, he meets a doddering old man who uses the title noun as an all-purpose substitute for everything: "Erloff," Joey deduces from context, is the woman singer in the club, and it is the club itself, and it is the ambiance of the club, and it is also Joey's date. "Everything was erloff with this decrept old bore," thinks Joey. Then the old bore, revealing himself to be Joey's theretofore unknown employer, offers him a big raise. Joining the cognoscenti, Joey closes his letter with the latest addition to his vocabulary: "The erloff Pal."

It is unfortunate that O'Hara, touchy to begin with, had to withstand *The New Yorker*'s close editorial scrutiny because, particularly with Pal Joey, disagreements over precise levels of intelligibility were bound to arise. In a letter reacting to one of Ross's rare rejections of a Pal Joey story, whose lingo was intended to seem charmingly strange to *New Yorker* readers, O'Hara complains that Ross seems "so damned un-understanding of the whole Pal Joey series that I wonder how any of them could have been bought." O'Hara is then forced to insist that his meaning, which is plainly intended to keep the reader guessing, is clear: "Joey on the surface was looking for advice, but isn't it obvious (what a weak word) that he wasn't asking for advice, but only using that form as an excuse to brag?" (*Letters*, 148). What is more than obvious to O'Hara is less than clear to Ross. O'Hara wanted his reader to collaborate with him in deriving his story's meaning, and he was plainly more willing to risk puzzling readers than Ross was.

In "A Respectable Place" O'Hara combines his penchant for codes with his penchant for surprises: A nasty off-duty cop comes into a bar one night and makes a tremendous scene, pulling his gun, faking suicide, and ultimately shooting up the bar's mirrors, sending some frightened customers out into the street. The bar owner calmly totes up the monetary damages and submits them discreetly to the local police. So far, these events seem to make sense, and the bar owner seems to be handling them adroitly. But then he finds himself being harassed by the police. On the verge of being driven out of business by their systematic persecution, he tries to contribute the settlement to a police charity but is accused of attempting to offer a bribe.

Late, too late, in the story, O'Hara's reader and the bar owner realize that he has badly misread the actions of the police. But when? Was there a better way to handle the drunken cop? Did the bar owner misinterpret the lieutenant's offer to pay for the bar repairs? Did he err in the *way* he offered to return the money? No, at all points, O'Hara takes great care to show him behaving properly, inoffensively, correctly, but in the end he is as thoroughly persecuted as if he had taken a full-page newspaper ad to publicize the incident. Any search for clues to identify the bar owner's awful mistake results in frustration because there are no clues. His mistake lies outside of the story: he thought he owned a bar in a democracy whose laws he understood, even when they were subtle and unwritten. But as Lionel Trilling wrote, comparing this story to Kafka's fables, his society instead "acts by laws of its own being which are not to be understood."[30]

"The King of the Desert" also concerns misunderstood social codes. Bored rather than malicious, two Hollywood sharpies are killing time by teasing Dave, a large, plain-spoken rancher, inventing an absurd scenario in which Dave strikes oil and the two let him keep about a gallon and a half. "Then multiply that," one of the Hollywood types says, "by forta forta forta times sibba sibba sibba, and what have you got" (*PN*, 76). Good-natured Dave endures the teasing, the double-talk, the assumption that he is a rube, but when the teasing touches on a subject Dave takes seriously—his pride in his ancestry—he simply flattens one of the jokers in midsentence. The unspoken code Dave lives by says, "Where I come from, we only talk for a while, and then we start to hit," and the way he notifies violators of the code is to hit them hard.

O'Hara dealt elsewhere with the clash between the mores of Hollywood and America. In a story collected in *The Time Element*, "The Professor and the Industry," an academic visits a studio whose corruption and self-absorption interest, amuse, and finally offend him. "The King of the Desert," however, is interesting because it fleshes out one of O'Hara's unique theories of composing short stories.

Explaining why so many of his stories mystify their readers, O'Hara claimed that it was his habit to

> think of two faces I have seen, make up a scene such as a restaurant table or two seats in an airplane, and get those two people in a conversation. I let them do small talk for a page or so, and pretty soon they begin to come to life. They do so entirely through dialogue. I start knowing nothing of them except what I remember of their faces. But as they chatter away one of them and then the other will say something that is so revealing that I recognize the sign of created characters.

O'Hara is equally mystified by the story as it unfolds, and he attempts to figure it out as it happens, just as his readers are doing. O'Hara explained that his usual practice is to create a story out of such a character-based start, but he claims that it only occasionally results in a finished story:

> If I become absorbed in the characters I can [write about them]. . . . But while I have written and published short stories that had such accidental beginnings. . . . [a]s a rule I don't even finish the stories I begin that way, and I deliberately destroy what I have done by giving one of the characters a line of atrocious dialog—humorous, profane, or completely out of character—that makes it impossible to continue—. (*Artist*, 7)

"The King of the Desert" may be an exception to this principle: it contains one line of dialogue so completely out of *any* character that the story's mood is destroyed, although O'Hara seems unaware of the damage. The Hollywood jokesters are still ribbing Dave, when one of them calls him by the wrong name—*his* own name: " 'I'm glad you came to me instead of one of those quacks on the next floor,' said Artie. 'Is it a woman, Artie? I mean Dave. My name's Artie' " (*PN*, 76–77). Though no speaker in literature—or in life for that matter—ever calls someone by his own name, authors sometimes mistakenly attribute the wrong name to a character, which is probably what happened here. But instead of crossing out the typo, O'Hara let it stand and then continued, the absurd mistake seeming plausible to him given the rapid patter of these particular characters.

More broadly, O'Hara's unusual principle of story composition shows his lifelong search for material to write about. Consciously, at least, stories did not come from O'Hara's ideas as much as the ideas latent in the stories developed from his absorption in his characters. O'Hara in this regard might be compared to a jazz musician noodling with a musical phrase, perhaps picked up from an arbitrary and uninspired source, and building it—sometimes—into an original and unique composition. The problem with pieces begun without conscious theorizing of any sort, however, is that more often than not the improvised riffs lead only to technical elaboration, and inspiration never comes.

By the early days of World War II, O'Hara's writing had foundered. He had ridden his naturalistic gifts about as far as they would take him. No longer merely re-creating scenes or styles of speech, he was developing tight if subtle plots and rounded characters, but as the 1940s progressed, he found that he simply could not produce stories as easily as he had before the war, nor as well.

The war itself impaired his productiveness. Admiring those writers old enough to have seen overseas action in World War I, particularly Hemingway, O'Hara found himself a bit too old to be a valued fighting man in World War II. (He was almost 36 years old when Pearl Harbor was attacked.) He tried joining the Office of Strategic Services, the predecessor of the CIA , partly because he knew some of its high-ranking officers. But for reasons of health he was rejected (a reminder that, some 20 years earlier, he was kept out of Yale, which many of his contemporaries in the OSS had attended). The shameful failure of his teens reappeared now in his thirties.

It is little wonder then, as World War II drew on, that O'Hara found himself, in a word, depressed. All of his biographers make that point. Though none use that clinical word, all support Bruccoli's contention that "the war years were bad for John O'Hara" (*OHC,* 170).[31] O'Hara himself described his condition in terms of depression's main symptom, the inability to work. He blamed this state on the effects of heavy drinking, telling the London *Daily Express* in 1967 that before the war he

> was dissipating all my energies in drink and high living. I was drinking
> a quart of whiskey a day, and that takes time—not just to drink, but to

have your hangover and to get better from your hangover. It was a
period when I couldn't write. (*Artist*, 221)

A few weeks later, he remembered that between

the invasion of Poland and the Japanese surrender, I found I could not
write anything longer than a short story. You might say that it took a
world war to keep me from my typewriter. (*Artist*, 113)

Depressed as he may have been, O'Hara resisted the lure—and the permanent cure—that so many depressives prescribe for their ailment, suicide, which became a frequent subject in his short stories for years to
come. O'Hara's wartime letters do suggest, however, that this blighted
solution did at least flicker through his mind: more in frustration than in
despair, he wrote in 1944 that he was so "sick of myself that it's a good
thing I don't use a straight razor. Or live in a tall building" (MacShane,
124). O'Hara's writing was in effect a war casualty. "It was impossible to
write during the war," he later observed. "Short stories that I could turn
out in a few hours were all I could manage" (MacShane, 126). In the
four years of the war, he published fewer than 20 short stories.[32]

O'Hara used his feud with *The New Yorker* as an opportunity to rethink
his career as a novelist, writing his postwar novels with a drastic change
in tone, in length, in scope, in subject, in technique, and in the very
purpose of the novel. And as these vast conceptual changes worked
themselves out in his consciousness, his decade-long neglect of the
short story makes perfect sense.

The 1940s mark a decline in O'Hara's short-story production—not as
severe a decline as in the 1950s but one without a simple explanation
like a break with his primary market. Numerically, O'Hara's short-story
publication differs widely from decade to decade:

Decade	Total
1920s	37
1930s	118
1940s	75
1950s	3
1960s	150
	383[33]

In the 1920s, 9.7 percent of O'Hara's 383 published short stories,
mostly sketches taking up a column or less in *The New Yorker*, appeared

in print; in the 1930s, 30.8 percent; in the 1940s, 19.6 percent; in the 1950s, less than 1 percent; and in the 1960s, 36.2 percent.

What is interesting about these numbers, both the ones dealing with the short stories and the following ones regarding the novels, is the surprising correlation between the two forms. One would think that they would have competed for O'Hara's attention, but in fact the opposite is true. The most productive decade for O'Hara's short stories, the 1960s, was also the most productive of his career as a novelist; and the least productive of the full decades in which O'Hara was writing short stories, the 1940s, also saw a low in his novelistic production.

Decade	Number of Novels
1930s	3 *(Appointment in Samarra, Butterfield-8, Hope of Heaven)*
1940s	1 (*A Rage to Live*)
1950s	3 (*The Farmers Hotel, Ten North Frederick, From the Terrace*)
1960s	7 (*Ourselves to Know, The Big Laugh, Elizabeth Appleton, The Lockwood Concern, The Instrument, Lovey Childs, The Ewings*)

As the following list indicates, O'Hara's collections included increasingly longer stories.

Collection	Year Published	Average Length of Story (in Pages)
The Doctor's Son and Other Stories	1935	7.9
Files On Parade	1939	7.8
Pal Joey	1940	8.6
Pipe Night	1945	6.5
Hellbox	1947	7.0
Assembly	1961	16.3
The Cape Cod Lighter	1962	18.3
The Hat on the Bed	1963	16.7
The Horse Knows the Way	1964	15.2
Waiting For Winter	1966	22.0
And Other Stories	1968	27.7

O'Hara's first five collections of short stories, published from 1935 through 1947, averaged under eight pages per story (with the collection written during the war containing stories with the shortest average length). Both quantitative measures (of average story length and of the numbers of stories published) taken together show O'Hara's much-reduced productivity in the 1940s. In his next six collections, the last six he would live to see published, the average story length nearly

tripled as the stories flew from his typewriter with ever increasing pro-
lificness.

Almost as visible a distinction as the quantity of pages is the tone of
the stories—the early ones are quick, brash, heavily steeped in the vernacular of their time; the later ones are much slower, more philosophical, and also steeped in the vernacular. Although the vernacular remains
the same, that of the 1920s and 1930s, the context changes: in the early
stories O'Hara is writing contemporary vernacular that, by the 1960s,
has—without changing—become a historical vernacular.

An obvious reason for the radical change in O'Hara's writing modes is
time itself. In the 1930s, O'Hara was a hard-drinking bachelor, an ardent
Democrat, and a masterful writer of brash, sharp contemporary fiction,
often criticized for its elliptical brevity. By the early 1950s, he had
become a good husband (twice), a loving father, a teetotaler, a cranky
and defensive convert to Republicanism, and a masterful writer who was
under fire for writing at ponderous length.

During the transition, his reevaluation of himself as a writer, which
began with the success of *Pal Joey,* continued. His novels were stagnat-
ing, at the least in the critics' eyes, and the only strong encouragement
he was getting was to produce more dramatic work, which he tried to
do, and more short stories, through which he was enjoying a reputation
as a master scene painter, human recording device, anecdote teller—all
descriptions he correctly took as backhanded compliments, because he
felt he could produce something much more ambitious than his output
to this point.

If O'Hara found his long fiction underappreciated in the 1940s, his
short fiction was overappreciated. While justly proud of his short stories,
he was ambitious to push them further. As early as the 1930s, critics had
acclaimed him "a master of the short story," which he found limiting: he
inscribed his infant daughter's copy of his 1945 collection *Pipe Night*
with the words "Your old man will be remembered as a short story
writer, if at all" (*OHC,* 179). Entering middle age, O'Hara sensed that
he needed to grow as a writer, that he needed to produce, and that he
was eminently capable of producing different, longer, more intricate,
less limited short stories and novels than he had produced to date, yet
he did not know which form his work would take. The 1940s presented
him with a midlife crisis of the most frustrating sort, one in which this
hard-working, sensitive, and gifted writer found himself abundantly
equipped to make a difficult journey if only he could find the door out
of his comfortable house.

Along the way, O'Hara's short stories branched out in several directions, none of them particularly fruitful. He was proud of the stories that led off and concluded *Pipe Night,* though it is hard to see them as advances in his work. Both "Walter T. Carriman" and "Mrs. Whitman" are essentially monologues, more skillful and subtle than those in *The New Yorker* in the 1920s but not much so.[34]

Searching for direction, O'Hara wrote, in addition to monologues and character sketches, more satirical stories in *Pipe Night* and *Hellbox.* He later reminisced about this period:

> I grew weary of the department in the *Reader's Digest* called My Most Unforgettable Character, or something to that effect. The M.U.C. usually was an old colored mammy who for years had been working secretly in her makeshift laboratory out back and had developed a cure for penicillin; or it was a town drunk who in his youth had swum the English Channel with anvils instead of flippers tied to his ankles; or it was Mother. . . . In due course I wrote a satire of the M.U.C. series and sold it to Ross's Folly. I called it 'Life Among These Unforgettable Characters,' thus announcing not too subtly that I was kidding the *Digest.*[35]

Aside from parodies, *Hellbox* contained the few stories O'Hara got from serving briefly as a war correspondent, including "War Aims," the best of these.

Hellbox also included such outré stories as "A Phase of Life." O'Hara described its subject as "a whorehouse in Harlem," which is why he thought *The New Yorker* had rejected it. It was also among his more elliptical stories, however, in which the relationship between the prostitutes and their customers, or the other characters whom the proprietors and clients discuss, is never made explicit. In the 1960s, O'Hara was boasting that this story was both clear and "pretty tame," but both points are questionable. He felt he had advanced beyond his "early struggles to get past [the] obtuseness and purity" of *New Yorker* editors, but the problem may not have been the obtuseness of his editors as much as it was the obliqueness of O'Hara's plots.[36] And he was quite consciously avoiding plot in his stories: "My fiction writing depends almost completely on characterization, situation, locale, dialogue, and practically not at all on plot or plot devices," he wrote accurately in the mid-1950s, and he seemed pleased at that late date with his doing without plot (*Sweet and Sour,* 148).

"Graven Image," however, is a tightly plotted story written during World War II. The locale—wartime Washington—is unusual for an

O'Hara short story, but the subject matter is not: the difficulty of transcending class lines. Two former Harvard classmates are having lunch at an exclusive men's club, one of them an undersecretary serving in FDR's cabinet, the other a wealthy blue blood seeking a high-level federal appointment. The Undersecretary (his name is never revealed), whose social status—or lack thereof—kept him from being invited to join Harvard's tonier clubs, asks Charles Browning if he still carries the tiny golden pig that betokens membership in Harvard's Porcellian Club. Producing the "graven image," Browning somehow—through charm, humility, and wit—manages to soothe the Undersecretary's still-seething resentment of Browning's social standing. Browning persuades the Undersecretary to sponsor him for the federal job, an act of delicate diplomacy that in itself shows how much Browning wants the job and how good he will be at it. But then, celebrating prematurely, Browning commits the faux pas of confiding that the Undersecretary never could have joined any important Harvard club "in a thousand years." Foot still in mouth, Browning cuts himself off—"but then I've said the wrong thing, haven't I?" Confirming this, the Undersecretary leaves Browning in the club alone, contemplating the error of his phrase.

This is a story—as Frank MacShane says of "Olive"—in which "there is not a wasted line or dead sentence" (108). Able to hit exactly the notes he wants, O'Hara controls the tone of "Graven Image" by doling out details sparingly, never distracting the reader, for example, with the name of the department the Undersecretary serves in, or which federal job Browning wants, or how he qualifies for it. With such seemingly crucial details omitted, the reader is allowed—indeed compelled—to search elsewhere in the story for significance. O'Hara does not even mention the presidential administration in which this story takes place; that must be deduced by one date ("I wasn't even for you in 1932," Browning confesses) and by one nickname (Roosevelt is called "The Boss" by both parties). All the details that are included, down to the Undersecretary's lunch order—peas, shoestring potatoes, lobster, and no cocktail—are significant. (Browning's instant agreement to "take whatever you're having" signals his subservience.) Every detail advances our understanding of the two men, and every omitted detail keeps pointing us where O'Hara wants us to look.

O'Hara often presents a likable character—Browning, Jerry the pool hustler, old Mr. Winfield in "Over The River and through the Wood— making a mistake and paying dearly for it. The epigraph to O'Hara's first novel, *Appointment in Samarra*, is in some ways the epigraph to his career because its theme is how, in trying to avoid making faux pas, people often commit them. (In the epigraph, taken from W. Somerset Maugham, a man, seeing the figure of Death waving to him, flees to the distant city of Samarra. After he goes, Death expresses surprise to have seen him here today at all, because he had an appointment to meet him tomorrow in Samarra.) In "Graven Image," Browning's fate, like Julian English's in *Appointment in Samarra*, is inextricably bound together with his character.

Bruccoli calls "Graven Image" the "archetypal O'Hara story of snobbery and exclusion," noting that both the Undersecretary and Browning are defeated, Browning because he cannot suppress his snobbery, the Undersecretary because he cannot rise gracefully above his persecutors (*OHC*, 171–72). Is the story primarily about a "small man" (as the Undersecretary is described) who cannot forget bygone injuries to his pride, or is it mostly about a supplicant who cannot suppress his boasting for an entire meal?

Like "Graven Image," "Bread Alone" shows O'Hara experimenting with settings and character. The back cover of the Bantam paperback edition of *Pipe Night* mirrors O'Hara's restlessness, sensationalizing the collection's varied subjects:

> FURTIVE ADULTERERS, RESTLESS HOLLYWOOD
> STARLETS, DISILLUSIONED ADOLESCENTS,
> BEAUTIFUL CON-WOMEN
> John O'Hara knows them all.

And he did more or less, although they are not equally worth knowing, nor can O'Hara tell each of their stories with equal insight. In *Pipe Night*, he is still casting his net widely, and some subjects are better catches than others. His best catch may be "Bread Alone."

"Bread Alone" takes up the theme of the character sketch "Pleasure" and develops it into a moving short story. O'Hara even reuses the language of "Pleasure," including the technique of the diminutive adjective: "But a man was entitled to a little pleasure in life" (*PN*, 81). Although he never again used a working-class African-American for a story's protagonist (as he never again used "Graven Image" 's cabinet-level inner circles of government), these two stories are wholly successful. They have the sharp edge but not the nastiness of O'Hara's satirical pieces, along with evocative and believable dialogue. Richard Wright wrote that this story was the only one he had read by a white author that used Negro characters who sounded like Negroes. Lionel Trilling, with somewhat less authority, agreed (*OHC*, 177).[37]

Subtly but repeatedly, O'Hara refers to his protagonist, a car washer named Hart, as "a man" (the passage quoted earlier, about a man's entitlement to pleasure, also refers to him as "a troubled man"), underscoring his struggle to maintain his personal dignity as a workingman and as a father. When Hart wins the baseball pool at work, he takes his son to watch a game at Yankee Stadium. Isolated from his white coworkers at the garage, Hart is also alienated at home: he cannot tell his wife about his winnings because she would confiscate them, and he cannot even tell the truth about the tickets to his son. "[F]rom the fifth inning on, Hart had been troubled," O'Hara writes, by his isolation, particularly from "Booker, the strange boy of thirteen who was Mr. Hart's only son. Booker was a quiet boy, good in school, and took after his mother, who was quite a bit lighter complected than Mr. Hart" (*PN*, 80, 82). Thus set apart from the people with whom he should be closest, "Mr. Hart wished the game would be over," because this pleasurable event holds such little pleasure for him (*PN*, 83). And then the unexpected happens.

The great DiMaggio whacks a home run near their section of the grandstand and, curiously, no one can locate the ball. At the game's end, Booker asks his dad to sit a while and, when the crowd thins out, Booker removes the souvenir from inside his shirt and gives it to his father. Hart's response is perfectly inarticulate yet perfectly expressive: " 'I'll be damn—boy, some Booker!' He put his arm around his son's shoulders and hugged him. 'Boy, some Booker, huh? You givin' it to me? Some Booker!' " (*PN*, 85). The sudden kinship, literal and figurative, between this decent man and his seemingly estranged son is powerful, and doubly so because of O'Hara's expert withholding of any hint of the ferocious loyalty the boy feels to his dad.

The small details, expertly dropped in, make the strong ending believable. The joy that Hart feels from his son's love is carefully set up: by Hart's loneliness, by Booker's implacable quietness, and by subtle descriptions of the racism the Harts bear almost instinctively: "There was a scramble of men and kids, men hitting kids and kids shoving men out of the way, trying to get the ball. Mr. Hart drew away, not wanting any trouble" (*PN*, 83). "Bread Alone," a fine and sad story most of the way, turns into an uplifting one at the end, because of the sadness.[38]

The New Yorker often pressed O'Hara to supply details it considered necessary for an understanding of his stories. In reaction to such a request for "Bread Alone," O'Hara complained that he was "trying to write decently and with some respect for the possible reader, figuring, as I occasionally do, that anyone who can read can get what I'm saying."

Apparently, Harold Ross had demanded more factual information about the minor character Ginsburg, who hands Hart his winnings, a request to which O'Hara reacted with typical sarcasm:

> I therefore was a little surprised that Boss Ross wanted me to draw a picture of a man with a Roman schnozz and a circumsized whang, with a social security number etc., also a driver's license saying he was Morton Ginsburg, 34, 1166 Decatur Ave., The Bronx, employed as a bookkeeper at the Elbee Garage because he had a cousin who knew one of the owners, etc. (*Letters*, 151)

Ross's relentless querying of O'Hara's stylistic spareness remained a minor irritant, but by the late 1940s the combination of major irritants and minor ones caused O'Hara to break relations entirely with *The New Yorker.*

When O'Hara used Jim Malloy as a narrator in *The Doctor's Son* collection, he evidently was dissatisfied with the result, because he dropped Malloy as a narrator of short stories for the next 25 years. (He did use Malloy to narrate his 1939 novel *Hope of Heaven*, which was not well received.) O'Hara experimented with other alter egos: Kelly in "Hotel Kid" and the nameless O'Hara manqué narrators of "The Man Who Had to Talk to Somebody" and "Portistan on the Portis." In *Hellbox*, his substitutes for Malloy are the narrator of "Ellie," also named Jim but biographically different from Malloy (and from O'Hara), and the narrator of "War Aims" and "The Skipper," a civilian magazine correspondent named Delaney, which happens to be O'Hara's mother's maiden name.[39] Both Delaney stories take place aboard World War II navy vessels.

"War Aims" and "The Skipper" are understated stories whose patriotic points become clear only in the last few lines. In "War Aims," a garrulous young navy flier engages the middle-aged war correspondent in conversation during a lull aboard a busy warship, telling him of his postwar plans to get married and open a law practice in a small New England town. He even speculates on who his closest friends will be and how he plans to decorate his office. As the flier's plans grow more elaborate, O'Hara's plan emerges, though Delaney never voices it: the young flier may not live to realize those plans. A general alarm sounds at the story's end. As he rushes off to combat, the implication is that it may well be for the last time.

"War Aims" embodies a principle of O'Hara's typical plot construction. In the first paragraph, O'Hara mentions that a rumor circulates aboard ship every afternoon at the same hour that a Betty, a Japanese warplane, has been sighted on radar. Because O'Hara does not emphasize the rumor, it seems like another piece of navy scuttlebutt, no more or less colorful than the description of the card playing in the wardroom, or the type of literature being reread by a petty officer. "If I take out the early reference to the Betty on the radar screen," O'Hara protested in response to a *New Yorker* request that he delete it, "the subsequent alarm becomes a deus ex machina" (*Letters*, 190). O'Hara wants to plant that crucial bit of information early, to inform his readers that such an event is always possible and yet to disguise it among the clutter of other seemingly insignificant details.

The strategy of "The Skipper" is similar to that of "War Aims." Early on, O'Hara plants the danger of even an empty oil tanker exploding but then shifts to the crew's loneliness and daily boredom, a description that makes the tanker seem almost like a floating men's club in wartime. But as Delaney prepares to leave the tanker, he asks the skipper if he can do anything for the men when he gets home. The skipper's answer, which ends the story, reminds us of the unspoken dangers: " 'Don't forget us,' he said, and the smile was gone. 'That's all. Don't forget us.' " In both stories, Delaney is present mostly to provide some civilian perspective, and his likely reaction to these situations would probably correspond to that of the reader.

"The Skipper" appeared in *The Time Element*, a posthumously published collection of stories written in the 1940s that also included some tales set in an actual men's club, told in the first person, by a narrator identified as Kerry. In both stories that Kerry narrates, he acts as a sounding board who puffs on his pipe and says, "Really, now?" and "Ahem," as his companion tells him men's-club anecdotes. These two stories suggest that O'Hara was trying out a new series of men's-club stories in the manner of W. Somerset Maugham, whose ubiquitous narrator Kerry strongly resembles.

"At the Cothurnos Club" starts with a Maugham-like frame tale, with Kerry listening to his luncheon companion describe another club member who amused himself for years by spreading malicious gossip about various actresses. Eventually and, O'Hara implies, inevitably, the name of the other club member's own actress-wife surfaces in one of these sessions, at which point he clams up and withdraws from club life. The same structure recurs in "Conversation at Lunch": same club, same

Kerry, same story structure. This time, the lengthy framing conversation concerns the dubious integrity of a successful club member who, as if on cue, comes to the table and is asked, delicately but clearly, for a loan that he can and should quite easily grant. He declines and, in the process, invents unnecessary lies, confirming his faithless character.

Had he continued writing short stories, O'Hara might have developed Kerry into his mainstay narrator, or he might have developed Delaney or even the narrator of "Ellie" into a greater voice in his short fiction. There are clear reasons for his break with *The New Yorker*, and there are mysterious ones, but the result of the rift was certainly that his short-story production for over 10 years virtually ended. But one of the major causes of the break was the fact that O'Hara's 1949 novel *A Rage to Live* got a harsh review in *The New Yorker*, which he took as such an act of gross disloyalty that he refused to contribute to the magazine until long after Harold Ross had died and O'Hara had been soothingly lured back by some old friends and some new editorial policies.

Brendan Gill (who wrote the offensive review) sees it differently, and there is some merit to his position. Gill declares that O'Hara had long been demanding to be paid much more than any other *New Yorker* contributor and had demanded to be paid on a basis that the magazine could not even consider. On the grounds that the stories he wrote with *The New Yorker* in mind were not saleable to any other publication, O'Hara wanted the magazine to pay him a regular salary, whether or not it published any of his stories. He asked the magazine to share some of the risks he assumed in aiming his work specifically toward their readership, but they refused. This fight was waged throughout the 1940s, and maybe earlier; if it had not occurred and caused such rancor, the Gill review might have been overlooked much sooner.

But an even likelier theory for O'Hara's renunciation of the short story is that he wanted a sweeping change in his writing, and *A Rage to Live* characterized this change as much as it caused the feud with *The New Yorker*. He felt he had revolutionized the short story but had been meagerly rewarded for his revolutionary work. For his short-story efforts, he was called a walking tape recorder, and such respected critics as Lionel Trilling, while praising his stories, said that he was avoiding his natural genre, the long social novel. That is what Edmund Wilson was calling for as well in his somewhat nasty 1940 article that urged O'Hara to return to Gibbsville for his subject. What Wilson meant was for him to return to *Appointment in Samarra*.

So the idea of revamping the thrust of his career peaked in the late 1940s, spurred along paradoxically by *Pal Joey*'s success and assisted by the sour reviews of *Hope of Heaven* and the backhanded praise his stories earned from critics, not to mention the effect of World War II and the possible clinical depression it brought on. After "1948, I had sense enough to take a look at my work as a body of work," O'Hara wrote, "and to look at my future. It did not happen overnight, but I came to realize that if I was going to leave a real, lasting mark, I could not do it with individual, isolated books. They all had to have a kind of continuity, a theme, a purpose" (MacShane, 208–9). And that overarching vision would be far more feasible if each book were an entire thematic unit. He felt that he needed to give up the writing of short fiction, with its varied themes necessarily diverging from each other, and devote himself to the writing of novels. That it happened after a decade of financial disagreements with *The New Yorker* and Ross's incessant querying of authorial decisions, coinciding with Gill's acerbic review, is happenstance. Given O'Hara's ambition, it was—to use his favorite word—inevitable that he should at some point abandon the short story.

For over a decade he entertained the idea that his reputation would depend on his writing long, detailed social novels, which, he wrote, he had been

> consciously, deliberately doing ... since 1947, when I was getting ready to sit and write A RAGE TO LIVE. Before that I wrote largely by instinct and from inside myself and from my own experience, but in 1947, or maybe 1946, or maybe even 1944—who knows when those things begin?—I consciously brooded about the novel, construction, technique, etc. (*Letters*, 283)

From 1949 through 1960, his next four novels were weighty tomes, differing from his previous novels not only in length but also in tone and scope.[40] Whereas his first three novels covered periods of days or months and were set contemporaneously, these four novels covered several lifetimes apiece and stretched from the nineteenth century through the recent past. (None of them extended into the present where virtually all his short stories were set.) This was new territory for O'Hara and was as far as he could get from his tight stories full of incidents and anecdotes. By the time he wrote the last of these novels in 1960, he had begun to explore the idea of writing some short stories again, stories of a different type. The best of these later stories are set in Gibbsville, and the best of those are narrated by Jim Malloy.

In four stories in *Hellbox* published in 1947, Malloy is a character but not the narrator. While these stories are not uniformly successful, Malloy's personality develops in them and when O'Hara resumes writing stories again in 1960, Malloy is his narrator. The *Hellbox* stories in which Malloy appears are "Pardner," "Transaction," "Miss W.," and "Conversation in the Atomic Age." These might be termed The Duesenberg Stories because they touch on Malloy's car, a long and fancy Duesenberg, which happened to be the same kind of car that O'Hara bought with his Hollywood earnings in 1941.

The best of these tales is "Transaction," in which Malloy buys the Duesenberg from an academic couple living in genteel poverty in Cambridge, Massachusetts. The ending of "Transaction" is particularly understated and particularly effective. After the car is sold, O'Hara concludes: "Hands were clasped, good wishes were exchanged, and the transaction was in general satisfactory," an ending so deliberately flat it signals the reader to look elsewhere for the emotional content of the story. "Transaction" is emotional and even accessible but only to a reader willing to interpret the story's many details: the well-bred wife looking unkempt when Malloy arrives, the ill-furnished apartment with "portly tomes" resting on the "tired" furniture "because there was no bookshelf" in the home of the patrician Van Buren family (*Hellbox*, 164). The very sale of the Van Burens' valuable and well-loved car to the newly rich Malloy suggests the young couple's financial straits, at least while Mr. Van Buren finishes law school. Malloy is taking advantage of their temporary poverty, which makes him feel guilty, "almost," he confesses, "as if I were kidnapping your child" (*Hellbox*, 165). But they are glad to have the money, glad to sell the car, and a bit perturbed to hear Malloy complain that the Duesenberg "isn't the car I agreed to buy" (*Hellbox*, 168).

The car, it turns out, has had a fancy spotlight added since Malloy saw it, and he insists on paying them $75 above the agreed-on price. The Van Burens have been wealthy and upper-class all their lives and will be wealthy again as soon as Mr. Van Buren finishes law school. (He is about to become the *Harvard Law Review*'s editor.) Malloy has been wealthy for a matter of months, but on this occasion he has advantages over the young couple, and it pleases him to behave generously towards them. The Van Burens' decision to accept his generosity, moreover, betokens their security, whatever their income happens to be. "Transaction" is obviously more than its bland title and very bland ending say it is. This story is a positive print of the negative "Graven Image": If the patrician Browning, temporarily in need of a favor from his former lower-class schoolmate, had continued to charm and support him—as he proved incapable of doing—perhaps the Undersecretary, like Malloy, could have continued to befriend him. O'Hara comes under much fire for his concern about the class system in American society, but almost all of what he wrote about social classes suggested that he was a genuine democrat who, nonetheless, observed the difficulties and possibilities of transcending the class system.

O'Hara's fiction seems to say, "Never assume you know anything." If the reader has been exposed to one view of the class structure in "Graven Image," the exact situation with different characters in "Transaction" teaches a different lesson. Even with the same characters at a different point, a story may not work out identically; and even if the two situations were back-to-back, the characters may have learned something from the first situation that they could use to reverse the second one.

Or they may not. As one character observes in "Last Respects," speaking of his brother's lifelong inexplicable behavior, "nobody ever really knows anybody else" (*TE,* 156). That story, written in the late 1940s, was O'Hara's first of many tales about returning home for a funeral. Such patterns that appear in his later short fiction start to manifest themselves in the late 1940s. Most of the later Malloy stories are stories of reminiscence, a theme that will predominate O'Hara's short fiction of the 1960s.

The reconsideration of the past and its odd ever-presence in the present will become his strong suit, and that theme, too, starts manifesting itself in these Duesenberg stories. In "Miss W.," as Malloy drives the car from Cambridge he rescues a college girl stranded in a ditch on a cold night. Returning her to her junior college, he finds that the headmistress is an old girlfriend of his. They settle in for a shared sandwich and some reminiscence. The ex-lovers acknowledge that time has changed their appearance for the worse. "I'm fat as a pig," Miss W. bluntly tells Malloy, "but so are you." Such clear-eyed assessments of middle age and the easy sharing of memories and food, O'Hara seems to say, almost compensate for the visions of youth and the ambitions and hungers that they replace. "Miss W." ends with a bittersweet acknowledgment that these former lovers are no longer who they were:

"It's not too bad," she said.
He said nothing.
She put down her sandwich. "Well, at least we can pretend it isn't."
"Right," he said.

This is a low-key version of Hemingway's famous despairing exchange between Jake and Brett at the end of *The Sun Also Rises* when he responds to her assertion, "We could have had such a damned good time together," with "Yes. Isn't it pretty to think so?" O'Hara's lovers have come down to earth more easily than Hemingway's, and their illusions are not as much shattered as they are slightly chipped.

Neither of the two remaining Duesenberg stories, "Pardner" and "Conversation in the Atomic Age," significantly advances Malloy's development. "Pardner" tells an anecdote about Malloy on his way to California in his new Duesenberg, encountering an obnoxious teenager who owns a restaurant in the Midwest. Malloy invents a clichéd identity, that of a rich Texas oilman, and foists it on the gullible youth, who desperately tries to assert his equal status with Malloy. Malloy is having none of it, which is why he is playing the mean trick on the youth. If the story does represent an advance, it is in Malloy's values, and in O'Hara's. Whereas in the 1930s, O'Hara found it hilarious to confuse his characters and readers with double-talk, such as "What do you hippum the mob?," everywhere he could, here he represents decorous behavior, while at the same time lampooning the youth's rudeness, his mistreatment of the waitress he employs, and his crust in presuming to ask Malloy personal questions. But O'Hara has at this stage in his career done as much as his lampooning can do.

So too with the sarcastic treatment in "Conversation in the Atomic Age."[41] Finally arrived in California, Malloy dines with a Los Angeles society woman, a friend of his wife. (In all four of these stories, Malloy has a meal or a drink, which may explain his weight gain.) Biographer Finis Farr cites this story as "a virtuoso performance in the manner of the Delphian sketches of 1928," emphasizing O'Hara's "mastery of the speaking voice" (Farr, 208). While that observation is perfectly accurate, Farr (who is far and away the least perceptive of O'Hara's three biographers) overlooks a real limitation of O'Hara hidden in those virtues, namely, that the technique of conveying spoken mannerisms is one O'Hara had been working on in print since 1928 and one that he had long since mastered. In the late 1940s O'Hara is, sadly, still relying on the same technique that served him well from his Delphian speakers through Pal Joey. So, in "Conversation in the Atomic Age," sitting across a luncheon table from his latest monologuist, an unperceptive, snobbish society woman, is Jim Malloy, who, like his creator, is bored silly listening to her rattling on, just as the husband was listening to his wife's prattling in "The Alumnae Bulletin" nearly two decades before. Malloy and O'Hara will, after a hiatus in the 1950s, be supremely equipped to develop this technique and move it, along with O'Hara's reputation, another notch forward. Or even two.

Return to Gibbsville

Brooding over his literary career in the 1940s, O'Hara finally decided to stop writing short stories and focus on the novel.[42] Having written four long novels by 1960, he then resumed writing short stories, publishing *Sermons and Soda-Water* that year and *Assembly* the next. These new batches of stories, however, differed from the short fiction he had been writing before, because he could apply to them the lessons in narrative techniques he had learned during his decade-long experiment with the novel. In musical terms, O'Hara's favorite analogy for fiction writing, he had determined to master an entire orchestra in writing those novels, learning each musician's strengths and limits, testing which instruments could produce which sounds, adding new compositions to his repertoire to see which ones fit with his orchestra; then he decided to apply these lessons to his other role as a solo performer.

In certain stories, the techniques O'Hara learned from writing novels are apparent: Jim Malloy's narrative tone derives plainly from the retrospective narration of *Ourselves to Know*, and the seamless transitions in "Flight" resemble those in *From the Terrace*, an 897-page novel consisting of one long chapter. All his late short fiction uses a greater quantity and variety of narrative tools than the earlier ones do. So much of the early fiction's techniques are gone: no more monologues, parodic writing, mood pieces, character sketches, or vignettes. The main technique of the early stories, the flat presentation of a single crucial, subtly significant scene, has been replaced by his use of several crucial scenes augmented by an often leisurely introduction, all stitched together by a series of mini-essays. Irving Howe complained mightily about this new discursiveness, calling O'Hara "pedantic, inserting passages into his stories which boastfully set other writers straight about" issues their writing got wrong.[43] In "Mrs. Stratton of Oak Knoll," his characters discuss at length F. Scott Fitzgerald's female characters and how they differ from the slightly bolder type of woman depicted in artist John Held's illustrations of Fitzgerald's magazine fiction. O'Hara may have originally observed this discrepancy in the 1920s when he compared Fitzgerald's stories with Held's illustrations, but if he did he certainly could not have fit a lengthy conversation about his comparison into his own stories until they became loosely structured. "His prose is no longer as terse as it once was," Howe goes on to complain in his review of *Assembly*. (*Assembly* would, as it turned out, contain O'Hara's tersest short fiction of the 1960s, and Howe's complaints would be among the more moderate of those critics who called for him to return to his earlier, punchier style.)

Clearly his novels had taught him, for better or worse, how to pace his writing, how to dole out description at a leisurely rate, and how to supply bursts of staccato dialogue that advanced the plot suddenly and in an unexpected direction. His previous stories, short and tightly focused, had no room to vary their pace; O'Hara realized from the novels written in the interim that a varied pace—and the introduction of strong plot elements—would enhance one of the themes of his later stories, unpredictability. So his later stories, with their varied and sometimes shocking twists of plot, encouraged critics to call them sensational. Their sexual content similarly encouraged critics to find them lewd. And admirers of O'Hara's bang-bang presentation of a single scene naturally found his longer, later stories discursive, digressive, disappointing, flaccid, and unreadable. Similar complaints were also directed, with some justice, at his last few ponderous novels. Such complaints are directed at most artists whose techniques grow more complex. Whatever limitations his later work had, O'Hara's crisis of the 1940s did change him from a craftsman into the artist he wanted to be.

O'Hara's artistry also coincided with his ever lessening regard for the commerce of publishing. By 1960 he was financially well-off and would grow far more so during that prolific decade, producing many more stories than *The New Yorker* or *The Saturday Evening Post* could publish. The income his stories produced, moreover, was far less than the income from his novels. So he, not the marketplace, established the length, subject matter, and language of his new stories. Coincidentally, as he became more financially independent, the publishing industry of the 1960s relaxed its puritanical standards, allowing him to explore racier material at exactly the time he felt most inclined to do so.

There were superficial similarities between O'Hara's short fiction of the late 1940s and the early 1960s. The men's-club settings of "Graven Image" and the Cothurnos Club stories reappear in his first two collections of the 1960s, in the story "In The Silence" in *Assembly* and in the novella "We're Friends Again" in *Sermons and Soda-Water*, both of which are narrated by Jim Malloy, the third-person protagonist of the four Duesenberg stories in *Hellbox*. But it is a more mature Malloy who tells these first-person stories, and they present a more mature view of men's clubs as well, with both coming from a far more mature O'Hara.

From his Hollywood and *Pal Joey* money, O'Hara was able to afford to socialize in men's clubs and even to be invited to join some of them, and it was obviously a heady experience for him, given his parvenu status and his interest in the rich and powerful. Looking out from a window of Manhattan's grand Metropolitan Club at the crowd below herding itself into a subway entrance one day in the late 1940s, he told fellow member Richard Watts, " 'They envy us, Dick.' Watts disagreed and said he believed the people only wanted to get home and couldn't care less who was peering down from club windows" (Farr, 207). But by 1960 he had enough money and had hung around in men's clubs long enough to see their glittery allure tarnished. No longer exotic places where the rich and powerful dangled prestigious jobs before each other, or where wealthy actors were asked for four-figure loans over drinks, the men's clubs in O'Hara's fiction became places for friends to unwind, or meet, or tell each other stories.

"In the Silence" is one such Marlovian story, told by Malloy to his friend Charles Ellis, about a fellow club member whom Malloy has not seen since his days as a young reporter in Gibbsville. The man Malloy remembers was an invalid, although Malloy never learns exactly what kind, married to an attractive woman. The young Malloy, invited to stay overnight with the couple in their remote hunting lodge, found himself attracted to the woman. The theme of Malloy's emerging sexuality pervades several of the stories he narrates, from "The Doctor's Son," in which the 15-year-old Malloy both sees and experiences passion, to "A Man To Be Trusted," in which a barely pubescent Malloy tries to express his confused sexual urges for another married woman. In all these stories, the straightforward lust he feels is tinged with shame and guilt and love and gratitude and anger and general confusion. Straightening out such an emotional tangle proves impossible for the young Malloy and, as he narrates the story years later, is still somewhat difficult for the older Malloy.

"In The Silence" ends with typical O'Hara irresolution, as he yields a clue, but not an answer, to the question of how to read the story. Acknowledging the sexual tension between her and Malloy, the woman thanks him for his understanding in not acting on it and gives him an old-fashioned silver matchbox as a going-away present:

I haven't the faintest idea what happened to the match box. It was very
good-looking. One side was a picture of a pack of hounds baiting a bear.
I think the other side was blank.

A trivial, even seemingly capricious point to end the story on, the matchbox underscores O'Hara's point about conflict: Some conflicts will always
be accessible and even obvious, such as the hounds baiting the bear,
while others will always remain inscrutable. Acting solely by instinct in
the cabin that weekend, Malloy decided that forcing his attention on the
woman would be less than appropriate, but he cannot be certain, and
he is unsure of his decision even when telling the story years later. The
woman praised him and indeed gave him the matchbox because of his
unusual sensitivity, but even now the relationship between the woman
and her husband and her reaction to Malloy is unknowable. The story is
about inconclusiveness but it is not inconclusive. It is a firm and positive
statement that certain knowledge is hard to come by. Sensitive people,
of whom Malloy is one, have to get by with their perceptions and must
learn to live with their doubts.

"Exterior: With Figure" also ends with the young Malloy's frustration
in his search for certainty. Through this first-person account of his
Gibbsville days, Malloy chronicles the Armour family and their sad end,
describing the difficulty of truly understanding the Armours, whom he
knew as well as anybody in Gibbsville. "It is a curious thing about the
old-fashioned small town," Malloy says, "where everyone was supposed
to know all about everyone else, that there were so many people whose
privacy was impenetrable" (*HB*, 52). That privacy remains intact at the
end, when Malloy recognizes how little he can ever know about the
family's benign patriarch:

> And Harry Armour. Henry W. Armour himself. Harry Armour. Henry W.
> Armour. Mr. Armour. He was—what? A man who stood and looked at
> nothing? I do not know. I wish I knew. I want to know and I never can
> know. I wish, I wish, I knew. (*HB*, 67)

Malloy refrains from making judgments about the people he grew up
with because he recognizes how much of everyone's life is private and
mostly unknowable, even to themselves. More than merely babbling
Armour's name redundantly, Malloy is reflecting in his concluding paragraph on what name to call him and, implicitly, who Armour was to him.
If *he* is uncertain, he implies, how can any observers comfortably draw
conclusions about people they think they know well?

The married women with whom the young Malloy flirts in "In The Silence" and "A Man To Be Trusted" are both flattered yet aware of how little control Malloy has over his sexual impulse. Both women consequently treat him with affection but also with condescension. Sexuality is a subject O'Hara was criticized for handling as often (his worst critics said "obsessively") and as honestly (those same critics would have said "vulgarly") as he did. But the appeal of that subject for O'Hara derives from its universality and the vague sense of shame his culture attaches to it.

Actually the subject of these stories is Malloy's humanity and only incidentally his sexuality. Malloy succeeds as a narrator because O'Hara, in developing him as a rounded character over the years, distinguishes him from the protagonists of the sketches and satires whose traits O'Hara isolates. Malloy is sympathetic and subjective where O'Hara's previous anonymous narrator was empathetic and objective. But O'Hara cannot reduce Malloy to a single set of primary characteristics; he must re-create the whole person, lingering on each detail long enough to address it fully but never suggesting that Malloy consists of only one or several details. Malloy is a rounded protagonist, and his confusion as he tries to make sense of a lifetime of static and changing emotions is his most human characteristic.

"Fatimas and Kisses" is a coming-of-age Malloy story, fully as effective as the first, "The Doctor's Son," written 32 years before, and less of a sketch involving setting and character. As focused as "The Doctor's Son" was on young Malloy's perceptions about adult life, its rambling structure allowed but did not direct the reader to follow Malloy's perceptions. "The Doctor's Son," while more developed than O'Hara's other narrative ventures at the time, still shared his early reluctance to spin a tight plot. Its relative plotlessness makes it resemble another (unidentified) 1935 story, which O'Hara described as "only a mood read" (*Letters,* 103). "Fatimas and Kisses" establishes a strong plot through the narrator's sensitive insights into the characters and setting.

A technical measure of O'Hara's mastery in "Fatimas and Kisses" is his skill in using dialect. Where he had earlier been a linguistic experimenter in displaying spoken mannerisms in phonetic detail—for example, in "I Never Seen Anything Like It" rendering Brooklynese with rich glottal detail in practically every sentence, including the title—here he practices restraint. One of his protagonists, a grocer named Donald Lintz, grew up as an uneducated Pennsylvania Dutch farm boy whose speech pattern the younger O'Hara would have taken as an open invitation for the use of wild and imaginative spellings. Here he limits his creative spelling to a word or two per paragraph. Instead of a constant stream of phonetic dialect, which must be appreciated in its totality, O'Hara encouraged his readers to mull over the occasional oddly spelled word, sounding it out in their minds or even aloud, making the rest of Lintz's dialect resonate even more sharply. When Malloy asks him how he came to join the Marine Corps in his youth, Lintz responds, "How I heart abaht the Marines?" A man who pronounces "heard about" like that would almost certainly pronounce "the Marines" as "da Mah-reence," but O'Hara relies on his readers to supply the vast majority of Lintz's dialect.

More than dialect is exhibited in that early conversation between Lintz and Malloy. The plot of "Fatimas and Kisses" is being served, again subtly: Lintz had been enticed by a recruiting poster to join the Marines. Much later in the story, when Lintz murders his wife and children, Malloy correctly figures out that he was clinically insane because Lintz's description of his wife's lover matched a cartoon figure in another poster Lintz saw every day at lunch.

Malloy's narrative growth and sensitivity are a result of his new reportorial role, which he fills much more comfortably than the role of a third-person *ficelle* listening to a foolish society woman in "Conversation in the Atomic Age." In "The Man with the Broken Arm," Malloy's strained involvement in the plot forces him to assume a Maugham-like, artificial, "I-am-the-narrator" archness, and in stories in which he is a central character (as in *Hope of Heaven* or "We're Friends Again") Malloy is too entwined in the action emotionally to give much of a narrative overview. It is in stories where he operates as both a plausible observer and motivated raconteur, like "Fatimas and Kisses" or "The Girl on the Baggage Truck" or "Exterior: With Figure," that Malloy is most effective.

Malloy explains the economic status of Lintz's store and at the same time shows how the store served Gibbsville's social needs and how it had an effect not only on Gibbsville but on Malloy personally. The significance of the store is revealed as early as the story's second sentence:

> If you wanted ice cream, by the quart or by the cone, you could get it at Lintzie's; you could buy cigarettes and the less expensive cigars, a loaf of bread, canned goods, meats that did not require the services of a butcher, penny candy and boxed bon-bons, writing tablets and pencils, and literally hundreds of articles on display-cards that novelty salesmen had persuaded Lintzie to put on his shelves and which he never seemed to reorder.

Part 1

This informative catalogue includes items that help explain the title. (When the adolescent Malloy tries to buy Fatima cigarettes to smoke with his girlfriend, Mrs. Lintz cannily treats him to several packs, in implicit exchange for his silence on *her* secret love life.) This description also includes plot-operative information on the Lintzes' relationship with salesmen: Mrs. Lintz is persuaded into bed fairly easily by a series of salesmen, one of whom Mr. Lintz shoots and kills just before killing his wife and children.

Malloy also shows his own marginal yet plausible involvement in the plot: he began observing the Lintzes' shop as a middle-class boy whose family preferred to patronize the tonier downtown stores. After the death of Malloy's father, however, the family comes to rely on the Lintzes' willingness to keep irregular hours, letting the Malloys and other poorer families stock their meager larders on short notice. The Lintzes, too, are willing to extend credit to poorer families, unlike the middle-class stores. (Pat Collins's garage in "Pat Collins" fills a need similar to the Lintzes' store in that both offer the same no-questions-asked policy to their sometimes disheveled clients, including "semi-emergency" service at all hours.) After a long expository section showing his changing personal relationship with the Lintzes, Malloy becomes professionally involved in speculating on the quadruple murder. As the local newspaper reporter covering the crime scene, he offers the best explanation of Lintz's motives. He understands Lintz's state of mind because of all the hours he spent drinking with the shopkeeper. (Again, this plot element is entirely plausible given Malloy's relative poverty at the time and Lintz's generosity in picking up bar tabs.) Through a lifetime of close observation of the Lintzes, Malloy is perfectly positioned to narrate their story, combining both a necessary involvement with the plot and a detachment from it.

The first-person narration, studded heavily with details, reads like a memoir, which suits O'Hara's new narrative style.[44] His former anonymous narrator could not plausibly linger over a detail or elaborate on a character's past without the reader calling into question his objectivity. But Malloy can reasonably indulge himself in personal, even idiosyncratic, observations with no radical change in the story's point of view. Of course, garrulousness and haphazard narration are not risk-free: should any observation fail to engage the reader, or any off-the-wall remark confuse the reader, or any chatty reminiscence veer off in the direction of pointlessness—all insurmountable barriers to O'Hara's detractors such as Irving Howe, Brendan Gill, Granville Hicks, Louis Auchincloss, and Gore Vidal, among others—then the stories fail.

But O'Hara's new style generally succeeds because Malloy's tone (and the tone of stories deriving from it) consistently entertains. Defensive and argumentative with critics and editors about his writing, O'Hara seems in practice to have gradually adopted the advice heaped on him by *New Yorker* editors to make his fiction more explicit.[45] In the 1960s he strove harder to entertain and correspondingly placed less emphasis on his stories' worth as terse brainteasers. Entertainment was a fairly low priority for the young O'Hara: he demanded that readers lift their share of the load and search for the meaningful details he carefully planted in the stories. Now he was prepared to plant more numerous and more prominent clues, making the reader's job less strenuous.

Almost as soon as O'Hara had invented the *New Yorker* short story, critics were rightly complaining about the limitations of his tight, oblique, plotless vignettes. Several stories in *The Doctor's Son* collection, one critic remarked, were "[m]ere portraits of futility [that] . . . fail in bringing out the significance Mr. O'Hara evidently feels to be latent in them."[46] Ten years later, reviewing *Pipe Night*, Lionel Trilling argued that short-short stories, at least those stories that Americans were writing, had run their course:

> [T]he very short story, with its well-taken bitter or pathetic point, is getting more and more tiresome, what with its situation so briskly set up and its insight so neatly given and the author skipping so nimbly out of the way, leaving the reader with the emotion on his hands to do with it what he can. Katherine Mansfield bastardized the great Chekhov to create this genre and we have all admired it for two decades while secretly we have been bored with it.[47]

Mansfield (as well as Hemingway) succeeded in writing the oblique Chekhovian story as a reaction against the very popular sentimental and plot-heavy stories of the previous generation's masters, O. Henry and Bret Harte. But now having joined, and even renovated, the bandwagon of Mansfield and Hemingway, and having driven it finally into the ground, O'Hara realized during his hiatus of the 1950s that he wanted to return in the direction of accessibility. To do so, he employed Malloy's tone, if not his actual presence, as his vehicle.

Because Malloy's leisurely tone eventually (though not invariably) introduces plot elements, readers no longer needed to maintain a steely eyed vigilance searching for minute details by which to understand O'Hara's stories. Now, he was quite deliberately making his stories more accessible to his readers: in a 1963 letter, he explained that "having been one of the leading practitioners of the oblique and the plotless, I have recently been putting action back into my stories" (*Letters*, 430).

One technique is the inclusion of a long expository section in which virtually no action occurs. Although plenty of background information, for example, about Malloy, the Lintzes, and Gibbsville is given in the first 10 pages of "Fatimas and Kisses," the first plot element is not introduced until halfway through the story:

> One afternoon, after the paper had gone to press and the other reporters had gone home, the phone rang on the city editor's desk and I went to answer it. "Malloy speaking," I said. (*WFW*, 100)

In the 1930s, O'Hara would have begun the story at this point, specifying the time (by inserting after "One afternoon" the phrase "in 1925") and location (substituting "the Gibbsville *Standard*" for "the paper"). But the development of Malloy precludes that terse structure. The emphasis O'Hara lays on Malloy is evident in the final few lines, after the police chief has accepted Malloy's view that Lintz was insane at the time of the killing:

> We walked in silence halfway to Lintzie's, then the chief spoke. "I thought a great deal of your father. What's a young fellow with your education throwing it all away when you could be doing some good in the world?"
> "What education? I had four years of high school," I said.
> "You were away to college," he said.
> "Away, but not to college."
> "Oh, then you're not much better than the rest of us," he said.
> "I never said I was, Chief."
> "No, you never said it, but you act it. Your father was better than most of us, but he didn't act it."
> "No, he didn't have to," I said.

Lacking Dr. Malloy's self-confidence, his insecure son will not be happy measuring himself against the challenges of Gibbsville. If he does not leave town soon, he will never know if he could have been more than just the best reporter in this "third class city." He understands that he needs a more adventurous life than Gibbsville can afford him and he realizes, in the final conversation with the chief, that it will be a long time before he grows up.

Another fictive structure that O'Hara develops in these late stories is the use of a frame around his central story. He used this structure sparingly before: "Bread Alone" begins with Hart at the baseball game with his son, miserable and apprehensive, and then flashes back to explain chronologically how Hart found himself in that uncomfortable position. O'Hara will go on to develop this frame tale, notably in long stories such as "James Francis and the Star" and "Pat Collins," both of which start with a curious scene late in his protagonists' lives, and then flash back deep into the past to show how such an odd scene could have come about. In *Sermons and Soda-Water* and elsewhere, Malloy begins or ends a story in the present, the 1960s, as he recounts an incident that happened in the 1930s. But "The Man with the Broken Arm," the narrative technique of which O'Hara soon abandoned, begins in medias res: on the morning after Malloy witnesses an appalling incident aboard ship, in which a well-known actress has humiliated her former husband, also a performer, on the ship's stage. She ignored him, laughed through his lines, and generally upstaged him. Malloy resolves to embarrass her in turn, but her ex-husband surprisingly helps her out of the jam Malloy creates. (Malloy's motivation for revenge is marginal at best in this story, which may have its origins in a transatlantic cruise O'Hara took in 1938 when he discovered his first wife was a fellow passenger.) The ship's purser, conspiring with Malloy, comments at the end, "It didn't work out quite as we'd expected." Malloy gets the last line: " 'What does?' I said."

Surprise became O'Hara's stock-in-trade in the 1960s. As he explained to a *Saturday Evening Post* editor, "I want Post readers to be constantly surprised. I do not want them to think that they know what to expect when they see my name on a story" (*Letters*, 430). But he usually took greater care than he does in "The Man with the Broken Arm" to motivate his characters plausibly.

Presenting himself as a hard drinker in "Fatimas and Kisses," for example, Malloy tells of drinking in a different bar from the one he frequented with Lintz, a bar where he overheard a conversation between two out-of-town salesmen about the availability of Mrs. Lintz to any salesman willing to "give her a dozen samples or shave your prices a little" (*WFW*, 99). O'Hara portrays Gibbsville as a small enough town that Malloy could plausibly spend time in both bars. (Set in a big city, such a coincidence would be implausible.) Yet the town is large enough that O'Hara rarely uses one particular bar as a setting for his stories.

In inventing a town to be used and reused in story after story, it would seem very tempting for O'Hara to limit the number of his settings and characters, but he avoids such recurrences. Several stories— "The Gunboat and Madge," "The Bucket of Blood," "The Gangster," "Pat Collins," "Imagine Kissing Pete," in addition to "Fatimas and Kisses"—are set in Gibbsville bars in the 1920s, but each story features a different bar. O'Hara also varied the names of Gibbsville's doctors, reporters, bankers, and citizens generally. Such divergence may make O'Hara appear repetitive or superficial to the hasty observer. "One of the critical platitudes about John O'Hara's writing," Guy Davenport observes, "is that he is repetitious. He is, on the contrary, one of the most varied of writers."[48] O'Hara's trick is to revisit a theme many times, varying the particulars just enough to make his readers reconsider the conclusions they drew the last time.

Sometimes O'Hara will reuse small details from story to story: assigning the surname Lundy to several minor characters in the Gibbsville stories "Fatimas and Kisses" and "Afternoon Waltz," for example, could be an oversight or it could be the beginning of a family profile that O'Hara never developed. But sometimes he clearly repeats a small detail deliberately. For example, the cop in "A Respectable Place" who fakes his suicide has the same given name as his maternal uncle, a needless repetition that beginning fiction writers are wisely cautioned against. Or in the later story "The Locomobile," the name of the story's antagonist is Arthur, which is also the given name of the protagonist's advisor. These repetitions are neither clumsy nor careless but evoke a sense of verisimilitude. In life, after all, when a given name crops up repeatedly, it is regarded as a simple coincidence and usually ignored. O'Hara is seeking to re-create that same circumstance when he repeats a name, either within a story or between several stories.[49]

Other times the connections are more overtly unifying: O'Hara tells us that Reese is a common name in the Welsh mining town in "The Doctor's Son," and he informs the reader in "Mrs. Stratton of Oak Knoll" of the background of artist Evan Reese, who comes from a Pennsylvania town much like Gibbsville. And sometimes there are figures who do appear in several Gibbsville stories: Malloy himself, of course, and Julian English from *Appointment in Samarra,* who appears fleetingly in several other O'Hara works, and the Stokes and Hofman families, who represent the upper crust of Gibbsville.[50] The Stokeses and the

Hofmans are mentioned by O'Hara's characters far more often than they actually appear. "Pat Collins" is about the Hofman family, as "The General" and "The Strong Man" are about branches of the Stokes clan, but more typically they appear offstage. O'Hara tries to create a town that is consistent and clearly recognizable yet is sufficiently inconsistent to evoke the unpredictability of life. For the most part, he succeeds at suggesting the endless variability of his highly stratified town.

Actually, the Stokeses and Hofmans are everywhere and nowhere: any attempt to derive a synoptic vision of their story or even to draw a simple family tree is more frustrating than fruitful, and this is probably O'Hara's intention. Rather than creating a history of the influence of money on Gibbsville, O'Hara is far more interested in creating the impression that some rich families control the town, though the Hofmans' and Stokeses' influence and even their identities remain murky. The secretive title character of "Clayton Bunter," though neither a Stokes nor a Hofman, is wealthy, but he is "not even the twentieth richest man in Gibbsville." Yet he is still sufficiently wealthy to dominate his family and acquaintances. Most of the Gibbsvillians wealthier than Bunter must be Hofmans or Stokeses, since we read about so many of them in O'Hara's short fiction. Among the Stokes women, there is Harriet Stokes Shields in "Afternoon Waltz"; Minerva (Minnie) Stokes who becomes Minnie Stokes McHenry in "A Case History"; Althea Stokes in "Mrs. Allenson"; Arielle Stokes in "The Strong Man"; Sophronia Stokes Hightower in "The General," whose unusual first name reappears in "The Skeletons," where Elsie Stokes marries into the family of one Sophronia Roach. All of these Stokes women inhabit Gibbsville in the first few decades of the twentieth century, but none of their names appear in each other's stories, leaving the impression that they have a large but faceless presence in the town. They are distant enough from one another to share little other than a name, with their large fortune allowing them to hold sway over other characters' lives.

The Hofmans are an even older and richer Gibbsville family. O'Hara first wrote about them in the early 1930s, in a lost novella entitled "The Hofman Estate." (Outside of the few early Malloy stories and *Appointment in Samarra*, O'Hara's interest in exploiting Gibbsville in fiction began in 1960 with *Sermons and Soda-Water*.) Whit Hofman appears briefly in *Appointment in Samarra* and significantly in "Pat Collins," but for the most part he and members of his family are discussed by other characters: "old Mrs. W. S. Hofman," Whit's mother, for example, steps from her horse-drawn carriage in "Claude Emerson, Reporter" to look for the title character, a scene that illustrates Emerson's contacts with the rich and powerful; in "A Good Location," set a few years later, the same "old Mrs. Hofman," now in her chauffeured limousine, visits the filling station of two co-owners who want to relocate their establishment to a more favorable setting, which is suggested by the title.

Unlike the fabulously wealthy inhabitants of Henry James's fiction, O'Hara's superrich characters do not exist merely to show what people would do if they had no money worries. Seen at a distance, their function is mostly to give O'Hara's poorer characters idealized figures about whom they can fantasize. When O'Hara actually depicts his wealthy characters, they often are as unhappy as his poorer ones, only about different things. Whit Hofman in "Pat Collins" wants to be loved for qualities besides his money, but he is not; Junior Williamson in "The Girl on the Baggage Truck" aspires to political office, but he understands voters so little that he talks to Jim Malloy without realizing that Malloy has no money and is visiting Williamson's estate as the hired escort of one of his guests. And the wealthy Mrs. Stratton of Oak Knoll has a secret that will surprise her family and friends when she is dead: she has spent all her money and has no estate to leave them, revealing the irony in the title "Mrs. Stratton of Oak Knoll."

This story, leading off the first of O'Hara's short-story collections of the 1960s, appropriately introduces his major late theme, compassion. Told in the third person, the story's narrative perspective is that of Evan Reese, a successful representational painter, who—like Jim Malloy—stands in for O'Hara in several ways. In 1960, Reese has long been married, and he and his wife have settled into a child-free domesticity. Born in Pennsylvania, Reese is a comfortably middle-class artist who served on a World War II naval vessel in the Pacific, the equivalent of O'Hara's stint as a war correspondent. Reese is proud of his British (although non-English) heritage, argumentative over matters he knows about, and—to the point of this story—is an expert in the field of oil painting. The grandam of the title has lived in her mansion next door to the Reeses for several years without ever inviting them to call on her. When her grown son pays her a visit, however, he happens to run into Evan Reese and they strike up an acquaintance, immediately after which Mrs. Stratton suddenly invites the Reeses to her house. During the visit, Reese looks at her art collection, which includes works by Van Dyke, Rubens, and Gainsborough, and discerns instantly that they are forgeries. Mrs. Stratton knows he knows her secret, and she apologizes for her past unneighborly behavior but trusts him to keep quiet, which he resolves to do. Reese connects with Mrs. Stratton emotionally, sympathizing with her need to keep up appearances; and, after a decade of living next door without a friendly word between them, they are able to talk to each other like old and trusted friends at the story's end.

Reese resembles Jim Malloy in more than mere biographical details— their connection is their humanity, their sympathy, their human decency, allowing them to understand other people's pain. Compassion was the quality O'Hara felt his stories had most in common with one another, and "Mrs. Stratton of Oak Knoll" abounds in compassion, all the more strongly because of its unexpectedness, extending as it does from the crusty, unsentimental Reese to the wealthy and haughty Mrs. Stratton herself.[51]

Compassion is also the quality that most prominently emerges from *Sermons and Soda-Water,* the final page of which concludes: "What, really, can any of us know about any of us, and why must we make such a thing of loneliness when it is the final condition of us all? And where would love be without it?" Loneliness gives meaning to love, O'Hara asserts, much as Shakespeare's sonnets assert that the emptiness of death gives beauty its meaning. This seeming contradiction also crops up when O'Hara conjoins inevitability with surprise, or cruelty with compassion.

The compassion that Reese feels for Mrs. Stratton, or that Malloy expresses for his good friend Charles Ellis, requires time and depth and scope to be declared adequately, three qualities largely absent from O'Hara's early fiction and omnipresent in his late stories. O'Hara's early stories about compassion usually point out how someone deserving of it—the protagonist of "Pleasure," or of "Price's Always Open," or of "Do You Like It Here?"—receives cruelty instead. In his late stories, O'Hara shows the positive form of compassion, which generally extends over long periods of time.

All three novellas in *Sermons and Soda-Water* are framed by the calm present but are about the riotous past, before Malloy had learned compassion and maturity, qualities that motivated him to tell these tales. The final novella, by far the weakest of the three, is a memoir of reconciliation, as can be seen in its title. "We're Friends Again" tells a whirlwind story of the young Malloy's casual sexual affairs, which ruined some marriages, and his witnessing of other people's sexual high jinks, which ruined others. Malloy and Charles Ellis, two formerly estranged friends, reconcile in the frame part of the tale: after Ellis's wife dies, Malloy consoles him, telling him, from sad experience, what he can expect from widowerhood. Isolated from the main part of the story, the frame would make a sober tale in itself about reconciliation and accommodation between the two, but all the details about the complicated events of the 1930s—sexual, political, artistic, even subjects as far-ranging as espionage, Catholicism, and men's clubs—interfere with the progress of the story line.

One of the story's more intriguing asides has to do with Malloy's analysis of his writing and its subject matter: anticipating the wireless phone, Malloy claims that, even if it is invented someday while he is alive, he still belongs to the era of the "thirty-foot extension cord . . . an era already gone." Malloy accepts that a "writer belongs to his time and mine is past. In the days or years that remain to me, I shall entertain myself in contemplation of my time and be fascinated by the way things tie up, one with another," which would in fact become O'Hara's chief subject in the remaining decade (*S&S*, vol. III, 65–66).[52]

Things tying up, one with another, is the purpose of reminiscence, making sense of events that are confusing up close. In "We're Friends Again," Malloy is too close to the chaos that reigns over his life to give a coherent account of the issues he wants to resolve, and "Imagine Kissing Pete" suffers from the opposite problem: in it Malloy is an effective, informed narrator who is too often absent from the events that he is supposedly reporting. The only one of the three novellas set largely in Gibbsville, most of "Imagine Kissing Pete" is written from Malloy's perspective in New York City. There he gathers the story's facts by entertaining Gibbsville visitors and sometimes by returning briefly to the town to talk to old friends about events he has missed. Sometimes this method works, but other times credibility is strained, as when he quotes verbatim dialogue between a husband and wife that he has not heard other than in summary form months or years after the conversation. The title character (about whom, right before his wedding, a bridesmaid says, "Imagine *kissing* Pete, let alone the rest of it") remains repulsive throughout the long story, degenerating into an eye-patch-wearing, philandering pool hall manager, a far cry from the youth who spent time with Jim Malloy in Gibbsville's country club and enjoyed his college days at Princeton. As he does in all three novellas, O'Hara provides an upbeat ending to this sordid tale of a disastrous marriage, as Malloy, along with Pete and his wife, cry tears of joy at their son's Princeton graduation. Pete's rehabilitation, and his degeneration for that matter, require more motivation and characterization than O'Hara supplies: throughout the story, Malloy is repelled by Pete, even though he is a member of Malloy's crowd, and he presents Pete, even at his best, as an unsocialized buffoon whom he wants nothing to do with. Malloy's unwillingness to empathize with Pete, coupled with his physical distance from the story's details, prevents the warm and emotional ending from seeming fully earned.

In "The Girl on the Baggage Truck," however, O'Hara places Malloy in the knowledgeable position he holds in "We're Friends Again," while providing him with some of the authorial perspective of "Imagine Kissing Pete." In this, the most fully realized of the three tales, Malloy, working as a New York press agent for a film company (as O'Hara did in the early 1930s), escorts a Hollywood actress around town; part of his job is to disguise her romantic involvement with Thomas Rodney Hunterden, a mysterious and shady businessman. "The Girl on the Baggage Truck" may have been O'Hara's conscious attempt to rewrite, and deromanticize, F. Scott Fitzgerald's *The Great Gatsby*, which also concerns a love affair between a wealthy woman and a shady tycoon. Both stories end tragically with a fatal car crash on Long Island, and both are narrated by a young man close to the woman (and rather more distant from the mysterious figure). The main divergence from Fitzgerald's story comes in Malloy's contemptuous attitude toward Hunterden (born Thomas Rodney Huntzinger), an attitude that contrasts sharply with Nick Carraway's reverent view of Jay Gatsby (born James Gatz). Another element that deromanticizes *Gatsby*'s plot is Malloy's sexual attraction to the title character, which leads to a brief affair between the two. In O'Hara's story, Chottie Sears, the girl on the baggage truck, survives the car crash that kills her businessman-lover. The story ends years later, when Malloy visits her in her California home and provides a leisurely and very down-to-earth account of her life after her beauty was destroyed in the crash. Malloy admires how she keeps her privacy, maintains her dignity, earns a living, finds a man who loves her—there is not much about her later life that Malloy does not admire.

Endurance and survival on a reduced scale are hardly Fitzgeraldian virtues. The practical solutions O'Hara upheld here answered fundamentally different questions than those eternal ones Fitzgerald posed in *The Great Gatsby*, and will distinguish O'Hara's aims from his. O'Hara admired Fitzgerald's gift for prose: "Fitzgerald was a better just plain writer than all of us put together," he wrote to John Steinbeck. "Just words writing" (*Letters*, 224). But O'Hara felt Fitzgerald's romantic vision kept him from seeing how interesting the real world was, and how varied. For O'Hara, "the interest of the human life in his mind's eye was so self-evident," John Updike suggests, that "he saw no need to *make* it interesting."[53]

In the final paragraph of "The Girl on the Baggage Truck," Malloy clears up the mystery of Hunterden's past with dismissive contempt. The mystery had been that although Hunterden had listed Gibbsville as his birthplace in his *Who's Who* entry, Malloy could find no evidence of this claim. He wrote to his friend, Claude Emerson, a Gibbsville reporter, to look up Hunterden's origins, and the resourceful Emerson could find no trace of anyone ever named Hunterden so much as visiting Gibbsville. Where Fitzgerald had swathed Gatsby's past in the attractive cloak of mystery, O'Hara presents the details of Hunterden's past as flat-out lies. Far from intrigued, Malloy is simply offended by them. The sexual rivalry between Hunterden and Malloy (there is no comparable situation in *Gatsby*), gives another, less idealistic motive for their mutual antagonism.

Much as he admired Fitzgerald's elaborate, almost poetic prose style, O'Hara employed a much plainer prose. Almost every other writer indulges in metaphors and descriptions more than did O'Hara. In his second novel, he addressed the inadequacy of metaphors, conceding that they "are all right to give you an idea" but ultimately divert the reader from the writer's goal of explaining people (*OHC*, 126). He saw them, as well as physical descriptions of characters, as a kind of cheating, of verbal trickery. Instead he determined to let characters' actions and spoken words move his stories along. His philosophy of prose demanded that it be utilitarian, with its primary goal being the clear depiction of his characters, however unclear the meaning of those characters' actions may prove to be.

The traits of his fictional characters did not necessarily signify O'Hara's moral acceptance or rejection of them. As much as he admired the ability of a writer to produce clear prose, for example, he wrote a story praising an execrable prose stylist, "Claude Emerson, Reporter." The title character is based on real reporters with whom O'Hara worked during his brief stay on the *Pottsville Journal*. Since Emerson begins as a sportswriter, O'Hara may have modeled him partly on Walter S. Farquhar, an older sportswriter O'Hara admired, but another *Journal* reporter, Percy Knowlton, seems a likelier model. Like Emerson, Knowlton earned O'Hara's backhanded praise for being "one of the most painstaking newsgatherers I ever knew."[54]

"Painstaking" is a particularly apt word for Emerson's approach to news gathering, since in the story he suffers a good deal of pain, mostly caused by several punches to the stomach while pursuing a news story. Emerson's comical limitations are emphasized in the beginning of the story, which nonetheless is finally an encomium to his reportorial skill. Among his limitations is the curious but not rare fact that, for a good newspaper man, Emerson could not write well. O'Hara uses the noun *newsgatherer* rather than *newswriter* because writing is merely the unfortunate end product of Emerson's true gift, which is getting to the truth. His writing skills, such as they are, are mentioned only to be ridiculed: excerpts are cited to show the excesses of his "ornate" style, such as "the festive board groaned under the weight of delicious viands," a particularly elaborate description of a buffet table (*CCL*, 66). Emerson's cliché mongering derives from honest impulses: "Claude Emerson had never intended to be a writer. He learned early that there was a set journalistic phrase for nearly every detail of every event that made a news item, and when he had acquired them all he saw no reason to originate another batch" (*CCL*, 76). Emerson more than compensated for his lack of creative skills, however, with a dedication and thoroughness that newspeople need even more than writing talent and that O'Hara himself sorely lacked.

Having been fired several times in his newswriting career for a lack of diligence, O'Hara knew that Emerson's industriousness was far more valuable than his own gift for crafting a sentence, which alone kept him on newspaper staffs for as long as it did.[55] Whereas Emerson is dull, comically dressed, and reliable, the young O'Hara was wild, spiffy, and thoroughly unreliable. On the *Pottsville Journal* staff, O'Hara "learned condensation (and padding, too)"—his skill at condensing matter down to smaller and smaller intelligible increments was responsible for his style, especially in his first few decades of short-story writing (*OHC*, 35). Newspaper offices prized that style for its efficiency rather than its pithy elegance, but O'Hara took from the experience what he found useful. "The newspaper influence is a good one for the writer. It teaches economy of words. It makes you write faster. When you're on rewrite as I was, you can't fool around at half-past nine trying to write beautifully lacy prose" (*Artist*, 183). Instead, Emerson's plodding ways earned him the simple but descriptive term following his name in the title. He was a reporter, and the story shows how a reporter works.

For a long stretch, the story is largely descriptive: it tells how Emerson dressed, how he got started in the newspaper business, what his work habits were, and so on. This slow exposition is a writing strategy that suited O'Hara's last decade of short-story writing. If O'Hara had written this story three decades earlier, he would have begun with its first action, skipping the long expository section entirely, and probably would have ended it before all the information cohered.

The story proper starts after 15 or so pages of a leisurely sketch of Emerson's daily life: on his way to work, he gathers some sketchy facts about an explosion, rumored to be fatal, that happened yesterday. Through skillful questioning, and more skillful knowledge of whom in town to question, and even more skillful knowledge of whom to question by bullying and whom by flattering, Emerson discovers a scandalous and illegal experiment by the town's largest employer that cost a young chemist his life. But by the time Emerson knows these facts, he has also taken a beating, and the story—with none of Emerson's juicy facts—has been buried inside the newspaper by Emerson's editor, secretly on the payroll of the chemist's employer. Indebted to advertisers and timid by inclination, small-town papers at their best, O'Hara suggests, hide the truth more often than they show it. "Claude Emerson, Reporter," O'Hara's eloquent rationale for leaving the newspaper game, is also a tribute to the dedicated people who try to write well for small-town newspapers.

As an indictment of corruption, the story is incomplete, but O'Hara's purpose is not to expose corruption as much as it is to chronicle it. Emerson's corrupt boss, publisher Bob Hooker, epitomizes small-town journalism at its worst, though O'Hara takes care to show how and why Hooker arrives at his beliefs. Hooker is a much more rounded villain than, for example, the headmaster in "Do You Like It Here?" For that matter, Emerson is a far less naive figure than the boy in that story, understanding perfectly why Hooker buries his story and, even from the beginning, that it is the kind of story that Hooker will quash at every opportunity. But it is also the kind of story that Emerson is trained to report, and he needs to try, even knowing that a punch in the stomach may be his only reward. In O'Hara's world, from "Price's Always Open" through the later stories, heroism is uniformly punished.

Although Malloy is absent from "Claude Emerson, Reporter," the reference to Emerson in *Sermons and Soda-Water* shows that they know each other. But Malloy's voice is present in the story. The easy familiarity, the tonal register, the fascination with details, the precise diction of "Claude Emerson, Reporter" are perfectly consistent with Malloy's voice and are consistent in all the Gibbsville stories, whether Malloy is mentioned implicitly or explicitly. O'Hara understood that precision matters, claiming that "Every average reader knows a little more about

one thing than he does about all others, whether his specialty be phila-
telics or philology. And when he comes upon a story dealing with his
specialty, he wants it to be right" (*OHC*, 88). Matthew Bruccoli (himself
a professor of English), for example, approves O'Hara's portrait of a
fussy academic type in "Pat Collins" (*OHC*, 293).

That long story also describes convincingly the daily operations of a
small-town filling station in the 1920s. It was convincing because
O'Hara had done extensive research into gas station operations: "When
I wrote *Appointment in Samarra* I established a dummy garage business,
took my papers to a guy I know who is a v.p. at General Motors (who
wanted to know when the hell I had run a garage)."[56] This kind of precision served him well not only in creating other garage settings, such as
that in "A Good Location," but also in describing other kinds of businesses. These included the bars and eateries in "It's Mental Work,"
"The Gunboat and Madge," "The Bucket of Blood," "Leonard," and
"The Portly Gentleman"; the banks described in "Clayton Bunter,"
"Jurge Dulrymple," "All Tied Up," and "The Man on a Tractor"; the bar-
bershops in "Goodby, Herman," "Frankie," and "The Cellar Domain";
the newspaper offices in "Claude Emerson, Reporter," "Horizon," "The
First Day," and "Fatimas and Kisses." O'Hara's thorough immersion in
the gritty details of such operations lent a stamp of authenticity to his
Malloy and non-Malloy stories alike.

Whether Malloy or O'Hara's nameless narrator (Malloy's tonal twin)
narrates a story, the ring of truth sounds authoritatively. Malloy does not
narrate "A Case History" in *Assembly*, but other characters discuss his
scandalous fictionalizing about Gibbsville inhabitants:

> "... that piece of tripe Dr. Malloy's son wrote a few years ago," said
> McHenry.
> "Oh, but that was a novel. Fiction. He made all that up."
> "But he certainly gave this town a black eye."
> "That's what I don't understand, Arthur. If it was all made up, what
> were people so sore about?"
> "He gave the town a black eye, that's what. And not one damn thing
> he wrote about actually happened."
> "That's what I said. But you as a lawyer, and I as a physician, we
> know things *like* them happened."
> "Oh, hell, as far as that goes, I know some things that if young Mal-
> loy ever heard about them. . . ."
> "So do I, Arthur," said Dr. Drummond. (*Assembly*, 429)

73

O'Hara, through Malloy (or through his other narrator, as in the wicked passage just quoted), insists that what he is telling is the truth (or a higher, Aristotelian truth) and that those pretending to be outraged or scandalized by his writing are simply annoyed to have the truth exposed. Behind closed doors, among themselves, they, like McHenry and Dr. Drummond, openly and easily admit to the veracity of his observations.

Malloy's narrative voice gravitates toward the polar opposite of the first voice O'Hara cultivated to tell truths about society. That voice was that of the pseudosophisticate who tells truths by telling lies so outrageous that we instinctively trust their opposite to be true. The young O'Hara was filled with rage at people's profound dishonesty, especially to themselves, with the result that his early fiction is filled with the voice of this reprehensible hypocrite. But his later stories accept this widespread dishonesty and simply treat his characters' failings and their virtues in a clear and generally calm tone.

"Pat Collins" is told in this tone and manner, though Malloy neither narrates it nor appears in it. (Whit Hofman mentions his name once.) Striking Malloy's tone of amazement at how varied and unknowable a town can be, O'Hara asks,

> Who has to know the town as a whole? A physician. The driver of a meat-market delivery truck. A police officer. The fire chief. A newspaper reporter. A taxi driver. A town large enough to be called a town is a complex of neighborhoods, invariably within well-defined limits of economic character. . . . Nothing strange then, but only abrupt, when Pat Collins ceased to see Whit Hofman. (*CCL*, 318)

One of the techniques O'Hara uses in "Pat Collins" to censure Whit Hofman is to cut off his point of view and eventually to drop him altogether from the story line. Most of the story is told from Pat's perspective (as evidenced in the clause "when Pat Collins ceased to see Whit Hofman," instead of "when Pat and Whit ceased to see each other"), but O'Hara gradually distances Whit from the reader in such small increments that, although readers sympathize with Pat, they have little idea why. As badly as Whit behaves in starting a ruinous affair with Pat's wife, Madge, he has his reasons: his own wife, Kitty, treats him unkindly, for example. But O'Hara denies us any interior perspective on Whit's problems, presenting them in Whit's spoken words, not in his inner thoughts. In contrast, he explains Pat's problems at great length, in language much clearer and more persuasive than Pat himself could have chosen. And when Madge makes what O'Hara calls "her true confession" to Pat about the affair, he cuts her out of his life completely, just as O'Hara drops Whit Hofman from the story.

O'Hara characterizes Whit as a villain not by any positive statement but by the negative act of focusing elsewhere. He refuses to let Whit's side of the story be heard, much as Pat walks out on Madge's confession before she is through confessing: "Are you through with me?" she asks, to which he answers with a contemptuous laugh, "Am I through with you? Am *I* through with you."

At the same time that Pat disengages from Whit, however, he finds himself missing him the most. Pat

> wanted the impossible, to confide his perplexed anger in the one man on earth who would least like to hear it. He refused to solidify his wish into words, but he tormented himself with the hope that he could be on the same terms of companionship with the man who was responsible for his misery. (*CCL*, 310)

Hofman has committed two simultaneous offenses here, pursuing Madge and forcing Pat into isolation. Hofman is shielded by his great wealth from the privations Pat suffers. Embittered, Pat becomes a drunk and his business is ruined. Eventually, he rejoins the middle class when another wealthy Gibbsvillian lends him money to open a smaller garage than he owned when he met Whit.

The story's structure is typical of O'Hara's late long stories. It begins in the present, when Pat and Whit have stopped seeing each other socially, but quickly flashes back to the 1920s when their unusual and close friendship began. Called the archetypal O'Hara story, "Pat Collins" examines the "well-defined limits of economic character" in establishing social class in America.

Pat Collins—young, charming, industrious, brave—leaps over social barriers when he befriends wealthy Whit Hofman. The barriers are breached, as they are so often in O'Hara's America, by the car. Specifically, Pat owns the new garage in town, and Whit cruises in to fill his Mercer phaeton's gas tank and to satisfy his curiosity. Declaring cars to be strong indicators of his characters' natures, O'Hara often used them emblematically. In a Puritan sense, O'Hara's cars form outward signs of their owners' inward, spiritual characters. Automotive analogies, which O'Hara loved to use, also allowed him to explain the behavior of the upper classes he liked writing *about,* in terms that the middle classes he liked writing *for* could understand. In "Pat Collins," cars are the initial bond in the friendship between the middle-class Pat and upper-class Hofman, and they soon go on to strengthen that bond, sharing confidences with each other that they would never think of sharing with their closest family:

> Whit, in his shorts and shirt, and Pat, in his B.V.D.s, pleasantly tired from their exercise, and additionally numbed by the gin and ginger ales, were in that state of euphorious relaxation that a million men ten million times have called the best part of the game, any game. They were by no means drunk, nor were they exhausted, but once again they were back at the point of utter frankness.... "I have too damn many cousins in this town [*Whit says*]. If I confided in any of them they'd call a family conference, which is the last thing I want.... Kitty hates me. She hates me, and I'm not sure why." (*CCL,* 284)[57]

Pat tries to help Whit with his marital troubles, making Whit's later betrayal so much greater. This portrait of a friendship is the most detailed in O'Hara's work. Alfred Eaton and Lex Porter in *From the Terrace* approach this kind of intimacy, but both of them share the prickly independence of almost all of O'Hara's protagonists, preventing the prolonged expression of warm feelings that appears in "Pat Collins." (The friendship of Charles Ellis and Jim Malloy is asserted several times to be affectionate and long-lived, but their affection typically remains unexpressed.) Pat's camaraderie with Whit is detailed at length in order to make their eventual rift tragic rather than merely sad. Whit is early on shown to be generous, in patronizing Pat's filling station and giving it his approval; decent, in welcoming Pat and Madge into the town's country club; fair-minded, in dismissing the Collinses' Catholicism as a bar to their social advancement; and seemingly worthy of Pat's trust, in his initial discouragement of Madge's flirtations. But when she persists, his resolve weakens, and the Collinses' marriage suffers. As Fitzgerald said of his wealthy antagonist Tom Buchanan, Hofman could merely "retreat back into [his] money . . . and let other people clean up the mess [he] had made" of their lives.

The collection in which "Pat Collins" appears, *The Cape Cod Lighter,* is the first example of O'Hara's idiosyncratic and perhaps arrogant manner of organizing his stories within collections. The usual arrangement used by poets or musicians in arranging their individual works within larger entities is one that O'Hara had used himself in previous collections, including *Assembly* a year earlier: the artist would decide which work would be a strong opener, which one would finish the collection powerfully, and then devise a pattern of alternating them—long with short, comical with serious, and so on. The underlying assumption is that the individual works can be enhanced by such an artful arrangement. O'Hara confronted this premise by denying it. Starting with *The Cape Cod Lighter*, he arranged his subsequent short-story collections *alphabetically* by title, implying his stories could not be improved or undermined by any arrangement. Whatever order they are read in, O'Hara strongly implies, their quality will emerge just the same.

The title *The Cape Cod Lighter* has been described as mysterious or cryptic (Matthew Bruccoli defines it as a device for starting a wood fire, though its symbolic application still seems hazy), and that became another quality of late O'Hara titles in general. Whereas his first few collections tended toward stories with flat or generic titles, some containing the names of characters, like "Walter T. Carriman," or others a bland description ("Mr. Cass and the Ten Thousand Dollars," "The Gentleman in the Tan Suit"), these later stories more often repeat a phrase from the story that can be either meaningful or cryptic (as in "It's Mental Work" or "You Can Always Tell Newark"). Some titles with characters' names still recur—"Pat Collins" being a handy example—but the strikingly peculiar titles often serve as clues to O'Hara's elusive themes.

Months before the publication of *The Cape Cod Lighter*, O'Hara had been promising a volume composed exclusively of long Gibbsville stories to be entitled *Third Class City*, a phrase O'Hara uses in several stories ("Imagine Kissing Pete," "The Weakness," and "Claude Emerson, Reporter" among them) to describe Gibbsville. "I plan to publish a book in the fall," O'Hara announced in the spring of 1962, "to be called THIRD CLASS CITY, which will be several long stories about guess where? ... I have finished two, and am finishing a third" (*Letters*, 393–94). *Third Class City* seems modeled more closely on *Sermons and Soda-Water* than on *Assembly*, his previous two collections, but when *The Cape Cod Lighter* came out that fall, it was a collection set only partly in Gibbsville, and its stories were of less than novella length.

Why did O'Hara change his plan to publish a volume exclusively about Gibbsville? A simple answer is that over the years O'Hara very confidently described many projects that never appeared: his letters from the 1930s and 1940s were chock-full of projected ideas—usually for novels or plays—described in enthusiastic detail, of which there remains no trace. *Third Class City* may have been one such project. But if

77

so, it was one that he could have easily completed. The posthumously published 864-page collection entitled *Gibbsville PA*, in fact, consists exclusively of stories set there, virtually all of which were written in the 1960s. Had he wanted to, O'Hara surely could have filled a volume of Gibbsville short stories with what he had on hand at any point in that decade. But doing so would have invited critics to compare the quality of his Gibbsville and non-Gibbsville stories, and O'Hara was particularly touchy about comparisons between his various works. Critics who praised his novels irritated O'Hara when they suggested that he wrote better novels than short stories, and vice versa. The ultimate tale about the dangers of comparing O'Hara's work to itself occurred during *Pal Joey*'s second run on Broadway, when a friend gushed that she enjoyed the play even more the second time around. "What was the matter with it the first time?" O'Hara snapped at her, sensitive as always to a dash of criticism within a flood of praise (MacShane, 156). Why give critics a chance to urge him to stick to Gibbsville stories or to refrain from ever writing one again?

No matter how long O'Hara wrote about Gibbsville, the town never aged. If anything, Gibbsville grew younger as O'Hara grew older, much as James Fenimore Cooper's Deerslayer novels were set further and further in the past the older Cooper grew. Many of O'Hara's later stories reflect on past events, often in a social setting—a wedding or funeral—that reminds the characters of crucial decisions they made in their youth and whether those decisions were, in hindsight, wise. Often the protagonists of such retrospective stories are elderly married couples meeting or hearing of a spouse's former lover and discussing how their marriage has worked out.

The title "The Properties of Love" suggests a way of interpreting one such story. The title is oxymoronic, describing love as if it were a subject capable of physical or chemical analysis. The story concerns the wealthy 52-year-old wife of an industrialist who one day hears the name of her first—and possibly only—great love, now a well-known medical doctor. She contrives to make an appointment with him, and when they meet they both immediately confirm the feelings they still have for each other; more importantly, the physician reveals that he is about to undergo surgery, which his expert diagnosis gives him very little chance of surviving, forcing the conclusion that their final meeting was prompted not by the chance occasion of her hearing his name mentioned after so long but by some quality of love itself alerting her to this last opportunity to speak with him. As a physician, he is used to speaking in scientific terms and seems to have no difficulty equating the scientific view with the mystical one he is propounding: "This morning you discovered that the man you love is going to die, and the only person in the world that also knows it is me. And how did you know? The only way you could know. The poet's way. The scientific way." His explanation fuses the two seemingly opposed ways of apprehending knowledge into a single perspective that acts as an antidote to materialism, the very issue that separated them in the first place, when he was a medical student with no immediate prospect of earning the kind of money that she knew she would require.

Both seem to have had satisfying marriages. The industrialist she married, Henry D'Avlon, also appears in "Exactly Eight Thousand Dollars Exactly," a story otherwise unconnected to this one; "The Properties of Love" could have easily been about another industrialist's wife. O'Hara's purpose in linking the two stories with the unusual name D'Avlon might be to underscore her husband's decency. In "Exactly Eight Thousand Dollars Exactly," Henry D'Avlon's character is juxtaposed with his brother's: the brother is heartless, cruel, and thoroughly manipulative of others' feelings, while Henry, who gives his brother the sum of money indicated in the title, is generous and caring.

Many of O'Hara's stories of the 1960s serve as retrospective analyses of young couples splitting up and marrying other people. In these stories, the pairs reunite to examine their choices: in *The Cape Cod Lighter* alone, "The Lighter When Needed," "A Cold Calculating Thing," "You Can Always Tell Newark," "The High Point," "The Compliment," and "The Old Folks" all touch on the theme of two middle-aged people considering the romantic choices they made in their youth. Far from repeating themselves, these stories show the variety in human relationships, the way each couple, no matter how superficially alike, has its own dynamic and how, at an early stage of development, each partner must make a decision to commit further to one another or, as with the couple in "The Properties of Love," to abandon their feelings for each other.

O'Hara does not judge these choices. In fact, he makes it hard for the reader to judge them. It would be easy, for example, to pass harsh judgment on Mrs. D'Avlon for having abandoned her medical-student lover. In the long run, after all, he turns out to have earned a shining reputation and a very comfortable living. Was she then a hard-hearted villainess who has sacrificed love and gotten nothing in return? O'Hara suggests the opposite. He shows her as a materialist but demonstrates how easily and comfortably her point of view meshes with the view of her

mystical yet scientific ex-lover. After his remark about the properties of
love, she is fondly reminded of the similar tones of their conversations
when courting: "She smiled. 'This is like our talks on the top of the
Fifth Avenue bus. Do you remember when I used to ride up to the hospital on the bus, and have to come home alone? Goodness, we used to
talk' " (*Assembly*, 296).

So this relationship, which could easily have turned into a good marriage, was founded on a congenial difference in outlook. Relationships
that turned out less well, like the miserable marriages in "Mary and
Norma," for example, concern spouses who seemed philosophically better fitted. Nothing can assure young couples of happiness, O'Hara
seems to say, and as he explores all the variations of marriage he shows
how, in different ways, each family creates its own unique happiness or
misery.

"Reassurance" paints a happy picture of a middle-aged couple's decision to isolate themselves. In their Virginia home, the Rainsfords are
hosts to another couple on their way from New York to Florida. When
the couple leaves, Mr. Rainsford begins his assessment of their annual
visit by remarking, "I love them dearly, but . . . ." A telephone call interrupts their discussion with the news that the husband has died of a
heart attack on the trip. Dutifully, they drive to the hospital to comfort
his widow, but soon after arriving, they return home. Seemingly willing
to extend themselves to help the widow, they retreat into their privacy,
a trait that has been the pattern of their married life. The story's theme
is emphasized by the inscrutable ending containing a seemingly irrelevant line of dialogue. On the drive home, the Rainsfords discuss their
discomfort with other people, and the husband interjects a non sequitur
about other drivers that also could be interpreted more broadly:

> "And we're going home."
> "And we'll have a fire," he said.
> "Yes, and you won't have to work on your speech."
> "And we won't have to like our friends."
> "No matter what age," she said.
> "These bastards never dim their lights," he said.

For the Rainsfords, mixing with other couples is a mistake, and the
events of the day clarify their position. They have withdrawn from society and in this story make great efforts to make a show of respecting
that society, but it is only the appearance of interest in social contact
that they maintain, not the interest itself. O'Hara's ending, like those of

many other of his stories containing such a non sequitur or an ambiguous moment, allows him to avoid the fulsomeness of the traditional final paragraph in which an author passes some kind of judgment on his characters' actions. O'Hara's greatest achievement, perhaps, is his stubborn refusal to provide that sort of patronizing conclusion.

It is important to O'Hara that his point be deduced, not stated explicitly. The pleasure of reading an O'Hara story is in fact similar to the pleasure O'Hara feels in creating a story: "the *work* of writing is fun," he points out in the foreword to *Assembly*, "and without the work the writing is not fun, pleasure, or a joy." His task, the way he sees it, is to reward the reader for thinking, and the challenge is to avoid rewarding the reader for doing too little thinking. O'Hara deliberately refrains from confirming readerly conclusions too quickly or too openly with an explicit statement. Unlike the sometimes impenetrable stories of the 1930s and 1940s, O'Hara's late work has a crustiness that seems to have softened in *Assembly* and the later collections, in which he doles out a few more crucial details, better enabling a hard-working reader to understand his stories.

O'Hara wrote comfortably about a variety of social classes: in *Assembly* he alternates between upper-class characters, mostly couples considering their marriages or lack thereof, and working-class couples doing the same. One story about the latter group, "The Free," is sandwiched between two stories about wealthy couples. O'Hara is neither condescending to his poorer characters nor overly respectful of his wealthier ones. The plot of "The Free" in fact is easily imaginable as a story about an upper-class couple: when a man is arrested for murdering his former lover, his wife leaves him not because she thinks he may be guilty but because he admits he had spoken with the murdered woman recently, breaking his promise to avoid her. Freed when the murder charge is dropped, he goes home, where he and his wife find that they are free from each other as well. The working-class details (he hustles pool for a living and eats raisin pie, she flicks her cigarette ashes in her saucer and pronounces subpoena "subpeeny") are as sharply observed as the characteristics of O'Hara's idle rich—more sharply, in fact, given that the brand names of the cars and the clothing of the rich attract attention, and those of the poor discourage it.

"The Compliment" bears an interesting relationship to O'Hara's earlier epistolary fiction, such as "Invite," a 1938 story in the form of a letter from a college student to a young woman inviting her to a dance. "The Compliment" contains but does not entirely consist of a long let-

Part 1

ter from an 18-year-old college freshman to a girl; its pontifications on world events suggest an intelligent if immature writer, and its personal remarks suggest a romantic impulse behind the letter. Considered on its own, the letter could have constituted an entire story by the younger O'Hara, whose reader would have been able to empathize with the letter's writer and to guess its possible outcome. But the older, less oblique O'Hara no longer withholds such vital information from the reader—instead of flatly presenting the letter as a document to be interpreted, he provides the context in which it is being read. The youth who wrote the letter is now a 62-year-old man, long since married to a woman other than the letter's recipient. Also 62, the recipient contacts the couple, asking if she could show them this now-ancient document. When she arrives, she presents it to the wife (the husband is delayed momentarily). After briefly discussing the letter, the husband, and the recipient's subsequent life, the wife thanks her for staying away from her husband during the past four decades. "The Compliment" epitomizes O'Hara's later fiction in the same way that "Invite" epitomizes O'Hara's early stories: where "Invite" catches the voice of a young man O'Hara only partly admires, "The Compliment" includes that same tonal tour de force in a larger, more meaningful, and more complex story with a real plot, not an implied one.

Most but not all of the stories in *Assembly* and *The Cape Cod Lighter* about reminiscence and regret feature middle-aged couples as the primary characters. In "You Can Always Tell Newark," a 50-year-old man has a quiet talk with an athlete half his age, reminiscent of the subtle and moving conversation between Stephen Dedalus and Leopold Bloom at the end of *Ulysses*. In both cases, neither man is as aware as the reader is of the symbolic connection between the two, as they discuss a serious subject in an almost casual way. (The older man in both O'Hara and Joyce is far more sensitive to nuance, however, than his younger counterpart.) Most of the minimal action in O'Hara's story takes place within the mind of the older man: while watching the young man play tennis, the older man meets a young woman who he realizes, after conversing with and then about her, is his own daughter. She is having an affair with the tennis player despite being not only married but also pregnant with a child of unknowable paternity.

In short, through an almost but not quite contrived coincidence (which could also be said of *Ulysses*), the older man finds himself sitting aboard a train next to a younger version of himself, whom he advises in a fatherly way without openly acknowledging their connection. "You

Can Always Tell Newark" is an almost dreamlike story in which the protagonist eerily meets his younger self in the same disturbing situation
he himself was in at that age. Contributing to the unreality of this thoroughly realistic story is a fine technique that O'Hara further refined in
the later story "Flight." Aboard the train, the older man thinks upon the
strange circumstances he has just learned about, in images that seem
increasingly abstract and hypothetical and that are, it turns out, formulated by his mind in a dream. Until he suddenly wakes up, there is no
mention of his having fallen asleep and dreamed. Flipping through the
newspaper, he

> turned to the Evening Chat column, which contained society news. At
> this moment some people he knew in Wynnewood were getting ready
> to receive guests for dinner: Mr. and Mrs. John Arthur Kersley will
> entertain at dinner this evening in honor of their daughter Willela Ker
> sley, whose engagement, etc. What if he knew the score of that dinner
> party, as he now knew the score of Ivers' tennis match? What if he
> could call up Jack Kersley and tell him for God's sake not to let John
> Jones sit next to Mary Brown, that before the night was over John
> Jones would say something to Mary Brown that would wreck their
> lives? What if he could call Mary Brown and tell her not to listen to
> anything John Jones said? And what if he had been able to speak to Rex
> Ivers and persuade him to default, so that he would not have gone to
> Philadelphia and seen Nancy. "My daughter."
> "I beg your pardon?"
> "Oh—I must have dozed off." (*Assembly*, 168)

The technique of withholding information crucial to the understanding
of a scene until immediately after the scene has passed is not uncommon in modern fiction but it is usually employed in physical rather than
psychological descriptions, as in Hemingway's short story "Fifty Grand,"
in which the increasing terseness of a conversation is explained, after
the fact, by the information that a noisy train had pulled next to the
platform where the conversation had taken place.

The tone of the climactic conversation in "You Can Always Tell
Newark" grows more surreal, even as its substance remains realistic: the
tennis player reveals (again, almost but not quite implausibly) to his
older acquaintance that he has determined not to break up his lover's
marriage, despite her wishes, for the sake of the child who, he acknowledges, may well be his. Her passion for him, he knows, will fade, and he
will have broken up a marriage and ruined the happiness of a child for a

few years of passion. At the end of this intensely personal confession to an almost total stranger, it is the confessor who thanks the penitent, ostensibly for trusting him with his confidence. Actually, as the reader understands perfectly, he thanks him for reassuring him about the wisdom of breaking up with the girl's mother a generation earlier.

In some stories, as in the ending of "Imagine Kissing Pete," O'Hara borders on sentimentality in his retrospective examinations of long-vanished times, and in others, like "The Girl on the Baggage Truck," he strips the past of its sentimental varnish. He keeps his readers very much on their toes, as they are never really sure if a story is about to take a turn into the realm of the hard-boiled or into the maudlin. The most sentimental story in *The Cape Cod Lighter* is the last one, "Your Fah, Nee Fah, Nee Face," which tells of a woman's love for her dead brother. They used to act out skits in public places, pretending to be siblings finding each other after years of separation. The first-person narrator catches their act in a hotel lobby and then, years afterwards, meets the woman socially. They discuss her brother, who has since drowned in a boating accident, and later discuss their unhappy marriages. In this story more than in any other, O'Hara paints a unblemished and idealistic vision of youth, free of the sordid concerns that permeate adult existence. Perhaps the ugliest moment in the woman's sad marriage comes when her husband implies that her love for her dead brother is essentially erotic. To dispel this notion, she tells a story—tinged with eroticism though ultimately innocuous—about the siblings' checking into a hotel as husband and wife, fooling the hotel staff and guests into thinking they were shy newlyweds. "We laughed for a whole day about that and then we used to do the same trick every time we had to drive anywhere overnight. Didn't hurt anybody," she says (*CCL*, 425). And her final memory, that of her brother's imitation of Fred Astaire saying "I lahv, your fah, neeface. Yourfah, neefah, neeface," moves her to tears. Her life, once touched by joy and innocence and love, is over by the time she is 30, and the narrator mourns the loss of her youth and of his own.

A much harsher look backward appears in "The Sun-Dodgers," less a story than a sketch of an era that to O'Hara's mind has been celebrated for all the wrong reasons. Here he sets the record straight, attacking Damon Runyon's image of colorful Broadway and its "benevolent bookmakers . . . [,] rogues and rascals." To the contrary, O'Hara claims, the "big shots and smallies that I saw—and I saw dozens of them—were unprincipled, sadistic, murderous bullies; often sexually perverted, diseased, sometimes drug addicts, and stingy. The women were just as bad, except when they were worse" (*CCL,* 361–62).

The wispy plot of "The Sun-Dodgers" is confused and confusing. O'Hara's narrator, excellent at providing lively and authentic details about Broadway nightlife, introduces several vivid minor characters but does not know what to do with them. At one point the narrator briefly describes a cop who, he promises, in "this chronicle plays a minor part, and having introduced him I will go on until I need him later in the story," a clumsy narrative device indeed and one that also proves to be inaccurate when, at the story's end, the cop has not made his return appearance (*CCL,* 361). A more immediately puzzling lapse comes when the narrator cannot adequately add the small numbers of seats around a table: "We hardly ever numbered fewer than five or more than nine, and eight was the most comfortable: four on each side of the table and two at the open end" (*CCL,* 363). Such crude and obvious mistakes suggest an unreliable narrator, but the story does not contain enough substance for him to be unreliable about. Moreover, the narrator of "The Sun-Dodgers" is supposed to be a successful professional writer, making such lapses unlikely. Far likelier is that they result from O'Hara's rare inattention to details. But the seamy underside of Broadway, ignored by Runyon and his ilk, is presented nonetheless convincingly.

O'Hara depicts Gibbsville, too, as a seamy place beneath its surfaces. He prefers to show corrupt or depraved activities rather than dwell on their results. "The Hardware Man" and "The Cellar Domain" tell of Gibbsville businessmen whose hard-heartedness and venality are finally the sum of their beings. The businesses that Lou Mauser and Peter Durant run are at the center of their lives, and their lives are nothing but business: competition, self-interest, and domination are to them virtuous principles. O'Hara gives neither Mauser nor Durant a minute of home life in either of these two long stories, showing only their activities in Mauser's hardware store or Durant's barbershop. The two titles also emphasize this point: "The Hardware Man" describes not only Mauser's business but also his utter lack of humanity. He behaves as if he were made of hardware. "The Cellar Domain" implies that Peter Durant, whose barbershop is located in a cellar, thinks of himself a ruler of a vast empire, isolated from lesser mortals and their feelings.

"The Cellar Domain" could also be paired with "Price's Always Open," for in both stories a small businessman favors an outcast among his customers, and his favoritism ends up costing him his business. These two stories reach opposite conclusions, the crucial difference being that Price's favoritism is motivated by his generosity toward Jackie Girard, while Durant's is motivated by his selfish appreciation of a boorish and mean-spirited customer.

Both of these stories end with a business in ruins, but "The Hardware Man" ends with Mauser triumphing over his competitor, the decent Tom Esterly, whom he has finally driven out of business. Mauser's lack of any life outside his store is contrasted with the family life of a longtime fellow worker whom Mauser drives to suicide. When Esterly makes this comparison in the story's last scene, Mauser does not understand what a happy home life has to do with business. He tells Esterly, "No wonder you're going out of business. You should of been a preacher." " 'I thought about it,' said Tom Esterly. 'But I didn't have the call.' " Mauser's failure to see the relevance of morality to the business world limits him severely, and he suffers for his limitation everywhere but in his pocketbook. O'Hara examines business success often because under close scrutiny it can reveal a character fulfilled as easily as it can signify, as with Mauser, a character stunted and deformed.

O'Hara's lifelong empathy with underdogs became more subtly shaded in his later stories, making villains such as Bob Hooker in "Claude Emerson, Reporter" and Whit Hofman in "Pat Collins" fully human, in a way he could not do for the antagonists of "Do You Like It Here?" or "Sportsmanship." In the best of the later stories, O'Hara creates a initial false sympathy for his overbearing protagonists, making their inhumanity more terrible.

In "All Tied Up" a self-important, authoritarian bank president, Miles Updegrove, takes umbrage at one of his bank tellers because he wears loafers, albeit ones invisible behind his workstation. If the story were told from the point of view of the oppressed bank teller, as "Do You Like It Here?" was narrated from the perspective of the unjustly accused boy, this small offense might have led to a fierce conflict, but "All Tied Up" derives its power from being told from the oppressor's point of view. Indeed, the bank teller scarcely appears in the story. The conflict takes place between Updegrove and the teller's supervisor.

The supervisor asks Updegrove if there is a reason he has been treating the teller with far less courtesy than usual. Through purposeful misunderstanding, Updegrove—never mentioning the loafers or his annoyance at them—escalates this discussion to the point where the supervisor is forced to quit his job. The monstrous Updegrove goes home, well pleased with his conduct in the argument. When the supervisor's wife appears at his doorstep tearfully begging for her husband's job, Updegrove tells her that he will reinstate him if he shows evidence of contriteness, which the wife assures him her husband will exhibit in abundance.

As the character from whose point of view "All Tied Up" is told, Miles Updegrove adds depth to the role of villain, a dimension lacking in his counterpart in "Do You Like It Here?"[58] Presented more flatly, Updegrove might have seemed more grotesquely stern, but his rigid nature emerges more insidiously as a fully rounded character. His abuse of authority is positively Nixonian, particularly in the conversation between the two bank officers in which Updegrove pulls the rhetorical trick of denying a charge (as in Nixon's famous "I am not a crook" defense) that is much simpler and more specific than the one he is actually accused of. When confronted with the supervisor's observation that Updegrove rudely ignored the teller holding open the bank gate for him, Updegrove inappropriately defends himself: "I didn't know I was supposed to do a curtsey when someone held the gate open for me" (*HKW,* 12). When the supervisor persists and keeps his temper, Updegrove ups the stakes by reminding him of how influential Updegrove has been in advancing his career. This rhetoric, superficially supportive of the manager, is obviously intended to intimidate him.

Updegrove's tactic in dealing with subordinates is to repeat unarguable and uncontested truisms and then to draw his own self-serving conclusions from them. Immediately upon praising the supervisor's abilities and by implication his own skill in noticing them, Updegrove spouts this truism: "But I have to remind you, Fred, that you're not perfect. Nobody's perfect. Not even you, Fred," and then cuts him off when Fred begins to protest that the issue is not his own lack of perfection (*HKW,* 13). Having established Fred's imperfection, he leaps to the conclusion that Fred has badly mishandled this particular personnel matter. Fred uses the psychological term "persecution complex" to describe accurately his first reaction upon hearing the teller's complaint against Updegrove. However, long after it has been established that this complaint is no distortion on the teller's part but Fred's own observation, Updegrove harps on Fred's use of psychological jargon, concluding that in his training "they didn't give you an M. D. degree," which Fred of course has never claimed to hold and the mention of which is entirely irrelevant.

Exaggerating, overstating, misstating, oversimplifying—all help Updegrove evade the simple truth of his own repressed annoyance at the teller. But the bullying rhetoric—the kind that O'Hara was recording with deadly accuracy since the Hagedorn and Brownmiller series of the 1920s—is secondary to the brilliant strategy of making the bully the story's focal character. For the first few brief paragraphs, O'Hara paints Updegrove sympathetically as an executive restraining himself nobly from pointing out an employee's annoying personal habit. But as with any micromanaging, self-important boss, no annoyance is ever too trivial to Updegrove. The only question is: In what Byzantine way will the trivial annoyance burst to the surface? The surest hint of Updegrove's flawed nature is that he himself points out his own noble restraint in not attacking his perceived enemies even more viciously and unfairly than he does.

Updegrove's marriage is crucial to the story, the plot of which concerns a business disagreement and which properly could have been told within the setting of the bank. In the first scene at the Updegrove home, he and his wife discuss the problem of the loafer-wearing teller, only to get sidetracked on several different points—the teller's family history, Updegrove's father-in-law's hobby of collecting quaint Pennsylvania Dutch expressions, the O'Haran staple of one spouse knowing the difference between *implied* and *inferred* and the other not knowing—so that the obvious solution to the problem, namely, having a discreet word with the teller's supervisor, never gets voiced. Instead, Updegrove gets more angry, concluding the talk with, "It makes my blood boil," an unreasonable conclusion that the wife supports: " 'Yes,' she said. 'Well, then you better find some way to get rid of him' " (*HKW,* 11).

Mrs. Updegrove is, in current psychological jargon, an "enabler" of her husband's misdirected rages. Her job, as she sees it, is to keep him on an even keel, with little concern for how the rest of the world copes with his fury. When Fred's wife turns up at her home, Mrs. Updegrove conspicuously absents herself and lets her and Updegrove talk privately, thus allowing him to bully Fred's wife more blatantly than he might with his own wife present. In this private conversation, Updegrove distorts events—his version is that he and her husband had been discussing "bank matters, and then all of a sudden out of a clear sky he started abusing me. Using strong language and making personal remarks that I couldn't tolerate." (The strongest language in the discussion, outside of a mention of the Deity's name, is Updegrove's reminding Fred to be "damn sure" to remember who the boss is.) Mrs. Updegrove then appears, more as Updegrove's servant than his spouse, to serve Fred's wife a glass of water and to remind them to summon her loudly "if you want anything else" (*HKW,* 16).

In the talk that follows, Updegrove—who was comically hostile to psychotherapy during the talk about the teller—manipulates Fred's cowed wife by seeming to treat her as a family therapist might. Pretending not to have a clue as to why Fred carried on at work, he asks her if she has noticed anything unusual about him lately. He notes that he does not "want to pry into anybody's personal affairs, but being's you came here, and you're naturally worried about him," he goes ahead and pries (*HKW,* 17). Digging up gratuitous but significant-sounding dirt about Fred's life—how much sleep he gets, how he disciplines his children, and especially how much coffee he drinks—Updegrove finally professes bafflement at Fred's irrational behavior but extorts from the wife a vow to leave Fred and to take their children with her if he does not apologize contritely to Updegrove. Satisfied, he shows her out and asks his wife if she has some coffee for him.

The more fully realized scenes and characters in his late stories enable O'Hara to develop the kinds of subplots that never appeared in his early one-scene presentations. The main plot of "All Tied Up," about a man browbeating a trusted subordinate and controlling his life in humiliating detail, makes a good story in itself but is etched deeper by the subplot's reiteration of the bullying that pervades all of Miles Updegrove's relationships.

In his wife, Updegrove has found a compliant woman who gets certain material rewards for enduring his pathological manipulations, so much so that she helps him mistreat those around him. Superficially, the Updegroves are a familiar middle-aged couple having an ordinary domestic chat, but when the subject of the husband's insane persecution of his employees comes up, his wife not only fails to question his conclusions but also supports and then advances them. Up to that point, while Updegrove has kept his twisted conclusions to himself, the reader may suspect that his wife will set him straight once she hears him voice them. But her part in supporting his pathology turns O'Hara's harrowing anecdote into a small tragedy.

O'Hara's interest in the bully's psychology continues in "Arnold Stone," whose title character is a more interesting bully than Miles Updegrove. A hard-hearted businessman of the 1920s, as is seen in his emblematic name, A. Stone, is first shown as a crusty and clever operator who has invented an imaginary partner in his theatrical production business, Hemphill & Stone, on whom he blames every nasty business dealing that Stone wishes to be absolved from. As a result of this "good guy–bad guy" routine, Stone accrues all of the firm's goodwill, and the fictitious Harold H. Hemphill is the target of the ill will of a small army of angry actors, set designers, theater owners, among others. Along the way, Arnold Stone becomes a millionaire.

The expository section of the story, explaining in delicious detail how Stone deceives, misleads, wheedles, and cons his clients and employees into satisfying the demands of the insatiable Hemphill, is a panegyric to Stone as an astute businessman, and the first part of the plot reinforces that impression: Stone gets summoned unexpectedly to visit a small-town theater. (The town is Gibbsville, but none of O'Hara's Gibbsville regulars makes an appearance, and this Gibbsville story could as well be set in any other town.) The Gibbsville theater owner tells Stone a tale of woe: all of his assets have been stolen by his mistress, and he begs Stone to lend him money to stay in business. Stone does but only after invoking the dread name of Hemphill to ensure that, despite Stone's own kindly inclinations, the terms of the loan will profit the firm. Up to here, this little drama seems to be the high point of Stone's con game, a practical example of his theory of business explained in the exposition: by hook or crook, Arnold Stone always gets a goodly bite out of somebody's hide.

But "Arnold Stone" turns out to be a tale of the biter bit. Stone goes home satisfied with his perfect comportment, like Miles Updegrove at a similar point in "All Tied Up," but he suffers a shocking comeuppance, most unlike Updegrove: instead of being conned, the Gibbsville theater owner has conned Stone. The thieving mistress is in fact in collusion with him; together, they have absconded with the original missing assets, plus several sizable loans gotten from private sources, of which Hemphill & Stone is one. Agitated, Stone throws an embolism on the spot and spends his final few weeks semicoherent in a hospital bed, from which he orders several nonsensical changes in his will, including the bequest of several thousand dollars to the theater owner's mistress. His lawyer and secretary agree to transcribe the changes to Stone's will but not to enter them in the will itself, thus making Stone the puppet of others instead of the skilled puppet master he has prided himself on being.

Unlike "All Tied Up," in which the puppeteer wins, "Arnold Stone" is an old-fashioned morality play in which the protagonist's sins are punished exactly. Rather than condemning villainy, O'Hara scrutinizes it.

He was fascinated by the spectacle of intentional mistreatment, especially of those who deserve better.

O'Hara, however, was more interested in victimizers than in victims.[59] In "All Tied Up," "Arnold Stone," "The Hardware Man," and "The Cellar Domain," his victimizers have lively conflicts to resolve, but sometimes he showed his victimizers without true victims. Obsessive self-interest combined with a great need for privacy fascinated O'Hara, and he built some plotless stories around secretive, morbidly self-interested characters. Lacking conflict, these stories risked dullness, a risk O'Hara was willing to run. Frank MacShane aptly described this "problem of conception O'Hara had to face—how to write interesting fiction about uninteresting people" (78). MacShane was writing more about O'Hara's character sketches of the 1940s, but one of their themes—the thought processes of limited characters—persisted throughout O'Hara's career. The churlish characters in "The General," "At the Window," and "Clayton Bunter" require strict privacy, causing O'Hara to wonder about their secretive lives. His speculations on his crass characters' secrets, often sexual, formed his final sketches. He tried to understand why people chose to thwart their own potential in such futile lives.

His Gibbsville stories generally, as well as his examinations of private lives in and out of Gibbsville, make his case that no one knows what goes on behind closed doors or inside people's hearts, often not even the people themselves. The sincerity of O'Hara's views may be seen in a letter he wrote to a close friend going through a divorce: "No outsider ever knows what is between a husband and wife. I will say that I am sorry about your own separation, because I think you two should have stayed husband and wife. But I know nothing. I know nothing" (*Letters*, 225). Politely professing ignorance of his friends' private lives, O'Hara felt professionally obligated to pry into such matters with his fictional creations, speculating, guessing, wondering, asserting, and attributing motives to their actions that, as Jim Malloy said of Henry Armour, "I want to know and I can never know. I wish, I wish I knew."

Return to Hollywood

The plots of O'Hara's Hollywood stories, showing national celebrities maintaining lives at great odds with their public personae, are as unpredictable as any he devised, and unpredictability was his strong suit.[60] It is a special joy to watch closely as someone reads a certain key passage in "Natica Jackson," because most readers actually react physically to reading it: they shudder, they gasp, they drop their jaws in amazement. O'Hara describes the most shockingly monstrous behavior being practiced by recognizably human characters. He does not always succeed because his challenge was to explain increasingly extreme behavior, some of which defies readerly compassion. But his starting point remained the same: he would witness some odd act—as mild as an out-of-work actor turning down a good part or as outrageous as a mother drowning her own children—and try to explain how that person justifies his or her behavior. O'Hara prided himself on understanding the psychology of his characters, which he did by first understanding how aberrant characters explained their actions to themselves.[61]

O'Hara alternated detailed stretches of plotlessness with startling bursts of plot advancement. He will describe, for example, the thought process of a character hanging and rehanging the suits in his closet, and he will describe it at far greater length than one would expect the reader's attention to stay engaged. Such passages are a kind of reverse tour de force in which O'Hara, instead of writing about a difficult subject with spectacular stylistic verve, writes at length about a humdrum subject in a bland style. After O'Hara has spun several serviceable pages out of almost no material and with no visible advancement of the plot, the tour de force becomes clear: through meticulous details and tiny revelations of character, O'Hara keeps his readers focused while his plot, for all intents and purposes, has left the room. By teasing his readers with tidbits of sudden plot advancement, O'Hara manipulates them into following some of the thinnest plots imaginable this side of metafiction.

When such passages were used as exhibits to support the criticism that O'Hara was an unimaginative thinker who valued the name brands of suits, automobiles, and other material possessions over the inner workings of his characters, he defended himself with the claim that he was deliberately serving his readers noun-rich passages as a kind of mental sorbet to cleanse their literary palates while he prepared the next course. Such a defense is suspicious (it is the first and most infuriating defense offered by every inept writer of fiction: "Yes, these passages are boring on purpose") but in O'Hara's case it is unusually persuasive.

In "John Barton Rosedale, Actor's Actor," the title character hangs and rehangs his suits immediately following a blowout argument with a Broadway producer, Norman Bahs, who offers Rosedale a juicy part for a good but not outstanding salary. Rosedale apparently rejects such offers routinely because by the time he arrives at his home he "was so unaffected by the encounter with Bahs that he neglected to give a report of it" to his wife. Rosedale's forgetting of Bahs's offer is O'Hara's only indication that the offer will figure significantly in the story.[62]

The details immediately following the heated argument are dull as can be. The argument itself, however, is one of O'Hara's liveliest, concluding with Rosedale's comment that $750 a week is an insult, which Bahs counters with, "Well, I can go to eight"; and Rosedale tops with "My dear fellow, you can go to hell," thus effectively concluding the negotiation (*HB*, 139). Rosedale and his full-figured wife, Millicent, settle in for a nice dinner (O'Hara specifies the soup, the main course, the earthenware china by name brand, and the wine by its varietal name) and an evening in front of the television. (This cozy domesticity, a frequent setting for O'Hara's couples, replicated his own practice in the 1960s of watching late-night movies on television with his wife. "Late, Late Show" in *Waiting For Winter* is another one of these stories, about a couple nearly reaching the breakup of their long-term marriage when the husband cuts short a conversation about his wartime espionage activities.) "John Barton Rosedale, Actor's Actor" can be regarded as set particularly close to home, literally, in that the Rosedales live in a Manhattan apartment complex where O'Hara maintained an apartment for many years (*HB*, 131; *OHC*, 143). In the story, when they find out that the excellent T.V. movie they are watching was produced and directed by Bahs, Rosedale tells his wife about that afternoon's argument and she tells him he should have accepted Bahs's offer. He then gets extremely nasty, saying, "I'm not broke. We have [enough] to eat—even for you" (*HB*, 143). Earlier in the conversation, he had assured her that her full figure pleased him, but her frequent reference to her weight suggests a self-consciousness that only a cruel spouse would exploit. John Barton

Rosedale has foolishly compounded his problems by attacking his one source of constant support.

When O'Hara looked into self-destructive behavior, he did not have to look far for examples: he was known to pick fights with his wives in public, even when they were supportive of him, and especially with his first wife, Belle, while O'Hara was still drinking, as the Rosedales are doing. Published in March 1963, the story dates itself to "easily ten years ago," well within Belle Wylie O'Hara's lifetime and O'Hara's drinking days, which coincided (*HB*, 140). O'Hara's response to cruelty or to rudeness—whether practiced by himself, observed in others, or simply imagined—was to explain its roots. Whether this story began with O'Hara wondering why an actor might turn down a well-paying role or why a man might turn on his patient and loving spouse matters less to the success of the story than O'Hara's seeing both behaviors as of a piece. Not only are the behaviors joined to each other but they are connected as well to John Barton Rosedale's vanity, anger, and self-destructive nature.

In a conspicuously long paragraph, Rosedale furiously denounces to his fellow club members the stock market in which he lost a fortune 20 years earlier: "He can be very angry about having been a near-millionaire, and they have all heard it before" (*HB*, 132). His audience's boredom notwithstanding, Rosedale recites his tale of vanished riches, and O'Hara spares neither Rosedale's listeners nor his readers a syllable of the tirade. The entire invective rendered into one tremendous paragraph does more than merely show Rosedale's speech patterns. His listeners wait patiently for the eruption to cool down, but in the passing minutes until it does, Rosedale establishes his inconsiderate treatment of others, an attitude with which he later oppresses his wife. (Though Rosedale bores his friends, the offense is less severe to O'Hara's readers who, after all, are hearing the story of Rosedale's stock market adventures for the first time.) Rosedale, as the story's first sentence tells us, has a certain "truculent style" to him, which may seem interesting and even charming at first but which over time demands patient forbearance. The story illustrates his methodical alienation of those who extend it to him and ends with his hurt and insulted wife closing a door on him, which will not be the last door to shut on John Barton Rosedale.

It is not only long descriptive paragraphs that yield sudden payoffs for O'Hara but the seemingly rambling conversations he wrote because he enjoyed writing them: "I *like* to write dialog; I like to hear my people talk," he once explained (*Letters*, 261). A conversation between an actor and his agent, for example, which for a good number of paragraphs has stood perilously close to the precipice of tedium, now without warning destroys their long-term relationship: Don Tally, of "The Portly Gentleman," the character alluded to in the title, is conversing with his longtime agent, Miles Mosk, in what seems to be their two-thousandth discussion about Tally's acting career, which has recently caught fire, and Mosk's style of managing it. Because of Tally's recent success, however, Mosk is perhaps overly sensitive to his client's not-always-good-natured ribbing. When Mosk says, "You know what you sound like, Don? You sound like a client that was getting ready to go over to another agency. Am I anywhere near correct?" Tally responds, with perfect sincerity, "Not so near. You got me work when I wouldn't go out and hustle a buck myself." But Mosk refuses to accept this assessment, a generous one from the self-centered Tally, and he worries that scab until it bursts: "I never solicited a client," Mosk protests at the end of the scene, "and I never hung on to one that wished to sever the relationship. Here's ten dollars for my cup of coffee. And don't you call me—I'll call you. You should live so long" (*WFW,* 343). Somehow, an everyday conversation has taken a terribly wrong turn, and O'Hara skillfully makes the disaster make sense.

In another show business story, also in *Waiting For Winter,* the title character of "Natica Jackson" has a similar conversation with her longtime agent, Morris King, who, with his wife, Ernestine, has deflected an anonymous producer's attempts to induce the movie star to do a Broadway show. King tells Natica, "The guy said it was a chance to prove what you could really do. And Ernestine said to him right to his face, 'Fifty million people go to the movies every week, and they're all that much further ahead of you, Mister.' " Natica responds by asking, "Mr. What?" Her interest in the identity of the producer could be construed as questioning her agent's wisdom. King indeed takes offense at Natica's interest. He tells her the name, virtually daring her to contact the producer, and for good measure gratuitously mentions that he knew the producer when he had a different name. "But what the hell," King observes, "I had a different name then myself, and Natica Jackson used to be Anna Jacobs if I'm not mistaken" (*WFW,* 286). As King reminds his very successful client of her humble origins, strongly implying his own role in Anna Jacobs's change of her unglamorous name and life for that of Natica Jackson, the air becomes charged, and O'Hara's readers ready themselves for the inevitable blowout—which never comes. Instead, the Kings go on to provide loving care for Natica throughout the scandal that subsequently develops and threatens her career, and she is grateful to them for it. So it is not only the twists of plot that lurk in the seemingly dull expository passages but also their potential to unwind. The tension in the conversations between Natica and King is powerful and no less so for the fact that it dissipates.

The ability to create this tension—between the expository passages and the explosive passages—is O'Hara's great gift. He exploits it by taking to the limit both qualities: O'Hara's expository stretches move the plot along less than those of any writer this side of Virginia Woolf or Nicholson Baker, but his plot twists, when—or if—they finally appear, tighten the story with the force of a James M. Cain or Stephen King.

O'Hara wrote about his technical manipulation of the reader, even down to what he expected the reader's eye to be doing as it perused a long catalogue of names or a snappy stichomythic exchange (*Artist*, 16–20). O'Hara's technical approach to his prose resembles a poet's use of various techniques: his turns of plot twist as suddenly and completely as a sonnet turns at its *volta*, the point at which a sonneteer reverses the argument and makes the opposite case. O'Hara's plots literally "turn" on some tiny event or, as occurred with Miles Mosk's estrangement from Don Tally, on a character's altered tone of voice. O'Hara himself was notoriously sensitive to nuances and to inferences. Known as the "master of the imagined slight," easily taken to offenses where none was intentionally given, O'Hara seeds his stories with voltas that, although tiny in themselves, turn a plot 180 degrees and in retrospect are far more significant than they seem. The theme of volatility, perhaps because of the superficial nature of the archetypal Hollywood relationship depicted in these stories, recurs in various forms in "The Portly Gentleman," "Natica Jackson," "The Way to Majorca," and "James Francis and the Star."

The title characters in "James Francis and the Star" have a friendship that, during the story's span the 1930s through the late 1950s, seems alternately genuine and manipulative. At the story's chronological end, which O'Hara describes in a prefatory frame, James Francis Hatter is dismayed to find that his old friend, Hollywood star Rod Fulton, has returned to California after three years abroad without so much as telephoning him. But the episodic quality of their relationship is such that, although Hatter's day is "utterly ruined" by the news of Rod's return, it is entirely possible the two will repair their relationship and breathe some life in it. "James Francis and the Star" is in this way less severely moralistic a tale than "Pat Collins" in *The Cape Cod Lighter*, a story that also begins with a retrospective opening and also tells the main story in a very long flashback. "James Francis and The Star" has numerous ups and downs, a quality that distinguishes it from "Pat Collins," which tells the story of a friendship that slowly and steadily deteriorated because of a marital betrayal.

A marital betrayal is also at the heart of "James Francis and the Star." Perhaps in the setting of midcentury Hollywood, infidelity is easier to overlook than in Gibbsville of the 1920s. These two very long stories do resemble one another superficially, the chief differences being the switch of the point-of-view character (in "Pat Collins" the husband and in "James Francis and the Star" the wife's lover), and the setting of each story. Taken together, these differences explain the vastly different outcomes: Jimmy and Rod's friendship survives while Pat and Whit's does not.

Jimmy and Rod's relationship begins somewhat like Pat and Whit's: a successful screenwriter, Jimmy Hatter, befriends a promising but unemployed actor, Rod Fulton. Rod eventually becomes a successful actor and then a movie star, while Jimmy's career hits a long plateau. During World War II, Rod serves with the air force in England, where he meets and marries a countess, Angela, whom he sends to Hollywood for safekeeping. Jimmy is charged with the responsibility of making Angela comfortable, which he does and then some. Jimmy and the countess come into heat more or less simultaneously. It is this kind of sudden and spontaneous lust, rather than the details of the sexual encounters themselves, that makes O'Hara seem salacious. This attitude implies, more than the rather muted sex scenes that typically followed, that sex is the top priority of every O'Hara character and that one spark of boldness is all that is required to ignite a roaring sexual fire.[63]

At first, Jimmy actively dislikes the countess and does not bother hiding his animosity, which she returns to him in full. But at a very early point, when he dutifully brings her war-rationed nylon stockings (purely, as he openly admits, out of his friendship for Rod), she equally dutifully invites him for a swim, promising she will not try to seduce him. "Why not?" Jimmy responds, and the spark is ignited.

> "Well, if you put it that way, I will . . . I don't suppose you and I will
> ever like each other, but you brought me those nylons, and the cigarettes,
> and the steak, without liking me. I think I'll sit on your lap. May I?"
> "Sure," Hatter responds. (*WFW,* 189)

A similar scene occurs in O'Hara's other brilliant Hollywood novella set in the 1930s, "Natica Jackson," in which Natica gets into a minor traffic accident and a major argument with a chemical engineer, who offers to drive Natica to her home after the accident. Woozy, she accepts and then, still full of acrimony, asks him what it means to be an oil company engineer. "Well, my job isn't the kind of oil you use," he explains. "I'm supposed to be developing certain by-products." Natica says, "Whatever that means. Wouldn't you like to make a pass at me?" And of course he would, and does.[64] Again, the actual sex is handled decorously: a few paragraphs later, "They went to her room and he stayed until eleven o'clock" (*WFW,* 257).

"James Francis and the Star" seems mostly sexual until Jimmy kills a tennis player with whom the insatiable countess has been dallying. Jimmy interrupts the tennis player stealing the countess's jewels and kills him in self-defense. The police are cordial to him, but everyone else—all of Jimmy's friends, acquaintances, and colleagues (except for Rod Fulton, who is on location filming a movie)—try to distance themselves from him. All that is known for sure is that Jimmy has killed a man and now, as O'Hara puts it (with a rare Biblical reference), he bears the mark of Cain. Everyone delicately shuns Jimmy , with no one telling him outright that they want nothing to do with him. Even the madam of a bordello where he goes to hide out does not reject him, merely remarking, "I kind of understand what they're all thinking." Jimmy responds belligerently, a reaction typical of O'Hara's oversensitive protagonists: "Do you want me to get out of here?" "No, no, no. You can stay," she says (*WFW,* 214). But when she asks him if he could just avoid being seen by her clients, he storms out of the brothel. Given O'Hara's notoriously oversensitive nature, such confrontations are rendered ambiguously, and each of them is subject to a highly individual reading. In this scene, Jimmy seems prickly but not necessarily wrong in taking offense. The brothel keeper is being delicate with Jimmy's feelings, but she is, after all, a brothel keeper, and the concept that her clients might feel uncomfortable associating with him is offensive by its nature. To be sure, Jimmy has been rebuffed by eight of his friends just prior to this latest rejection, but he is not wrong to take it as a rejection nonetheless. Other characters in O'Hara's short stories who take offense at small provocation—such as Miles Mosk, John Barton Rosedale, Jim Malloy, and Judge Buckhouse (in "The Cellar Domain")—may be overreacting, but Jimmy Hatter is not clearly doing so.

Up to the killing of the tennis player—who is named with atypical emblematicness Slaymaker—the story is told through Jimmy Hatter's point of view, but after that incident the perspective shifts and the story is narrated through the often myopic eyes of outsiders. Suddenly, Rod is said to have divorced "Angela Somebody" (whose last name Jimmy, of course, would have known perfectly well), an announcement that is followed by a parade of details, some hilarious (Rod's status as an actor rises sharply, despite his "one bomb, in which he played Plato"), some sad (Rod's second wife, whom Jimmy dislikes, dies of cancer) (*WFW,* 215). The next few decades are summed up swiftly, the most important detail being the changed nature of the relationship between Jimmy and Rod: Jimmy's status in Hollywood is damaged by his involvement in the shooting, while the man who benefited from the killing, Rod, the absent husband, sees his status rise. Rod and Jimmy "could function as friends if there was a tacit understanding that the once dominant James Francis was now the dominated" (*WFW,* 220). Instead of asking Jimmy's permission or advice to go places, as he would have when he was a nobody living in Jimmy's house and washing his car in lieu of rent, Rod now travels and socializes without even telling his old pal. Sometimes though he switches from using Jimmy to treating him kindly, as when Rod, "as unpredictably considerate as he was carelessly tactless," throws a gala party to celebrate Jimmy's fiftieth birthday (*WFW,* 221). The story's final mood is pleasant, as the two former—and, it now seems, future—best friends are kidding each other while Rod prepares for his lengthy trip abroad. It seems that Jimmy has even regained the upper hand briefly, as he ribs Rod in the story's final lines about the menial tasks Rod once gladly did for him, but the jovial ending is undercut by the story's opening paragraph in which Jimmy is depressed by Rod's failure to contact him on his return to the U.S.

No matter the length of his stories, O'Hara needed to keep their endings unresolved. In "James Francis and the Star"—which is a very long story—he leaves the ending open by shifting the point of view near the end. The long section told through Jimmy's perspective reveals his relative sophistication and his skepticism of celebrity life. But after the murder and the accompanying shift of perspective, Jimmy is rendered objectively. His insights now hidden from the reader, Jimmy is clearly damaged by the trauma of killing a person, but the emotional impact of that trauma is far less clear.

In his late stories, O'Hara often used this distancing tactic. Immediately following the dramatic climaxes of "The Brain" and "Mrs. Allenson," for example, the narrative suddenly detaches from a reliable perspective that reveals the thoughts of the protagonists, shifting to the point of view of a new character who is a stranger to the events of the story as a whole and who predictably skews the facts of the story badly.[65] Implicitly, such tactics direct the reader to correct the skewed version and disentangle its errors.

In O'Hara's two completely successful long Hollywood stories, the tactic works brilliantly. In "James Francis and the Star," the personality of Jimmy Hatter, one of O'Hara's most completely realized creations, directs the sensitive reader to empathize with Jimmy even after the perspective has shifted away from him. In "Natica Jackson," the tactic of shifting perspective is even more brilliantly employed.

"Natica Jackson" tells how the actress falls deeply in love with the chemical engineer she goes to bed with. Throughout most of the story, we know he is a married man, although his wife and children do not appear. Then suddenly O'Hara picks up the narrative from deep within the consciousness of the engineer's wife, and it is a strange consciousness indeed. The wife, without a single rational signal, senses—entirely correctly—that her husband is cheating on her, and she decides to get revenge without ever trying to confirm her suspicions. Readers might not regard her revenge as excessive if she were to have an affair herself, or file for divorce, or even murder her husband or Natica. But she crosses the border into psychosis when she murders instead her own two young children, whom she drowns in order to blight her husband's life. She wants him to mourn these slaughtered innocents for the rest of his life, and she wants to remind Natica—whose name she never knows and whose existence she only infers—of the grave consequences engendered by her adulterous act, creating such agony in the adulterous pair that they can no longer take pleasure in each other's company.

The wife's wholly irrational thinking is shown at the same time to be perfectly conceived: after O'Hara leaves her consciousness and returns to Natica's, Natica in turn intuits the wife's twisted plan to make her husband distasteful to Natica: "I don't want to see him," Natica realizes, "and maybe I never will want to again, with that damn crazy murderess looking over his shoulder at me." A few minutes later she realizes, too, that his wife, who is about to give birth to a third child who will grow up in the husband's custody, plans to make Natica permanently repellent to him:

"As sure as we're sitting here, he's never going to see me again. He'll want to, maybe, but the kind of man he is, he'll have a ghost, too. Not only his wife locked up in an institution, but a child to raise. And he'll never try to see me. And all of a sudden I'm beginning to realize that that crazy woman knew what she was doing. . . . Just as if she called me on the phone and told me. Maybe she doesn't know my name even, but I get it inside me. . . . She's saying 'This is what you have to live with. Ann Jacobs or Natica Jackson, or whatever you call yourself, this is what you have to look forward to.' "

Her listener, Ernestine King, concurs: "It's the only thing to believe that makes any sense" (*WFW,* 317–18).

The child-murdering wife typifies O'Hara's late ability to understand the strange, hateful, permanently warped minds of psychotics without condoning their actions. In the 10 pages O'Hara spends inside her head, he reveals not only her thinking but the philosophy behind that thinking, and he almost makes a reader admire its strange purity. She is a poet and a homemaker, and he uses those roles to explain her thoughts: "But everything in the room had been given its carefully selected place, and once given its place had never been put anywhere else." O'Hara implies that her rules of behavior, taken individually, merely indicate a sense of neatness but in their totality, point to rigidity and a systematic shutting out of the opinions of others, including her husband, of whom she is plainly contemptuous: "Beryl Graham could not have lived any other way, no more than she could have permitted herself the fifteenth line of a sonnet. Sometime in the first year of her marriage she had arrived at a personal ritual of lovemaking, with limits beyond which she would not go, and the ritual remained constant throughout the succeeding years" (*WFW,* 301).

As O'Hara scrupulously avoided mentioning the home lives of Lou Mauser and Peter Durant to emphasize their inhumanity, here he omits one crucial detail from Beryl Graham's conception of lovemaking: her husband. O'Hara explains (at much greater length than is given in this excerpt) her philosophy of sex, which includes the male role only to diminish its importance. Even the phrasing ("of *her* marriage" and "a *personal* ritual of lovemaking") implies a purely mechanical function for her sexual partner. When Beryl Graham makes love, *she* is making it and *she* is receiving pleasure, and it makes as much sense for her to consider Hal Graham's pleasure as it would for her to consider that of a dildo. The absence of emotions, to say nothing of the absence of love, in her lovemaking is a testament to her supreme self-centeredness. Egocentricity is precisely the philosophy of this monstrous woman, who even denies her husband the chance to achieve climax with her: "It was quite enough for him to be a partner to her climax. He must be satisfied with that intimacy, and he must then go to sleep, gratefully" (*WFW,* 302).[66]

Having provided detail after detail of this woman's self-worshipping existence, O'Hara moves into his jaw-dropping plot twist, the murder of her children, and makes it seem, as Ernestine King remarks, to make sense. Beryl Graham is fully human, at least as far as psychotics ever are, but she is also a perfect example of a harpy. Using techniques that have been compared to those in Euripides' *Medea,* another story of infanticide, O'Hara manages to evoke some sympathy for Beryl Graham by demonstrating a convincing psychology that, on its own terms, justifies drowning one's own children.[67] O'Hara also foreshadows the horror by a neat piece of American (as opposed to Greek) phrasing: when Hal Graham warns that if his wife catches on to his affair with Natica there will be "bad trouble," Natica responds, "Bad trouble. What other kind is there?" (*WFW,* 295). But neither she nor he knows quite how wise Graham's distinction between everyday trouble and bad trouble will prove to be. There is a certain amount of foreshadowing here, including the reiteration of the redundancy "bad trouble" in several characters' mouths, and other characters warning Natica of things to come, including her agent Morris King saying, "I'm trying to warn you." To him Natica responds, "I've been warned. By Graham. I'll take the consequences" (*WFW,* 300). But she does not yet have any idea how grave the consequences will be.

Immediately following Beryl Graham's abandonment of the two swimming children several miles out at sea, O'Hara tells the next section of the story, a single long paragraph, in the voice of the dockhand who meets her boat. Here the device of switching to a stranger's perspective at a crucial point in the narrative, which was awkward and confusing in "The Brain," is powerful, juxtaposing Beryl's point of view with the normal perspective of a stranger.

John Updike cited O'Hara in his late stories as "virtually a feminist writer. Throughout his fiction, women occupy the same merciless space his men do, with an equal toughness" (Updike, 185). Updike correctly reads the fascination O'Hara had for people different from himself, even in ways as fundamental as a difference in gender. "The disadvantaged position of women," Updike goes on, "and the strength of the strategies with which they seek advantages are comprehended without doctrine, and without a loss of heterosexual warmth." O'Hara saw women—as he saw homosexuals and businessmen and murderers and Englishmen and drunks—as intriguing because of their variation on his own patterns of behavior, but he afforded them their right to that variation without diminishing their humanity.

O'Hara undermined this feminist tendency by extending his fascination with difference to a fascination with the outright bizarre. Certainly, a demonic character like Beryl Graham, however human the skin tones O'Hara used to portray her, constitutes a difficult bit of evidence to support his feminist sympathies; such female monsters (the small army of male monsters roaming through his work notwithstanding) are not quite offset by such fully rounded female characters as Natica Jackson and Ernestine King.

Cissie Brandon, another movie star and the protagonist of "Yucca Knolls," is an even more folksy, completely human Hollywood figure who is overshadowed by one of O'Hara's monstrous horde, a very colorful male movie director who takes over the story. "Yucca Knolls," finally, is not much more than a character sketch of this director, Earl Fenway Evans, as seen through Cissie's eyes. The story lumbers along for a long while toward a faintly realized point, suggesting that O'Hara started "Yucca Knolls" with only a vague idea of his characters, discovered Evans's fascinating evil halfway through and then tried to force the story around his character. O'Hara's lifelong interest in malevolence, regardless of gender or origin, often served him badly in his last few books, where he pushed the limits of taste and judgment in outdoing his previous book's monsters, sometimes arriving at a caricature instead of a character.

Unlike the retired film stars in "Yucca Knolls" dealing with Earl Fenway Evans's sexual and artistic extravagances, the elderly film stars who inhabit "The Glendale People," "The Private People," and "The Answer Depends" deal with adjusting to retirement, albeit one from a more glamorous life than their fellow retirees. Still, they are constantly challenged by having to reconcile their new reality with their old lives—in all three stories, the protagonists are rather bookish ex-film stars who have been misperceived as empty-headed glamour-pusses by their contemporaries. Jack Dorney, the 63-year-old star who moves to Manhattan to become one of "the private people," finds himself patronized by New Yorkers who express amazement that he can read books. "Ned was never bothered by subtleties and nuances, and I don't suppose he ever read a book in his life," complains the film-star narrator of "The Answer Depends," which is less a short story than an internal monologue containing one old actor's reminiscences about another (*HKW,* 29). The retired film star in "The Glendale People" is even writing a book, although he will never finish it because its contents would be too emotionally charged for his readers, the Glendale people of the title—non-Hollywood middle Americans whom O'Hara describes in a passage similar to Nathanael West's shriller and more grotesque descriptions in *The Day of the Locust.* These and other stories, particularly those in *And Other Stories,* bring out a theme common to O'Hara's work over the years: you can never understand people and when you think that you do, you can be absolutely sure you are wrong.

Lesbians and Other Human Beings

"I began to see that I had got into a bad habit for a writer," Jim Malloy confesses in O'Hara's final long story, "A Few Trips and Some Poetry." "I was attributing to people a capacity for long-lasting emotions that were impossible for them to sustain. I would happen to catch a man in great sadness, and I would expect him to remain sad a year later." Conveying the whole of a person, as Malloy—and O'Hara—realized, requires the selection of traits even as they are evolving. The achievement of painting a convincing portrait of a genial lifelong pal, as Malloy does with his friend Horse McGrath in "A Few Trips and Some Poetry," is that much greater if Malloy can show that friendship changing to animosity and (maybe) back again. "Perhaps the only true wisdom was doubt," Malloy asserts, "and I could now begin to acquire wisdom by doubting the instinct for understanding human beings that in my complacency I attributed to wisdom" (*AOS*, 116).

The difficulty of understanding people, coupled with their built-in capacity to change the moment they are understood, explains O'Hara's final group of stories. The ever changing stream of private thoughts, largely sexual, that runs inside O'Hara's most outwardly placid characters runs wilder in the late 1960s; he examines private lives that sometimes seem implausibly bizarre and other times seem right on the money. In every decade of his career, O'Hara consistently tested the limits of what his publishers permitted him to write about, and the 1960s were an exception only in that publishers' prudery in general suddenly and, it seemed, completely relaxed.

Coincidentally, just as publishers became willing to let O'Hara and other authors discuss homosexuality, orgies, and promiscuity (all of which figure in the plot of "A Few Trips and Some Poetry") with increasing frankness, O'Hara became far less dependent on magazines to buy his stories. Whereas he had exerted maximum effort to tailor his early stories to fit *The New Yorker*'s sense of propriety, now he earned most of his income through his novels and collections of stories and hardly cared how—or if—magazines chose his work or rejected it. (Most of his letters to magazine editors from the 1930s touch at some point on money, a subject that almost never comes up in the 1960s.)

The new standards let him describe sex in all its forms—private and public, thought and deed, heterosexual and homosexual, adolescent and sexagenarian—explicitly, sometimes in perplexing detail, as if to titillate his readers or himself, and sometimes quite naturally and refreshingly. In "A Few Trips and Some Poetry," he allows Jim Malloy, whose humor had been mostly arch and pithy in previous stories, to make quips that bring out for the first time his ribald adolescent charm. "I slept the sleep of the just," Malloy remarks, "The just-laid." The remark is in keeping with Malloy's sensibility, his relative youth, and the sexual content of the story, but it is doubtful that O'Hara would have permitted himself (or been permitted) this remark earlier. Later in the story, when a character, describing Julian and Caroline English (the main characters of *Appointment in Samarra*) says, "She sucked the life out of him," Malloy responds, "A nice way to die" (*AOS*, 94–95). Such small liberties with language, considered unforgivably obscene earlier in O'Hara's career, enliven his late prose.

The sexual appetites of O'Hara's late characters seem not only larger than those of his earlier characters but more varied. For example, a superb 1946 short story, "The Decision," describes a young medical doctor, about to embark on a promising career, being informed that since his parents both died in mental institutions, he would be best advised neither to practice medicine nor marry. The story does not dwell on the doctor's anguished reaction to this devastating news and mostly describes his leisurely way of killing time, by drinking and reading, while he waits to go insane. Later stories that took up this theme of a senselessly wasted life—such as "The General," "The Engineer," "Jurge Dulrymple," and "The Skeletons"—repeat the structure of "The Decision," showing first a character's empty life and then providing a surprising explanation for it, but the explanations in the later stories are more than just surprising. They are sensationally so: the title character of "The General" is a transvestite, that of "The Engineer" is homosexual, the women in "Jurge Dulrymple" are lesbians, and the daughter in "The Skeletons" is a lesbian child molester. By no means does O'Hara imply that heterosexuality is a sure route to fulfillment. The protagonist of his 1967 novel *The Instrument* is virtually inhuman, extracting emotions in an almost clinical sense from his frequent heterosexual encounters. It is not any one sexual act, practice, or philosophy that marks O'Hara's final works as much as it is the frankness with which he links sexuality to humanity. His nonjudgmental accounts of characters' private lives in the 1960s let him explore the humanity of various sexual patterns and tastes, perhaps too fully for some readers.

Connection itself is one of the themes that ties together O'Hara's stories. The final story, alphabetically, in the last collection published in his lifetime, *And Other Stories,* concerns the improbable connection between a wealthy young lesbian and her stable hand, an impoverished middle-aged Irish drunk. For much of "We'll Have Fun," Tony Costello, the stable hand, is seen as obsolete. The story is set in Gibbsville of the 1920s, when America's dependence on the horse as a mode of transportation was at an end, a reality that Tony resists accepting. Gibbsville's garages are quickly replacing its stables, and there are only a few stable owners left who will let Tony bed down in a stall on a cold night in exchange for his knowledge of horses, which is no longer needed. When the young lesbian turns up late in the story, Tony teaches her about caring for her horse properly. In the process, he discovers that she has been misunderstood and marginalized as much as he has but for vastly different reasons, and these two unlikely friends connect. Responding to Tony's invitation to buy a new horse, she ends the story with its title line, "We'll have fun," and it seems likely that they will.

Unlikely connections take place all through O'Hara's final collection. In "The Farmer," a young woman gets thrown by her horse and rides back to town with a farmer in his truck. She is wealthy and idle and he, as he tells her on the trip, must break his back to break even. Feeling sorry for herself, she puts her problems in perspective after hearing how this decent fellow found himself stuck in a repetitive and stultifying life. Articulate and self-reflective, the farmer blames no single person or system for his woes, even extending empathy to those trapped with him, like his uneducated and largely unaware wife. His own education consists of one year of college; when his older brother died, he had to return home to run the farm. Like Tony Costello, he is the last in a long line of men in an honorable profession about to become obsolete, and he does not have many options open. Also like Tony, who confides that he is tempted to cut his throat on "days I just as soon take a razor in me hand and let nature take its course," the farmer is drawn to suicide. He restrains himself only because his family would not get any insurance settlement, and his very long speech about his despair ends this way:

> "Last summer one day I was so disgusted, I was out in the field getting in the hay, a thunderstorm was coming. I said to myself, what was the

use of it all? And I stood there with a pitchfork in my hand and I held it up in the air for the lightning to strike. But it didn't. It hit a tree on my neighbor's farm, but not me. If I took a shotgun and blew my head off, they wouldn't get the insurance, but if I got hit by lightning they would. They'd have been all right, and so would I. Are you ready to face Dr. Jones?" (*AOS*, 40–41)

His final question, juxtaposing the young woman's minor problem with his profound despair, illustrates his compassion for her, a sentiment that she returns to him.

O'Hara's compassion extends beyond those lives ruined by sex, by drink, by poverty, including even those so completely cut off from any possibility of future pleasure that their own deaths beckon to them. Some of these seekers after death merely feel neutral, nothing, zero. In "Zero," the title of the final (alphabetically arranged) story in *The Horse Knows the Way*, when his angry and jealous wife threatens to kill him, the despairing protagonist just says to her, "Go ahead, you'd be doing me a favor," and he requests it so sincerely that she suddenly knows how passionately he longs for death.

O'Hara's characters threaten—or commit—suicide so often that critics saw it as an another form of his sensationalism and of a piece with his penchant for describing sexual acts, substance abuse, cruelty, and other extreme behavior that readers would find titillating. But his stories of suicide—including but by no means limited to "How Can I Tell You?" "Andrea," "The Jet Set," "Our Friend the Sea," "Nil Nisi," "I Spend My Days in Longing," "The Bonfire," and "The Last of Haley," in addition to many of those mentioned in this section (and his novels *Appointment in Samarra* and *The Instrument*)—extend his compassion to those who see no reason to go on living.[68]

He wrote well about depressives, probably because he had been one himself. From the 1920s through the 1950s, his letters are punctuated with remarks about his own impending suicide. While some of these threats have a deliberately self-dramatizing (or even semicomic) tone to them, their total effect is literally dead serious. His instinctive response to the prospect of extended pain, psychological or physical, was to consider ending his life. This strange yet terribly common response put him in touch with the most severe depressives, who are pitied or scorned rather than understood by those around them. O'Hara understood suicides and would-be suicides because he had felt their despair sharply for most of his life.

He also was deeply moved but publicly silent about the 1961 suicide of his friend Ernest Hemingway, whom he once called "the most important author since the death of Shakespeare." After hearing of Hemingway's suicide, O'Hara told his daughter, "I understand it so well" (MacShane, 198). Although he never elaborated directly on what he understood so well, he did publish a cryptic little story, "How Can I Tell You?," the next year, which describes some of that almost indescribable impulse toward self annihilation.

In addition to the proximity in time between Hemingway's suicide and O'Hara's story, the method of suicide hints at the famous writer's death: O'Hara's protagonist attempts suicide by placing in his mouth a double-barreled shotgun, which was also Hemingway's weapon of choice. His protagonist, Mark McGranville, does not succeed, at least not yet, because Mrs. McGranville happens to interrupt him in the act. There are additional parallels. McGranville is, in his small way, as pre-eminent in his field as Hemingway was in his. McGranville is a very successful car salesman who on the day of the story has sold three cars. "On the sales blackboard at the garage his name was always first or second, in two years it had not been down to third," he thinks as he lies awake at night beside his sleeping wife, fully aware of how admirable his life appears. "Nevertheless," the story continues, "he went to the hall closet and got out his 20-gauge and broke it and inserted a shell" (*HB*, 122).

Probably like Hemingway, whose work met near-universal acceptance, McGranville reviews a life filled with outward virtues but empty of inward meaning. The horror of that inward meaninglessness for him is that he cannot express, to anyone who does not share it, his sense of it and, worse, he knows he never can. Before his wife falls asleep, he tries articulating to her this feeling, summed up in the story's title. He cannot tell her what he feels, he cannot begin to articulate it in a way that anyone else can understand, and this futility, as much as any other frustration, impels his need to take his life. He feels cut off not only from those he loves and who love him but also from their ability to understand the pain he is in.

The final connection between McGranville and Hemingway has to do with O'Hara's method of linking his reality to his work. When he wrote *Appointment in Samarra*, also about a man, Julian English, who tries to commit suicide, and who succeeds, he based his characters on

> real people, people who have lived and are living. . . . then I put them
> in different locations and times, and covered them up with superficial

109

characteristics. . . . In the case of Julian English, . . . I took his life, his psychological pattern, and covered him up with Brooks shirts and a Cadillac dealership, and so on, and the reason the story rings so true is that it is God's truth, out of life. You would be surprised to learn who some of my principal characters are. (*Letters,* 401–2)

O'Hara wrote this letter to Gerald Murphy (himself a putative model in some of F. Scott Fitzgerald's fiction) in the summer of 1962, some five months before "How Can I Tell You?" appeared in *The New Yorker.*

The late appearance of McGranville's wife in the story might be taken as a hopeful sign, signaling a belated connection in the nick of time, or it might betoken mere postponement of his inevitable death by his own hand. The ambiguity stresses the delicate balance in McGranville's mind: he knows his life seems fine but he feels death's allure. Whether this is a story of a vital connection between the McGranvilles or a deadly misconnection is uncertain. Jean McGranville understands her husband's mind just well enough to know that she does not really understand it, but she knows she wants him to live. So when she pleads, "Don't. Please," at the end, she is providing an emotion contrary to the one he feels so strongly. She does not try to reason with him, however, because reason has nothing to do with his impulse. O'Hara hints at but does not state their connection, and he leaves open the question of whether it is strong enough to save McGranville's life for long.

The fulcrum of O'Hara's strongest stories often rests on an ambiguous point, unknowable from the story and possibly unknown to the author, such as the McGranvilles' marriage. There is no way we can know—or the characters can know—if their marriage will save McGranville's life, but that question is crucial. In "The Strong Man," characters from an earlier novel (*Ten North Frederick*) appear, and again O'Hara reuses his Gibbsville characters purposefully: Arthur McHenry and Joseph Chapin, law partners in both the story (set around 1930) and the novel (mostly set later), have a pivotal discussion about McHenry's love life, which is in disarray. A good husband (and "the strong man" of the law firm, Chapin assures him), McHenry has fallen in love with one of the firm's clients, a widow seven years his senior. Chapin tries to argue that this is far from love, that McHenry is experiencing some sort of personal crisis, and pleads for him to come to his senses. "Edith and I haven't had a perfect marriage," Chapin admits, "But I've never done anything I'd be ashamed of and I've never done anything that would cause her embarrassment. And I never will. I'm not a puritan but if people like you and me don't follow certain rules, how can we expect other people to?" This would be a more convincing speech if O'Hara's readers did not know that in the earlier novel (set a few years later, however, than "The Strong Man") Chapin himself will emphatically break the rules he is now arguing for, falling in love with a woman who provides the only pleasure of his last sad years. So his straitlaced speech here is tinged with an irony known only—but known well—to O'Hara and to many of his readers.

All of Chapin's talk about the rules is reminiscent of another of O'Hara's previous novels, *A Rage to Live*, in which a self-righteous husband rejects his adulterous yet penitent wife, delivering a peroration about the unforgivable sin of violating the rules. But as Chapin here reminds McHenry, it is the critical times, not the smooth ones, in a marriage that test its strength. "The test of a marriage isn't when you're enjoying each other's company in the bedroom," Chapin tells McHenry, speaking like the puritan he claims not to be (*AOS*, 300). The fact that this virtuous tone is struck by Chapin, only a few years away from violating the moral code he preaches, underscores the theme: None of us understands what motivates us. Though our behavior may be a far cry from our ideals, mostly we fall short by failing to understand ourselves sufficiently, not by hypocrisy.

Some of O'Hara's finest late stories concern a moral stand that may or may not be sincere. In "The Weakling," a rich man is asked to contribute to a fund for a woman who in her youth had slept with all the fund's founders. The man refuses to contribute until he makes it clear that he has never slept with the woman, despite her claims to the contrary. By placing his perspective outside of either the man's point of view or the point of view of the fund's representative, O'Hara leaves ambiguous whether the representative truly believes the wealthy man's claim or whether he is pretending he does in order to get his contribution. A similar point is made in "I Know That, Roy," in which a man's daughter comes across a wartime photograph of Pacific island women having their breasts fondled by a group of U.S. soldiers, one of whom, the daughter claims, strongly resembles her father. He denies the charge and eventually has to insist that his daughter and his wife stop referring to the soldier in the picture as "you." When the husband is alone with his wife, he assures her of his absolute fidelity to her the entire time of their separation during World War II, and she settles any outward questioning of her beliefs by assuring him in turn, "I know that, Roy." Her inward beliefs, however, are anybody's guess.

Curiously, outside of the title and the final line, he is hardly ever referred to by his first name in the story. Throughout, he is called "R. G. Hanwell," a rather formal name for a character who is depicted in his own home, not in a boardroom. Since Hanwell is the only male character in the story, O'Hara could have easily used a neutral *he* to refer to him, but O'Hara repeats his formal name several times, contrasting it with the wife's informal "Roy." The implication of the excessive formality may be that his denial is also merely formal, reiterating a lie he told his wife earlier to spare her jealousy. And, for her part, Marian Hanwell is, just as formally, going to maintain her belief in his flimsy but unassailable defense. As the title of another O'Hara story (also about digging up events from the dead and buried past) puts it, "What's the Good of Knowing?"

O'Hara reflected on his trait of referring to some of his characters by their full names, which he does with Hanwell here, with Peter Durant in "The Cellar Domain," with Jack Dorney in "The Private People," and with George Denison in the paired stories "The Locomobile" and "The Man on the Tractor." "I want to *control* the reader as much as I can," he explained, "and I make the effort in all sorts of ways. (Punctuation is one of them). . . . The repeated use of the full name, George Denison, George Denison is not accidental" (*Letters*, 422). Much more than varying the pace of the story, which the full name does but only a little, the full name stresses that character's formal standing in a way that his first name alone tends to diminish.

In "The Private People," for example, Jack Dorney is a prominent film actor who retires with his wife to live in New York. He is so famous that when someone asks who he is, Dorney's companion does not supply his name but merely asks if the questioner is an American citizen. The questioner then looks Dorney over again and says, "Oh—Jack Dorney?" (It is suggested, by a reference to Dorney's role in a famous Civil War movie, that he is comparable in fame to Clark Gable.) The first part of this story is filled with phrases such as "said Jack Dorney" and "Jack Dorney came." After five pages of such usages, O'Hara begins to refer to him merely as Jack, a technique that is in keeping with the story's theme, the humanizing of a celebrity. While it is true that Dorney is a great film star who deserves the attention he receives from the strangers he meets on his daily walk, he is also a husband, a reality the story recognizes as the references to his name change from formal to informal. Dorney has dragged his wife, Celeste, across the country to live in Manhattan, where she is so desperately unhappy that she becomes a drunk.

Miserable, she flees to California, where she creates embarrassing public scenes, so stressful that their repercussions are felt on the East Coast. Dorney flies to Los Angeles where, with his lawyer, he rescues her from the lockup in which she has been confined by a quack psychiatrist. The real significance of this dramatic rescue scene lies in the conversation between the Dorneys at the end of the story, where the dignified and almost reverential tone of "Jack Dorney" no longer resounds. In this section, the Dorneys work out a compromise to resolve their separation, across a gulf literally as wide as the continent that divides them. California is Celeste's home but, as she learns in the middle of the story, it is only a real home if her husband is with her, and he is adamant about his desire to live out his retirement away from Hollywood. He knows she will be a drunk wherever they live, so Dorney forces himself to tolerate her drinking and agrees to live with her as peaceably as he can. In the end, Celeste must fall asleep drunk every night with a light on in her room, but as O'Hara's lovely final line notes, "Oh, it is not a very bright light."

The ambiguous revisionism in "The Weakling," "I Know That, Roy," and "What's The Good of Knowing?" also appears in "All I've Tried to Be," in which a middle-aged man agrees to identify the figures in an old group photograph that someone has mailed anonymously to the local newspaper. He does so for the benefit of the pretty young reporter who brings it to his office, and then he asks her to dinner. Is he the anonymous supplier of the photo? When she asks him point-blank, he gets up on his high horse, asking her why she thinks he is the sort of person who would do such a thing, how can she suspect him, of all people, considering "all I've tried to be," and so on. She believes him, or says she does, and agrees to go out with him. These protests of his merely make the point—contrary to their content—that he is exactly the sort of attention-mongering lecher who would mail in such a photo and then, when a lovely young reporter inquires about it, would manipulate her into going out with him. But there is also the smallest chance that he is merely a long-winded blowhard innocent of premeditation. Either way, the story puts the reader in the young reporter's shoes, trying to interpret behavior without knowing the thoughts that impel it.

The withholding of crucial information is O'Hara's forte, and in his late fiction he does it so well and so often that his sudden supplying of information can manipulate readers into going where he wants them to go. Sometimes he withholds information within a character's point of view because that character has not quite yet synthesized his or her emotional reaction. In such stories, readers experience the emotional intensity simultaneously with the character. "The Windowpane Check" describes a scene in which a passenger on a train notices that a distinctive jacket he had donated to charity is being worn by a fellow passenger. The jacket conjures up intense associations with his late wife; he gave it away because he wanted to avoid the emotional turmoil he is now experiencing. The wearer of the jacket sits next to him and confesses that he knows the man donated the jacket; the jacket wearer continues to talk, forcing him to discuss the painful subject at length. Here O'Hara has constructed a nightmare scenario: not only is a man seated on a crowded train next to a bore droning on about a painfully emotional subject but also the bore is himself a widower who chatters on about his lonely life and his fears of his own impending death—in short, every subject his trapped auditor wishes to avoid.

The volta in this story comes late, and it comes fast: as the train pulls into Philadelphia, where the two men can at last go their separate ways, the man asks the jacket wearer to have dinner with him at his home. Against all logic, odds, and the entire thrust of the story, the realization hits the man as the train slows down: their deaths are impending only if they remain stuck in their mourning periods. Gimmicky a technique as it may seem, O'Hara has thoroughly studded the story with the man's warm reminiscences of his wife, making them just powerful enough to advance the notion that he needs a life richer than his present existence. At the very end, the jacket wearer asks the other man about a painting hanging in his house, and the man responds, "We still have it. That is, I have," a correction that marks his advance into the next stage of his life.

As the bored and the boring make a surprising connection in "The Windowpane Check," and as the heterosexual and lesbian do in "We'll Have Fun," so in "The Friends of Miss Julia" do the young and the old. A lonely widow, Mrs. Davis, is befriended by the young receptionist at her Los Angeles beauty parlor; the two go out to lunch, where the older woman confesses her unhappiness at living on the West Coast just to be near her daughter, married to a Hollywood executive. "Then go," the younger one advises Mrs. Davis after hearing her sad tale. "Just tell your daughter and your son-in-law that you're leaving next Tuesday" (*HB*, 85).

The widow protests (she will hurt their feelings, she does not know how to tell them), but her new young friend is having none of it, and soon Mrs. Davis is convinced that she must move back home to the Bronx. The connection between these two friends is tenuous at first (among everyone in the beauty shop, they are the only ones who react decently to news of the death of their friend, the Miss Julia of the title), but their difference is what allows the young woman to jump to such a sweeping conclusion for her older friend.

This story can be coupled with "The Private People" in that a move between the East and West Coasts provides the conflict in each story: Celeste Dorney moves to New York from Los Angeles and convinces herself the decision was a mistake, but she is wrong; after Mrs. Davis moves in the opposite direction, she convinces herself her move is a mistake, and she is correct. More than mere nay-saying, O'Hara has shifted crucial details to justify drawing opposite conclusions. Celeste Dorney's Los Angeles friends do not care for her, while her East Coast husband finally does; Mrs. Davis's New York friends really do care for her, but her family in Los Angeles wants her there only as a kind of ornament. The theme of so many of O'Hara's connection stories can be summed up by the title of one of his first such stories from *Hellbox*, "Somebody Can Help Somebody."

Judged by title alone, O'Hara's stories often seem to cry out to be taken in pairs: "The Weakling" and "The Strong Man" (both of which turn out to be ironic titles); "Justice" and "No Justice"; "Exterior: With Figure" and "Interior With Figures"; "In the Silence" and "In the Mist," among others. But more meaningful pairings can be discerned in the stories with plots that are nearly identical until they diverge late in the narrative. Both "The Gunboat and Madge" and "The Bucket of Blood" concern a Gibbsville outsider—Jay Fitzpatrick in the first story and Jay Detweiler in the second—who arrives in town as part of a shady deal. Fitzpatrick is involved in a fixed fight, after which his opponent is knifed to death, and Detweiler is employed as a carnival shill until he is stricken with an appendicitis. When their initial schemes go wrong, each of them works in and eventually buys a Gibbsville bar that he runs efficiently. Each story ends with Jay attracted to a woman: Fitzpatrick to Madge Devlin, a crooked bookkeeper, and Detweiler to Jenny, a whore who wants to ply her trade out of his bar. It is hard to believe that O'Hara could have devised two such similar plots within five years of each other without being aware of the more obvious similarities.[69]

At this point in their plots, however, "The Gunboat and Madge" diverges from "The Bucket of Blood" (which, despite the title, is the less violent story). Jay Detweiler breaks up with Jenny over her scheme, while Jay Fitzpatrick marries Madge after she rejects a dangerous scheme at his business. In the coda of "The Gunboat and Madge," Jay and Madge are an old couple retired to Florida, indistinguishable from their fellow retirees, who know nothing of their more colorful past. As in "The Glendale People," the protagonists' lives have been so fraught with excitement that there is no point in convincing the other characters of that fact. (However, unlike Dale Connell, who must retell his stories to himself to be understood in "The Glendale People," Jay and Madge have each other.)

If O'Hara had had only a single plot to tell, he probably would still have been able to spin variations on it to fill a thick collection of stories; happily, he had more than one plot to tell. His tales of cruelty are not much different from his tales of compassion, his tales of loneliness are similar to his tales of love, and his tales of inevitability are often hard to distinguish from his tales of sensational surprise. Even a close reader will be occasionally hard-pressed to tell the differences, though that close reader will much more than likely want to try.

Notes to Part 1

1. O'Hara described his early models for writing in the introduction to the 1956 Modern Library reprint of *Appointment in Samarra:* "[M]y short stories, the early ones, did owe something to Hemingway, Dorothy Parker, and Lardner until, as Wolcott Gibbs pointed out, I got going on my own. What the stories owed Hemingway was form; what they owed Mrs. Parker was point of view, and what they owed Lardner was my discovery from him that if you wrote down speech as it is spoken truly, you produce true characters, and the opposite is also true: if your characters don't talk like people they aren't good characters."

2. Brendan Gill, *Here at The New Yorker* (New York: Random House, 1975), 265. Subsequent references will be cited in the text.

3. Morris Freedman, "By O'Hara Besotted," *American Scholar* 66, no. 4 (Autumn 1997): 585–90.

4. Charles W. Bassett, "John O'Hara's 'Alone': Preview of Coming Attractions," *John O'Hara Journal* (Winter 1982–1983): 18–24.

5. Bruccoli plausibly suggests that this idea originated in the structure of Faulkner's *The Sound and the Fury*, published in 1929. Hemingway's 1924 *In Our Time* is an equally plausible prototype.

6. The use of a telephone exchange as a title anticipates O'Hara's second novel, *Butterfield-8*, some seven years later.

7. Thomas Wolfe, in the 1935 story "Only The Dead Know Brooklyn," and Tom Wolfe, in his 1987 novel *The Bonfire of The Vanities*, demonstrate their command, such as it is, of Brooklynese. Standard Brooklynese orthography also appears in Mailer's *Tough Guys Don't Dance* and in McBain's *Long Time No See*.

8. Gore Vidal, "John O'Hara," in *United States: Essays, 1952–1992* (New York: Random House, 1993).
9. O'Hara often compared story composition to musical composition. He referred constantly to his technical similarity to a music composer in his letters, for example, in the 1931 note asking an editor if he had received O'Hara's "opus number one" and in the 1963 letter comparing his stories to George Gershwin's compositions: "You take a tune like MINE, for instance. That's like one of my short stories; it could easily (with a lot of hard work, but easily) become a long piece, but instead of a fugue we have a rich little tune that is only one of many. . . . When you have mastery of your medium that George had (and that I have, let's not kid about that), you simply must not let easy popularity keep you from the big things" (*Letters*, 415).
10. James Thurber, *The Years with Ross* (Boston: Little, Brown, 1959), 13.
11. A 1928 letter to Harold Ross pitching a profile of Governor Al Smith's son ends, "Herewith are two pieces which I believe are in the New Yorker manner. I hope these will find favor. Sincerely, John O'Hara." He was, in other words, trying to learn how to adapt his areas of specialized knowledge (he had attended prep school with Smith's sons) to produce what Ross and his staff wanted. In 1929, another O'Hara query to *New Yorker* editor Katherine Angell closed with a self-introduction: "I've worked on almost as many papers as Mr. Ross, so I know pretty much what it's all about. Other dope on myself are: My father was a doctor, I am just twenty-four years old . . . ." Later that year, he wrote Mrs. Angell with more story ideas: "Good Ole Will O'Hara has put on his thinking cap for Profile ideas and here are some of the results."
12. That would have been O'Hara's real-life answer, too, of course (he claimed that everyone mistook him for a Yale man, because he tried to dress like one), suggesting that this sketch derives from O'Hara's early years of working odd office jobs around New York City while freelancing at night.
13. O'Hara lived in a Pittsburgh hotel while editing a local magazine for a few months in 1933.
14. Bruccoli's description of her as a "Shenandoah beauty" resembles an earlier reference to a nameless girl whom O'Hara got pregnant and whose abortion he borrowed money to pay for (*OHC*, 45). O'Hara's guilt over these events may account in part for his continued interest in the Mary character, whose name is given by Finis Farr as Mary Shuckeleitis, which was changed to Shuck, and by Bruccoli as Mary Stukitis, which was changed to Stewart (Stukitis and then Stewart are the names O'Hara assigns the character in *The Way It Is*).
15. The *New York Times Book Review* of 24 February 1935 contrasted the "excellent reporting" of "The Doctor's Son" (and "It Must Have Been Spring," another early Malloy-narrated story) with the rest of the collection, calling the latter "slick . . . thin, trivial, synthetic" stories that appear "monotonous [because] he has no viewpoint to offer, [because] he records rather than judges,

Part 1

[because] he synthesizes characters instead of ferreting out their depths."
Twelve years later, the *Times Book Review* was still harping on O'Hara's amoral,
cynical stance: "O'Hara seldom finds any human activity worth even faint admiration and he consistently ... finds much to sneer at, to be cruelly sardonic
about, and to condemn with a savage finality" (17 August 1947).

16. He had a literary reason, too: as is typical of first-person narrators,
Jimmy Malloy in "The Doctor's Son" is several years older than his creator.
Compare the birth years of bildungsroman narrators to those of their authors; as
a rule, the fictional counterpart will be two to five years older, a small concession
to the idealized self. John Peale Bishop also confuses Malloy's biography with
O'Hara's, claiming on the basis of dates in "The Doctor's Son" that O'Hara, as
well as Malloy, "was fifteen at the time of the Armistice," when in fact O'Hara
was 13. John Peale Bishop, "The Missing All," *Virginia Quarterly Review* 13 (February 1937): 120–21. As O'Hara aged, those two years became less significant,
allowing him to merge identities with Malloy.

In *Hope of Heaven,* Malloy's life differs from O'Hara's in several small
particulars: Malloy describes his ex-wife as "rich, and older than I and divorced,"
while O'Hara's first wife, Helen Petit O'Hara, was neither older than he nor previously divorced. And as late as "Imagine Kissing Pete," a story published and
narrated in 1960, Malloy claims to "still see [his ex-wife] once in a while,"
although both of O'Hara's former spouses had died in the early 1950s. These
trivial points aside, there is no meaningful distinction to be drawn between
author and narrator of the later short stories.

17. O'Hara had done some work in the film business, first as a publicity
writer in New York City for R.K.O. pictures and, after the success of *Appointment
in Samarra* in 1934, as a screenwriter based in Hollywood. His 40-odd Hollywood stories (and one novel, *The Big Laugh*) constitute a thoroughgoing, almost
sociological analysis of all strata of Hollywood society. The character Sidney
Goldsborough may be modeled on Samuel Goldwyn, for whom O'Hara worked
briefly.

18. Edmund Wilson, "The Boys in the Back Room," *New Republic,* 11
November 1940, 666.

19. One story with a character's name in its title is "Olive," which Frank
MacShane argues is an interpretive title because of its focus on a minor character; and MacShane provides O'Hara's view of its meaning: "On the surface, the
story seems merely a sad anecdote, but it is really about the destructiveness of
people with limited imaginations; that is why it is called 'Olive' and not 'The
Colonel and Miss Bishop' " (MacShane, 108).

20. There is no evidence that either author ever read or knew about the
other's story.

21. Exceptions include Bob Hooker in "Claude Emerson, Reporter," Dr.
Merritt in "A Family Party," Slaymaker in "James Francis and the Star," the title
character of "Arnold Stone," and Mr. Price in "Price's Always Open." In using

the name Price emblematically, O'Hara (no doubt unconsciously) echoes Jane Austen, who, in her novel *Mansfield Park*, also names her protagonist Price with emblematic intentions. Both O'Hara and Austen usually avoided such easily accessible symbols in their characters' names.

22. Sheldon Norman Grebstein, *John O'Hara* (New York: Twayne, 1966), 124.

23. Lionel Trilling, in his introduction to *Selected Short Stories of John O'Hara*, was the first critic to note O'Hara's similarity to Kafka, despite the fact that "there are no two writers who at first glance must seem more unlike and less likely to sustain comparison than O'Hara and Kafka" (xiii).

24. George Monteiro, "All in the Family: John O'Hara's Story of a Doctor's Life," *Studies in Short Fiction* 24 (Summer 1987): 308.

25. The eight Pal Joey stories not included in *Files on Parade* found their way into print in *Pipe Night*, making every story in the Pal Joey series collected in at least two books, a scheme Pal Joey himself would have approved.

26. In the introduction to *Five Plays*, O'Hara's estimate of Ross's encouragement was numerical: "Harold Ross . . . urged me to write a hundred of" the Pal Joey stories (ix).

27. In the middle of writing the series in 1939, however, O'Hara presents a slightly more hostile Rossian take on the series. Following a *New Yorker* rejection of a Pal Joey story, O'Hara submitted his next installment with the warning, "If you don't like this one, the series ends—and maybe if you do like it. You [*New Yorker* editor William Maxwell] might pass this on to Ross, though, with this reminder: that he said to me in '21' last Fall, when both of us were sober, that if I wrote him ten Pal Joey pieces I could say the hell with Hollywood." And, O'Hara's irritation at that one rejection aside, Ross did publish 12 of the 14 Pal Joey stories O'Hara eventually collected, showing his genuine appreciation of the series (*Letters*, 148).

28. As far back as the 1920s, O'Hara's ear for dialogue caused some observers, including the theatrical producer Jed Harris, to express the belief that he was "the greatest natural playwright in America" (Farr, 120).

29. The narrator is plainly O'Hara himself and his friends are equally thinly disguised: Jimmy Cannon (the well-known sportswriter, called Jimmy Shott in this piece) and the fight manager Hymie Caplin, whose name is not altered.

30. Lionel Trilling, introduction to *Selected Short Stories of John O'Hara* (New York: Random House, 1956), xiii.

31. These remarks followed hard on the repeated rebuffs of his attempts to join organizations performing useful wartime service. According to various accounts, O'Hara tried the army, the marines, the navy, and the Civil Air Patrol; he also considered joining the army specialist corps, the merchant marine, and the Red Cross, in addition to serving briefly with the OSS and the Inter-American Affairs office, where he supervised scripts for U.S. propaganda films.

These rejections were especially painful to O'Hara, who placed great importance on being accepted by the best of such organizations.

32. When O'Hara claims that in the early 1940s he "couldn't write" or that World War II kept him from writing, or when MacShane cites 20 stories in four years as a sign of decreased production, one can only infer that he could not write up to his own standards of quantity and quality. The fact of the matter is that this was an unproductive period *for John O'Hara*. For most writers, this period would have been considered productive and, for many, even a high-water mark of productivity.

33. The listing of O'Hara's short stories is based on Matthew J. Bruccoli's chronological numbering in *John O'Hara: A Checklist*, corrected to include the publication of 12 additional O'Hara stories from the 1960s.

34. O'Hara's undue pride in "Walter T. Carriman" and "Mrs. Whitman" is reflected in his inclusion of them in various "best of O'Hara"- type anthologies. See *Letters*, 221–22, and *OHC*, 233, for some of those selections.

35. John O'Hara, *Sweet and Sour* (New York: Random House, 1954), 145. Subsequent references will be cited in the text.

36. By the 1960s he was singing a different song: "Having been one of the leading practitioners of the oblique and the plotless, I have recently been putting plot back into my short stories," he wrote to Don Schanche in 1963. (An excerpt from this letter appears in Part 2 of this book.)

37. Lionel Trilling, "John O'Hara Observes Our Mores," *New York Times Book Review*, 18 March 1945, 1.

38. O'Hara felt that *The New Yorker* was too quick to reject stories about baseball. "I happen to know," he wrote a *New Yorker* editor after "Bread Alone" was accepted, "that Ross has an old hate on baseball, claiming that New Yorker readers don't know or care anything about it. But I also happen to know that Ross is so wrong in that" (*Letters*, 152). Elsewhere, O'Hara uses baseball for its metaphoric value: in the 1964 story "The Brain," he describes a business mistake by citing an axiom that John McGraw, former manager of the New York Giants, had about fining players for mental mistakes, never physical ones; in the 1960 story "The High Point," a character quotes Leo Durocher's observation about nice guys finishing last; and in "It's Mental Work" of the same year, the bartender who takes control of the bar in crisis is compared with "Bill Dickey, you remember who used to catch for the Yankees? A take-charge guy." Baseball also helps to date "The Gangster" (in *And Other Stories)*, which ends with one character remarking on the probable pennant winners that year, the Senators and the Pirates, a combination feasible only in certain years, although O'Hara may have been violating his own principles of factual accuracy here and merely generalizing about the period when both teams were contenders. "Bread Alone," however, represents O'Hara's only effort to use baseball as the central metaphor. *The New Yorker*, as his letter implies, was much more receptive in its pre–Roger Angell days to stories about football (compared to those about base-

ball). O'Hara did write several football stories, notably "Lombard's Kick," about a housewife's exasperation with football talk, and "The Tackle," about a college star's bizarre attempts in later life to discourage dwelling on his football days.

39. O'Hara had adopted Delaney as a pseudonym to sign a column he wrote in the early 1930s reviewing radio programs.

40. He also published two slim novellas in the 1950s, *The Farmers Hotel*, a prose version of a play, and *A Family Party*.

41. This story is the only one of the four not to refer specifically to his Duesenberg, but much of the meaningless California chitchat is on the general subject of cars, one of O'Hara's favorite methods of characterization.

42. O'Hara's decision to concentrate on writing novels was not, of course, purely philosophical. He and Random House president Bennett Cerf at times blamed his hiatus from writing short stories on *The New Yorker*'s deliberate alienation of him by allowing Brendan Gill's review of *A Rage to Live* to stand unretracted. Aside from the issue of O'Hara's mercenary motives in breaking with the magazine (for years, he had been complaining bitterly about the lowly sums *The New Yorker* paid him, as Gill himself points out in *Here at the New Yorker*), he was too devoted to his writing to allow any mere editorial policy to suppress for 11 years a genre he found completely fulfilling. On some very real level, O'Hara wanted to write novels and, for most of the hiatus, the feud with *The New Yorker* allowed him to do just that.

43. Irving Howe, "The Flaw in John O'Hara," *New Republic*, 27 November 1961, 16–17.

44. For example, Gilbert Highet wrote of his "embarrassment" at the tone of *Sermons and Soda-Water*, which to him resembled "fragments of an enormous autobiography." O'Hara's autobiographical tendencies in all the Malloy stories, as Bruccoli comments, are salutary ones since "he is usually most effective when dealing with his own deeply felt experiences" (*OHC*, 265).

45. O'Hara's widely noted vitriolic hypersensitivity to criticism and to hostile critics was remarkably inconstant. Although he raged when Arthur Mizener's afterword was printed in a 1963 edition of *Appointment in Samarra* and demanded Brendan Gill's head on a platter as his price for returning to *The New Yorker*, O'Hara was also pleased to include in his books introductions by Wolcott Gibbs and Lionel Trilling, who were far from uniformly uncritical of his work. Indeed, Gibbs's preface to *Pipe Night* belittled some of O'Hara's previous work as "monotonous," "rather tough reading," and mere "finger exercises." After Trilling was no less tough on him, referring in print to *Pipe Night* stories in which O'Hara was "not always at his best" and to stories that fell "into the pit of easy and all too well known sentiment," O'Hara invited him to introduce his volume of selected short stories in 1956. In that introductory essay, Trilling commented on O'Hara's sometimes "excessive" details (a comment that usually infuriated him) and noted that O'Hara's "passion for accuracy is out of control" in parts of *A Rage to Live*, the very work that led O'Hara to rail against Brendan Gill for

pointing out its "discursive and prolix" qualities. Trilling's review of *Pipe Night*, with its recommendation that "for O'Hara's talents the novel is the proper form," may have caused O'Hara's temporary leave of absence from the short story more than Gill's review did.

46. Edith H. Walton, review of *The Doctor's Son and Other Stories*, *New York Times Book Review*, 24 February 1935, 7.

47. Lionel Trilling, "John O'Hara Observes Our Mores," *New York Times Book Review*, 18 March 1945, 1.

48. Guy Davenport, "And Other Stories," *New York Times Book Review*, 24 November 1968, 5. Davenport shows the variety of the collection *And Other Stories* despite its being "a cycle of twelve stories on a single theme."

49. Certain repeated names are clearly and unfortunately accidental. The title character of one story, "Aunt Anna," has the same name as a clearly different major character in the novel *The Instrument*, Anna Phelps. And in "The Skeletons," the unusual given name Sophronia crops up without comment, though O'Hara had in the same collection given that same name to the wife of the title character in "The General." Perhaps the strangest repetition in O'Hara's work is the surname Minzer, which recurs in "A Good Location," "Yostie," "Barred," "The Gunboat and Madge," "A Few Trips and Some Poetry," "Imagine Kissing Pete," "John Barton Rosedale, Actor's Actor," "Christmas Poem," and the novel *Lovey Childs;* the name belongs to a different minor character in each case and each time is associated with sleazy, immoral, illegal, unattractive, or insane behavior. O'Hara seems to have known no one named Minzer, although he seems to have had a motive to malign critic Arthur Mizener, who had attacked *From the Terrace*. (One Minzer is called crazy Artie; the others are named Johnny, Sally, Daisy, Eddie, Muriel, and Ed. The Minzers in *Lovey Childs* and "Christmas Poem" are given no first names. All of these works postdate Mizener's review.)

50. Philip B. Eppard, "Julian English outside of *Samarra*." *Colby Quarterly* 32 (September 1996): 190–95.

51. "[C]ompassion is probably the one element most common to the 300 or more short stories I have written," O'Hara wrote to his friend Barklie Henry on 30 November 1963. Manuscripts Division, Department of Rare Books and Special Collections, Princeton University Library.

52. "[T]he sweetness of my early youth was a persistent and enduring thing, so long as I kept it at the distance of years," O'Hara has Malloy say in "Imagine Kissing Pete" (*S&S*, vol. II, 71–72). Malloy continues: "It was not nostalgia, which only means homesickness, nor was it a wish to be living that excitement again. . . . I wanted none of it ever again, but all I had I wanted to keep. . . . In middle age I was proud to have lived according to my emotions at the right time, and content to live that way vicariously and at a distance. I had missed almost nothing, escaped very little, and at fifty I had begun to devote my energy and time to the last, simple but big task of putting it all down as well as I knew how."

53. John Updike, "The Doctor's Son," in *Hugging the Shore* (New York: Knopf, 1983), 185.

54. O'Hara applied the same description, "a Mayflower descendent," to both Knowlton and Emerson. O'Hara credited Knowlton for teaching him "to respect A Fact, and to spell names correctly" (*Pottsville Journal*, 2 October 1950, 5, quoted in *OHC*, 35).

55. See Charles Bassett, "Naturalism Revisited: The Case of John O'Hara," in *Critical Essays on John O'Hara*, ed. Philip B. Eppard (New York: G. K. Hall, 1994): "Elderly *Journal* staffers recall O'Hara as something less than a dedicated researcher (he was unhappy at home, drank excessively, and loved a young woman he could not marry)" (156).

56. Letter to James Forrestal, 17 December 1946, Pennsylvania State University Library Collection.

57. O'Hara is probably unaware here that he is quoting from his own 1928 *New Yorker* short story, "Tennis."

58. See Joseph McElroy's essay in Part 3 of this volume for a critique of the antagonist's role in "Do You Like It Here?"

59. Victimizers appear even more prominently in O'Hara's late novels than in his short stories: the protagonist of *Ourselves to Know* is a murderer; that of *The Big Laugh* a heel; that of *The Lockwood Concern* an egocentric miser; that of *The Instrument* a human automaton, to name only a few.

60. O'Hara's Hollywood stories are not necessarily limited to that part of California. Some of those classified as Hollywood stories here are set on Broadway, for example. The classification could be stretched to stories depicting include upper-class life on the East and West Coasts, even that of characters outside of show business, provided they project a public persona. The suburban settings O'Hara employed in the 1960s, for example, are clearly used to tell stories that would not make sense in Gibbsville, with its long-established family histories. (Indeed, most Gibbsville stories are set in the past, and the few Gibbsville stories set in the present—like "The Locomobile" and "The Man on the Tractor"—look back in time for their content.) Kathryn Riley's essay, "The Suburban Vision in John O'Hara's Short Stories," (in part 3 of this volume), thoroughly discusses the themes of many suburban stories (mainly how families get torn apart and how they sometimes surprisingly become reunited); and so these stories will be largely overlooked here, though they do share one primary characteristic with the Hollywood stories. However they are defined, the Hollywood stories all share the element of surprise.

61. O'Hara especially enjoyed hearing authorities confirm his psychological insights, as when he was informed that a psychologist "reads everything I write, and has said that I never make a mistake about the psychological treatment of my characters. He is not the first to say that, by the way" (*Letters*, 413).

62. The play Bahs offers Rosedale is entitled *Perihelion*, a title that recurs in the late Hollywood-Broadway stories as often as the title *Strange Virgin* recurs in the earlier

show business stories: *Perihelion* appears in "Papa Gibraltar," "The Man with the Broken Arm," and the play *Veronique*, as well as in "John Barton Rosedale, Actor's Actor."

63. Bluenoses like Louis Auchincloss are alarmed by O'Hara's mere mentioning of sexuality, censoriously observing that "[e]ven the character from
whom one might expect some degree of reticence—the rich dowagers, for
example—will discuss sex on the frankest basis with the first person to bring
the subject up. And in Gibbsville or Fort Penn the first person to bring it up is
the first person one meets"—Louis Auchincloss, "The Novel of Manners Today:
Marquand and O'Hara," in *Reflections of a Jacobite* (Boston: Houghton Mifflin,
1961), 149. Not troubling to cite asexual rich dowagers like Mrs. Stratton of Oak
Knoll, O'Hara typically responded to such oversimplifications by equating the
proportion of sexuality in daily life with the relatively small proportion sexuality
takes up in his writing.

64. Again, Auchincloss oversimplifies this trait in O'Hara when he writes,
"The most casual meeting between a major and minor character will result in
either an ugly flare-up or a sexual connection or both" (Auchincloss, *Reflections*,
149). In fact, the flare-ups and sexual connections work, for the most part, precisely because they are relatively rare, and O'Hara's readers never quite know
when to expect them, or when an encounter that has great potential to become
an argument or a seduction will dissipate into nothingness.

65. "The Brain" resembles "The Sun-Dodgers" in its confusing structure:
the title character of "The Brain" gets himself fired from his job, although
whether the second distanced perspective is a retelling of the first up-close version or a continuation of those narrative events is completely unclear. We can be
sure that the story's facts are skewed because the names of certain characters,
such as the Brain's secretary, are slightly different in the two sections of the story.

66. This self-centered sexual philosophy is reminiscent of "the virtue of
selfishness" espoused by Ayn Rand, whom O'Hara met in 1962 and, after a long
conversation with her, concluded "that I am diametrically opposed to her philosophy" (*Letters*, 413). Where her writing glorifies and extols the ego, O'Hara's
demonstrates how the excesses of egoism consumes human lives.

67. See John Wright, "Natica Jackson and *The Medea*," *John O'Hara Journal*
2, no. 2 (Summer 1980): 64–68, for a flawed but stimulating look at parallels
between O'Hara's story and the play by Euripides.

68. The last five stories listed concern suicide by drowning, a method of
self-destruction that held a special morbid fascination for O'Hara. He was
frightened by deep water and, despite owning a beachside cottage for several
decades, refused to swim. Other stories that deal with drowning but not suicide
include "Natica Jackson," "Your Fah, Nee Fah, Nee Face," and "Alone."

69. One such strange occurrence, for example, involves two stories in *Good
Samaritan*, "The Journey to Mount Clemens" and "The Mechanical Man,"
whose endings O'Hara in his last years mistook for each other. See page ix of
Albert Erskine's introduction to that collection for the full account.

Part 2

THE WRITER

From Addresses to the Students of Rider College in 1959 and 1961

I think I was the first to use the expression, a tin ear, in connection with the writing of bad dialog. The tin ear has always meant the inability to carry a tune, but an author who has a tin ear is one who forces his characters to say things they would not say, in ways they would not say it; and most authors have tin ears. This would not be so bad if it was an isolated fault, but it seldom is. Let me give you an example.

Some years ago, when I was writing a great many short stories for a magazine, I was called in by an editor to discuss a story in which one of the characters was an upper-class New York girl, a Spence-Chapin-Brearley type girl. I had given this girl a line of dialog which went something like this: "Robert didn't come with she and I." I repeat the line: "Robert didn't come with she and I." Now obviously the girl should have said "with her and me." The preposition *with* governing the objective case. The editor, a college graduate and a Junior League type herself, maintained that the girl would not have made the grammatical mistake I had her make. But the editor was an editor and not an author, and she had never written any dialog. She was also, let's face it, a bit of a snob, and she was trying to tell me that people like her did not make such mistakes. My point, however, was that just such a mistake was made all the time, and that it revealed more about the girl than a hundred words of descriptive matter. Girls who went to fashionable schools would not say, "Josephine is prettier than me." They would have had drummed into them the rule that the verb to be takes the same case after it as before it, and they would go through life correctly saying, "Josephine is prettier than I." But while learning that one rule they also were developing what might be called an elegant resistance of the objective pronouns. I therefore stubbornly refused to make the change

From Matthew J. Bruccoli, ed., *"An Artist Is His Own Fault": John O'Hara on Writers and Writing* (Carbondale: Southern Illinois University Press, 1977). Reprinted by permission of Wylie O'Hara Doughty.

that the editor suggested, and the story appeared as I had written it. The incident had a happy ending. A few weeks later I saw the editor again and she said to me: "You were right about *she and I.* They say it all the time, even my niece says it." Well, I knew that, or I wouldn't have written *she and I,* but I was pleased that I had been able to teach an editor to listen for the peculiarities of speech that occur in all classes. Whenever an author can teach an editor anything he has not only done himself a favor, but he has just possibly made it a little easier for other authors.

This theory of mine, that I could be persuaded to call O'Hara's Law, that an author who does not write good dialog is not a first-rate author— is not something I stumbled on, or arrived at overnight. I have indicated earlier that a line of bad dialog can destroy a character, even for the non-professional reader who does not know why the character has become unbelievable. I discovered O'Hara's Law in my own laboratory. I love to write. When I am not writing I am really wasting my time, and when I no longer can write, I will soon die. Now one of the many experiments I have conducted in my laboratory—and I hope you realize that I am not being serious when I refer to it as my laboratory—is to put a sheet of paper in the typewriter, think of two faces I have seen, make up a scene, such as a restaurant table or two seats in an airplane, and get those two people into conversation. I let them do small talk for a page or two, and pretty soon they begin to come to life. They do so entirely through dialog. I start by knowing nothing about them except what I remember of their faces. But as they chatter away, one of them, and then the other, will say something that is so revealing that I recognize the signs of created characters. From then on it is a question of how deeply I want to interest myself in the characters. If I become absorbed in the characters, I can write a novel about them and so can any other novelist. A fine novel can be written about any two people in the world—by a first-rate novelist. A great novel could be written about any man or woman that ever lived—by a great novelist. But while I have written, and published, short stories that had such accidental beginnings, I do not approach the writing of novels in such casual fashion. As a rule I don't even finish the stories I begin that way, and I deliberately destroy what I have done by giving one of the characters a line of atrocious dialog—humorous, profane, or completely out of character—that makes it impossible seriously to continue. . . .

. . . It is one thing to admit or claim that I write credible conversations, naturalistic speech. But it is something else to say I have a phonographic ear. My dialog is good because I never allow a character to say anything he would not say, that is not a product of his social and educational background and of the occasion on which he is speaking, relaxed, under stress, drunk, sober, tired, or whatever the occasion may be. But most importantly his social, that is to say his social and economic background, and his educational background govern the way he expresses himself in words. Well-educated men and women—and I have listened to them in high society and in parties at the Institute for Advanced Study—disobey the ordinary rules of grammar whenever they open their mouths, and they do not speak in sentences. They do have better vocabularies than the uneducated or the less well educated, and they finish their thoughts. But if you have ever taken a taxi from Penn Station to Grand Central you have had to listen to a taxi driver finishing his thought, whatever it may be—usually his idea of how to solve the traffic problem or the conduct of the United Nations or the way he would run the Yankees in 1960. So perhaps I am overemphasizing the virtue of finishing a thought, and should only make the point that the great brain at an Institute party expresses himself more graciously than the hackie, and a good dialog writer can create the speech of both convincingly without using a tape recorder.

Control of dialog by an author means not only his getting the speech down so that it seems real. Control also can be useful in other ways. For instance, in the writing of a scene between a man and woman who are parting after a love affair it may be the author's intention to create a mood of sadness, grief at the prospect of parting, but without getting maudlin. Here the author can make his man and woman talk away for a couple of pages, saying the homely, ordinary things that make up the most of human speech. But he can stretch out the conversation, if he has complete control, so that just the length of the conversation and the banality of it can convey a sense of the agonizing experience the two people are going through. He must know precisely where to end it, and God knows he must know where to begin. Later on I am going to take up the hypnotic effect of type, to demonstrate how effectively type can be used in subtly influencing the reader, but for the moment I only want to point out that the quick, short sentences that would appear in such a scene as I have described are part of an author's control of dialog that goes beyond his editing of the words. . . .

. . . [T]he significant detail really does have significance.

In 1930, three years before I began to work on my first novel, I wrote a short story in which no human being appeared. I described in detail, significant detail, the contents of a hotel room. The story was about a thousand words long, which is not long for a short story, so the details had to be the right ones. When you finish reading the story you know that the man who had been occupying the room had been on the town the night before, that he had quarreled with his girl, and that he had committed suicide by jumping out the window. The story was, of course, experimental and a literary tour de force. It was almost bought by a magazine, and the reason it was not bought is macabre in itself: on the day I submitted the story a member of the magazine staff committed suicide by jumping out the window. Now I have just given you a beautiful example of insignificant detail. The fact that coincidentally a member of the magazine staff committed suicide has no place in this lecture, although it has a certain amount of interest of itself. Significant detail does not at all mean that you take one or two items—a silver cup, say, and an old riding crop—and try to get your effect with the minimum of detail. Sometimes it is desirable to do so. The famous cuff links made of human teeth in *The Great Gatsby* come quickly to mind, and you can supply your own favorite examples of the single significant detail out of your own reading. But the complaint against me in recent years is that I supply too many details. It is not a valid complaint. Many times I have described the contents of a room, or the bric-a-brac on a mantel, and the hasty reader misses the significance of the items I have mentioned. Fortunately I don't give a damn for the hasty reader; if he pays $5 for one of my novels and he wants to throw his money away by skipping or skipping over, that's his loss and not mine. I have done an honest, complete job. If he only wants to listen to the trombones, it's all right with me. I know the violas and cellos are there. I put them there. But detail has to be handled with care, even when the detail is there in abundance. For instance when you are describing a man's clothes you must get everything right, especially the wrong thing. . . . I once described a man who was perfectly dressed except for one small item. He was wearing a double-breasted suit from a good tailor, which meant that it was well cut and fitted him nicely, the material was quiet but distinctive, his shoes came from London and were just right, his necktie was a small-figured one, his shirt was a quiet stripe, from a London shirtmaker. The man was beautifully turned out except for one thing: in his collar instead of a gold safety pin he was wearing a miniature hunting horn. That one detail was significant among all the others and made all the others significant as well. Here was a man with plenty of money, who got his clothes at the best places in New York and London and in all respects but one his taste was correct. But the miniature hunting horn itself was all right; it indicated that he was probably a fox-hunting man or he would not have owned such a pin. The significance was in his wearing the pin with the wrong outfit, and the fact cast doubt over the soundness of his taste. The genuine fox-hunting man would not have worn that pin anywhere but in the field, and certainly not in an outfit that was so carefully and expensively chosen for town wear. The guy, in other words, was a bit of a phony. He could not resist that one vulgarity, and because he could not resist it, he inadvertently proclaimed his dubious standing. The significance of the detail was that everything else was perfection.

Now that kind of detail might not seem important to a great many readers, to most readers, but it was important to me, and because it was important to me, important enough to state it, it could become important to a reader who would ask himself why this author had bothered to include it. My novels are full of such items that I know full well are overlooked by readers, professional and otherwise.

Not longer than a week ago I heard it said over the air that a psychiatrist could tell a lot about you by what kind of car you drove. Well, it's nice to have the head-shrinkers catch up with us, no matter how long they take to do it. Novelists have known for forty years that you could do that. Sinclair Lewis was very good at that. In his day the Buick was as much a badge of your social and economic standing as a Rotary Club button, as the Shriner's ring, as the Elks tooth; and just to make sure that you got the point, Sinclair Lewis would mention the car and the insignia. But if he had wanted to make a subtler distinction, he could have used the Franklin as a characterizer. To most of you the Franklin is not even a memory, but there was a time when it was as effective for the novelist's purpose as the Buick. In the twenties if you said a man owned a Franklin you would not be talking about the kind of man who owned a Buick, although some Buicks cost the same amount of money as some Franklins. The Franklin-owner would not be wearing an Elks tooth nor a Rotary Club button. He might wear a Masonic pin, but not a Shriner's. The Franklin-owner was more likely to be a tennis player than a golfer, a doctor than a real estate agent, a college man than a noncollege man, and a much more independent thinker than the Buick owner. He would also be likely to own more securities than the Buick owner, whose money would be tied up in personal enterprises. Now why is all this so important to the novelist? It is important because character is so important; it would be out of character for a Buick type man to own a

Franklin; it would not be quite so much out of character for a Franklin man to own a Buick. In any case, the novelist has told the reader that Jones owns a Franklin, therefore Jones will behave as a Franklin-owning Jones will behave. And if he behaves in a way that is out of character, either the novelist has been wrong in providing him with a Franklin, or he, the novelist, must explain and make credible the acts that are not in character for the Franklin-owning Jones.

The soundness of the novelist's use of the automobile as a characterizer is not, I think, open to question. It is accepted. . . . [T]he significant detail was not merely an arbitrary rule of composition that had been created by the academicians. As an author I have been fascinated by a detail that my wife reported to me last week. She saw a station wagon being driven by a young nun. The little nun was driving along with her arm out the window and her hand resting on the roof. From that one detail I could almost construct a short story, and it would certainly be very helpful in a novel.

A while back I mentioned the hypnotic effect of type, and this seems to be as good a time as any to dwell on that topic. I have discussed dialog and detail, somewhat sketchily, to be sure, but there is a book that I have no intention of writing that would concern itself solely with dialog, and it could be followed by another book, likewise not on my schedule, about detail, and both dialog and detail are related to what I call the hypnotic effect of type, or what might also be called the use of type in mesmerizing the reader. . . .

. . . I have always used italics in dialog more than most authors do, for the reason that a composer uses shaded and unshaded notes. But it is impossible to do more than an approximation of the rhythms and tones of speech, and even as I use italics in dialog I am admitting defeat. If you try to write phonetically you are in danger of writing phony, as do the people who think they are being naturalistic when they spell you, y e w. In my never-to-be-written book on dialog I would make the point that in dialog you could spell the second person pronoun that way, y e w. But only if the speaker came from New Jersey, Maryland, Eastern Pennsylvania, Central Ohio, and certain other parts of the country where you is not pronounced *yoo* but is pronounced *yew*. Perfect naturalistic representation is impossible of attainment and to attempt it in a novel or short story is not only to waste your time but also to risk the loss of the ideal reader's attention. If you doubt me, and if you have a good enough ear to make the experiment, try to write a line of dialog phonetically as it would be spoken by an upper-class Englishman. There simply is no way to put down the upper-class Englishman's enunciation of the full vowel sounds. The reason, of course, is that the Old Etonian does not employ the full vowel sounds. When he says "how do you do" he says neither *how* nor *do* nor *you* nor *do*. What's more he probably doesn't give a damn how you do. And regional sounds in this country can at best only be indicated, the classic example, of course, being the Virginian's four-syllable pronunciation of the word mule. Even I, with my built-in Penn-sylvania twang, cannot reproduce in speech or writing the Philadel phian's way of saying "downtown Philadelphia."

So I keep my readily recognizable tricks with type down to the barest minimum. However, I know the potentialities of type, and I am about to demonstrate to you the ill-known fact that the writing of a novel is far from being all there is to the creation of it. The creation and production of a novel has what might be called its own logistics, and I'll go into that later, but first this matter of type.

... [W]hen I first read Ernest Hemingway's *A Farewell to Arms* I was so impressed by his paragraphing that I remembered it photographically, and then when I read *The Autobiography of Alice B. Toklas* I realized that in at least one respect the people who said that Gertrude Stein had been an influence on Hemingway were quite correct. My theory was that a reader who did not read English, who looked at the Caporetto retreat passages in *A Farewell to Arms* and at many pages of the Alice B. Toklas book, would be led to believe that both books had been written by the same person. Both books were, of course, published before I wrote my first novel, and while I do not now recall that I made any use of the Hemingway-Stein technique in *Appointment in Samarra*, I am free to admit that beginning with *A Rage to Live*, which I published in 1949, and which I regard as the first novel I wrote in which technique was more than merely construction, I was quite conscious of the effectiveness of that particular Hemingway-Stein technique. I refer especially to the use of great blocks of type that are much too long to be called paragraphs. And here let me say that this technique has no relation to the sentences and paragraphs of William Faulkner, which are another matter entirely. Hemingway, and others before him, including Washington Irving and Sinclair Lewis, instinctively or by design, presented the reader with massive blocks of type that by their massiveness prepare the reader for a great collection of facts even before the reader has had a chance to read the words and sentences. This is a splendid device. For several hundred years the spoken word in novels has had all the typographical breaks, by reason of the fact that said-he and said-she are kept separate and thus subtly the reader is directed to break his attention from he to she, which is what the novelist wants him to do. But in descriptive passages, whether they are descriptive of the contents of a room, or of a fistfight, or of a stream of consciousness, most novelists have been timid about risking the long, unbroken block of type. Consequently they paragraphed descriptions that should have been kept intact. For instance, and to invent a case in point, during the Second World War I visited an atoll in the Pacific after it had been secured by our forces in an action that was said to be one of the most destructive, from the standpoint of shellfire, of the war. To me the only way to describe that island and the effect of that shellfire would have been to put it all in one paragraph or block of type, no matter how long it would run. It was the way I saw it, and I know my job well enough to have picked out the significant details, even if there were hundreds of them, ranging from a single marine's boot lying in a ditch to a lone coconut palm tree that had completely escaped the tons of heavy artillery. . . .

. . . I do not tailor my stories to suit any commercial publication requirements; I don't have to. Nearly everything I write gets printed, and it gets printed the way I want it or not at all. I have been publishing fiction for more than thirty years, and in that time I have acquired a reputation and with the reputation, a following, so that while my books enjoy varying degrees of success, none of them nowadays is a total flop. If that were not so, I might be inclined to knuckle under if a publisher suggested that I stretch out some manuscripts and cut down some others, although I doubt it. I have always been rather independent, which is the understatement of the evening.

What, you may ask, determines an author's decision as to the method he is going to use, and therefore the length a story will run? Well, if you want to know what determines William Faulkner's decisions, you'll have to ask him. But I'm here, and I'll try to tell you what influences my decisions.

I'm afraid that the truthful answer is not an altogether satisfactory one, but truthfully, the method I use on a given story depends first of all on author's instinct. I don't know whether you're born with it, or you acquire it through years of creative writing, but I do know that somewhere along the line you become aware of it, and if you have enough self-confidence, you learn to trust your instinct. It's almost always right.

Out of somewhere you get an idea for a story. Frequently, at least with me, it is not a story idea but a character idea. This is old stuff to those of you who have heard me before, but I reserve the right to repeat

134

myself and even to contradict myself. That's the kind of lecturer I am. So I get a character idea, and that is often all I need to get started on a story. As I told you in, I think, my second lecture, I get my character placed somewhere and start him talking to someone, and pretty soon the character takes form, for the dialog, if it is true, is self-revealing right away. The dialog establishes the economic-social-educational status of the character, and very soon establishes the circumstances of the scene in which he is speaking. Before I have finished two pages of manuscript my author's instinct has told me how much I want to tell about this character, and thus the length of the story is dictated by my wish. You understand, of course, that I employ this method in writing short stories, which vary in length from 1,500 to 15,000 words, which is quite a variation.

From Letters to Don A. Schanche and William Maxwell in 1963

To Don Schanche, 18 May 1963

In the modern short story there has been practically an abandonment of action—for which, I admit, I am partly responsible. Every time I write a story I do some experimenting; it may not be apparent to the reader, but it is in there to some degree. I know it's there. In the past thirty or forty years there have been very few first-rate short stories that contained action or plot; we who wrote the stories have been influenced by Chekhov, among others, and have been reacting against the junky plot stories that Littauer at Collier's and Rose at the Post, among others, have insisted upon. That reaction was okay. The plot stories did bear little relation to truth and life. But having been one of the leading practitioners of the oblique and the plotless, I have recently been putting action back into my stories. Vide, for instance, two stories that come to mind that appeared in The New Yorker: one called THE BUCKET OF BLOOD, about a carnival hustler who buys a speakeasy in Gibbsville, Pa., and another called IT'S MENTAL WORK, about an itinerant bartender in NY. I sold those stories to The NYer because the emphasis was not on the action, but the action was there aplenty. THE LAWBREAKER is in the same genre, but I sent it to you first because you are entitled to first look at anyway half my stories and because I want Post readers to be constantly surprised. I do not want them to think they know what to expect when they see my name on a story. New Yorker readers now know that they *don't* know what to expect from me, and that is good. You have had a nice mixture so far, and I am going to continue to mix them up.

From Matthew J. Bruccoli, ed, *Selected Letters of John O'Hara* (New York: Random House, 1978), 422, 430. Reprinted by permission of The Pennsylvania State University Libraries, Marybelle Schanche, and Wylie O'Hara Doughty.

To William Maxwell, 4 April 1963

I am always, always, experimenting.

Because I write plain, but without the jerkiness of Hemingway-plain, most of what I do of a technical nature is not noticeable. For instance, what I do about blocks of type, or paragraphing. I have been working on that since 1930, which is the year I read A FAREWELL TO ARMS, and I still work on it in every story and all my novels. It would take too long to tell you about it, and it wouldn't make very fascinating reading, but it has to do with the technique (mine) of mesmerizing the reader. . . . I want to *control* the reader as much as I can, and I make the effort in all sorts of ways. (Punctuation is one of them.)

The repeated use of the full name, George Denison, George Denison, is not accidental. It would be a damned sight easier just to say George or Denison or he said, or said George, etc. But here again I am fixing that name in the reader's eye, and I am borrowing from, among others, the 19th Century Europeans. Ivan Ivanovitch, a Russian writer would say, every time, as the Irish, in dialog, address each other as John-Patrick, Francis Xavier, etc.

There are times when I want to slow down the reader, almost imperceptibly, but slow him down. I can do that by saying George Denison, in full. I can do it for a greater length of time with a big block of type, like the Caporetto retreat. I can make it easier for the reader by filling up that block of type with nouns—rifles, machine guns, tanks, motorcycles, ambulances, and other non-think words—but the reader is still being slowed down. He picks up the pace, is forced to, when I go back to dialog. But since most of the stories I write for The New Yorker are in dialog, I have to use other tricks, and another trick I use is to dispense entirely with the attributive tag. The full name will do that, if used sparingly. By which I mean, George Denison, but not a whole bunch of full names. One of the things that make Hellman unreadable and instantly identifiable is too many proper names, too many capitalized words. Eustace Seligman, Frederick B. Adams, John Hay Whitney, et al., attending a dinner of Les Amis d'Escoffier at the John Dillinger Room of the Hotel des Artistes. I am well aware of that danger.

Finally, I prefer "said John Smith" to "John Smith said," for a number of reasons. It is easier on the eye to follow a comma and close-quotes with a small *s* than with a cap *J*. And "John Smith said" is abrupt and full-stop where I don't want it to be.

Part 3

THE CRITICS

David Castronovo

"The Doctor's Son" is a signature short story that contains O'Hara's best chip-on-the-shoulder realism. It tells the story of 15-year-old Jimmy Malloy, a boy pressed into service as a driver for his physician-father during the influenza epidemic of 1918. The first-person narrator—in an abrupt, matter-of-fact, but distinctly sarcastic style—drops the reader into a confusing world of class distinctions, sexual betrayal, and sudden death. Genteel Gibbsville and working-class Collieryville are the settings for Jimmy's awakening to the complexity of adult life. An initiation story of sorts, O'Hara's grim journey through a disease-ravaged town is something else as well: a thorough and steady account of the nature of a community. The boy registers his reactions to the sick and the well, the decent and immoral, the beautiful and ugly, the classy and the downtrodden. The shape and style of the story tell a great deal about O'Hara's future as a writer: his lifelong desire to expose human weakness, his obsession with what he was fond of calling "social conditions," his rejection of focused satire in favor of sarcastic chronicling.

The design of the plot is actually O'Hara's style writ large: an offhand, unliterary plunge into reality, precise about details, yet vague about their significance. Jimmy begins with a perfectly neat account of how doctors get sleep, fend off suffering hordes of patients, and employ threats of violence when things get desperate. He unpacks these drastic measures like so much inventory, like goods laid out for inspection; once they are in place he turns to what happens when Dr. Malloy collapses from exhaustion and young Dr. Myers is summoned from the University of Pennsylvania to carry out his grinding schedule. Jimmy drives Myers on his rounds—from the prosperous home of mine superintendent David Evans to the squalid "patches" where ragged and angry "Hunkie" and Irish miners live. The young substitute—he has not quite finished his studies—does his job well but combines medicine with romancing Evans's pretty wife. Mrs. Evans's daughter, Edith, as it

"The O'Hara Attitude" is published here for the first time by permission of David Castronovo.

happens, is Jimmy's girl. This, it should be said, is the only circumstance that complicates the plot. Two young people who are secretly in love—and very innocently sharing furtive kisses—watch two adults engaging in a cheap little affair. The subterfuges of the amorous doctor and eager patient are paralleled by Jimmy and Edith's strategies of spying. The atmosphere of a plague year can be seen in everything from the breakdown of routines, to the unlikely affair, to the the children excused from school, to the general drunken abandonment. Late in the story, Evans has been out to get Myers at a local tavern where the doctor is treating people wholesale. He is worried about his wife, soon reassured (ironically) by Myers that she is well and—with a sense of relief—swigs booze from a bottle that has been contaminated by plague-stricken patrons. Within two pages Jimmy is reporting on Evans's death, on Myers's return to Philadelphia, and on Edith's departure for boarding school and subsequent elopement. The last line, "Now I never can remember her married name," complements the abrupt manner of the opening passage about Gibbsville in crisis.

The bitter edge of this final line certainly echoes Hemingway's tone in stories from *In Our Time* and earns O'Hara a definite place in the fictional chronicling of the Great War. Jimmy's voice—a register of the horror of things, the dead children, the squalor of the patches, the moral chaos—is as resentful and as precise about what has happened as the voice that reported on the quai at Smyrna ("You remember the harbor. There were plenty of nice things floating around in it") or the battlefields. O'Hara has adapted and modulated that famous tough-but-compassionate voice of Hemingway for his own kind of story—basically a social survey rather than Hemingway's moral fable. Lacking Hemingway's cosmic sense, his deep reach into souls, his vision of a crumbling civilization, and his despair about the nature of things, O'Hara developed a social-materialist slant on the American condition. (Hemingway took a glancing look at this part of life—often a careless and stereotypical one as in the portrait of Robert Cohn in *The Sun Also Rises*.) Yet O'Hara, the master in his own territory, adopts the Hemingway attitude—the nasty edge, the sarcasm, the bits of tenderness—to put a charge on his social themes.

"The Doctor's Son" is saturated with class consciousness. As the story moves toward death and loss, it does so in the language of social class—and often with an ironic spin. People are shown within a tangled web of gentility. Before the action of the story is allowed to move forward, O'Hara gives us a breathless sociological account of Gibbsville—com-

142

plete with the pecking order, the colleges attended, and the nationalities of the town's best. In one scene Dr. Myers, a man who talks openly about his poor background, nevertheless sneers at a poor, obese Hungarian woman; this contrasts oddly with the fact that he previously bought her a drink and interrupted his schedule by making a house call. When Jimmy accompanies Myers to the patches, nothing is more important than the politeness and consideration and respectfulness (or the very occasional lack thereof) of the patients. Decorum, even in the face of death, is highly valued currency. Or, as the rough tavern owner, Kelly, puts it in his remarks to the sick who have gathered at his place, "And any lug of a lunkhead that doesn't stay in line will have to answer to. . . ." This of course does not mean that O'Hara lets phony politeness stand for the real thing. Everything about Mrs. Evans is stilted, overdone in dress and manner—and O'Hara has already pointed out that she was a Collieryville Polish girl who never quite fit in with Jimmy's mother, a boarding school product and bridge player. The snobbery of these characters, so natural to O'Hara, does not detract from the story: actually it is an honest account of how things were. O'Hara does nothing to glamorize his own class: his impulse is purely reportorial.

Be sure—he seems to say on every page—that you realize where you are: in a nouveau riche woman's dining room, in a University of Pennsylvania medical school graduate's office, in a Cadillac or a Ford or a Buick. And when you know where you are . . . even then you will be surprised by people's unpredictable behavior. Somehow it helps to know what backdrops and standards people are acting in reference to; and yet such referents—the surgeon's pride, the barkeep's affability, the upper-middle-class matron's politeness—do not give us access to the depths of character. We end up, like Jimmy, with a kind of well-informed bafflement, a resentful state between superficial knowing and genuine recognition. And this may help define the problem of O'Hara's fine but limited art: most often he is the social chronicler without a satiric purpose or a guiding philosophy, the writer with a fabulous command of actuality but a fairly predictable attitude—sore-headed and knowing—to bring to bear on it. His famous precision—for all its brilliance in defining groups and creating memorable people—provides a meager yield of general meaning. What, after all, has Jimmy learned? The answer can only be that he has combined his almost instinctive knowledge of social class with a heightened awareness of the nasty side of sex and the brutal face of disease and death. He has learned that Myers is a Penn man who plays around while saving lives; he has learned that Edith is a lovely girl who knows about sex and who finally retreats into her class strong-hold, probably because she is ashamed of the secret they once shared. He has learned about the bitter, contradictory, chaotic quality of adult experience.

The narrative fault in this awakening story is, regrettably, a matter of basic logic. Early on, Jimmy pinpoints his own attitude and situation in the line, "All the little kids at dancing school called me James, and the oldest girls called me sarcastic." He is no longer a little kid; he is worthy of respect. Once again, there is O'Hara's characteristic whiff of status and sexuality. "The Doctor's Son" is about someone who is knowing and world-weary at 15—and was so, it must be added, before he ever encountered Myers or death or loss. While the story is an unforgettable piece of scene painting and a tough-and-tender slice of social chroni-cling, it does not quite resonate as an emotional experience because the recognition is there from the start.

Guy Davenport

John Henry O'Hara was a very great American writer who has thus far eluded inclusion in any school, movement, or other category. He was a realist, we say with some confidence, and when we put him tentatively beside other realists, he is still distinctive and seems to have little in common with them. He makes James T. Farrell seem primitive and strained. He pairs well with Dreiser, who shared his disillusions, but makes Dreiser appear to have a lot yet to learn about American men and women. The inevitable comparison with Hemingway shows up Hemingway's romanticism and radical immaturity. We could sustain comparisons: what would keep turning up is O'Hara's mastery of writing not to write, like Hemingway, for a particular effect, or like Faulkner, to keep inventing prose styles, or like Eudora Welty, to find the perfect phrase to fix a character or moment, but to put down information about human beings. O'Hara's prose is as invisible as the spokes of a turning wheel.

He had the instincts of a writer: relentless curiosity, a perfect ear for the vulgate (of which he was justly vain), the gossip's memory, and that acute gauge of spite, jealousy, resentment, and uneasiness that made him (and Proust, and James) the great writer he was. This is temperament: that felinely feminine nose for hidden emotions of which Hemingway knew no more than an infant. O'Hara tells us things about people that a lifetime of observation cannot equal.

And here we run into the paradox of O'Hara. He was wise to people, but not wise about them. He is not a satirist, as he has no moral program to examine (like Graham Greene). He is not particularly a critic of his society. Obviously he is a moral writer, with a sharp distinction in his own mind between right and wrong. But he never acts as plaintiff or judge or jury. He suspends his characters in a glare of intelligence, much as James did. He tells us what their values are, he shows us what these values do to the people who have them, and leaves the matter at that. I would place him among the philosophers if I could imagine a philoso-

"On O'Hara," *John O'Hara Journal* 3, no. 1–2 (Fall/Winter 1980). Reprinted by permission of Guy Davenport.

145

pher who set out to describe real people in the real world, satisfied that such a picture is sufficient activity in itself.

Reading O'Hara is a full engagement with narrative at its purest. He always had something to tell, and knew perfectly how to tell it. This is a far rarer art than we suppose. We can say this of Maupassant, but not of Proust; of Chekhov but not of Turgenev; of James but not of Conrad.

There are writers (Maupassant, Chekhov, James) who find the world with their imagination, and writers (Proust, Turgenev, Conrad) who find the world in their imagination. O'Hara found the world with his imagination. That pot of white bean soup that had been on the back of the stove for years and years: it is real. So is everything else in O'Hara. He was probably temperamentally incapable of making anything up. And what he observed, he kept clean of any contamination from the traditional coloring of literary tones. He frequently worked with all the elements of tragedy, but never allowed them to take tragic shape; he is always close to the comic but never exploits it. His mind is ironic; he never makes irony the point of a story. He likes to discover moral abscesses behind respectability and pretense, but is not indignant when he does.

And yet he is not that ideal thing, the neutral, dispassionate observer. For one thing, he likes people, and likes them because he knows them well. For another, he is a sympathetic, forgiving man, a man, as we used to say, of heart, and a large heart, at that. He knew that there was no distance between himself and the people he wrote about. He had no Tolstoyan aloofness, no Flaubertian detachment. I know at least one O'Hara character plucked just so from life and worked into a novel; I found him uninteresting, a local joke, a man whom I knew in the course of everyday business and about whom I knew, like everybody else, that he was a ridiculous womanizer with no known conquests. But in O'Hara he is extraordinarily interesting. I have a feeling that O'Hara probably never met the man, that he heard about him, asked about him (questions I would not dream of asking about anybody), got all the dirt, and then stashed him away in his memory until a novel came along where he would serve as a minor bit of very human weakness and nastiness.

That's life and literature for you. Novels direct and clarify our attention to the world (to isolate one thing that novels do). I live in a John Cheever neighborhood islanded by people from Flannery O'Connor and Harry Crews. I appreciate (and am stabilized by) these imaginative frames. O'Hara's whole concern as a writer was to make accurate transcriptions of such framing, delineating forces. He did a lot more, but we will have to wait to see what it is. I suspect that he made the most interesting picture of city and suburban life that we have, and that this picture contains information of all sorts that we cannot yet see. In his later work he was exploring sexuality in a way that transcended what science was doing. Compare O'Hara and the volumes from the Kinsey Institute. Knowledge uncontrolled by sympathy and understanding is not yet knowledge.

O'Hara's concerns will be tabulated by the scholars. I can imagine dissertations on ambition in O'Hara, on ingratitude in O'Hara, on the rapacious male, the unfulfilled woman, on status consciousness, on character deterioration, and so on. No one has as yet made a clear statement as to what he achieved. I think he is as accomplished as Henry James, and is something like a James for our time. Instead of James' subtlety and refinement he had a boldness (perhaps bluntness) and accurate articulation of the vulgar tongue.

He has a tradition. He descends from Edith Wharton and Howells, and from Harold Frederic. That is, from the plain observers who found the world sufficient to their needs as storytellers without the imposition of a musical style (like Faulkner and Wolfe) or a stance that attitudinized their subjects (like Hemingway or the current batch of extreme modernists, Pynchon and Barthelme, for examples).

O'Hara has, in a sense, not yet arrived. He was read in his lifetime because his stories and novels were good to read. I think critics were a bit appalled and baffled by them, because the integrity of his art prevented their putting him down, and yet they could find no handy way to tame his energy. The average English teacher is stymied for a way to "teach" an O'Hara work. Where does the man stand? Are these symbols? What's his message? That telling about people because they are interesting to talk about, and that telling a good story well is a thing that can be done masterfully, is all the critical apparatus you need with O'Hara. He will do the rest.

Charles W. Bassett

An outstanding example of O'Hara at his early best is "Alone," a short story originally published in *Scribner's Magazine* in December 1931 and reprinted in *The Doctor's Son and Other Stories* (1935). O'Hara was hardly an unknown writer when *Scribner's* editor Kyle Crichton bought "Alone" for $75 (some 73 O'Hara stories had already appeared in *The New Yorker*, beginning in May 1928). Still, O'Hara believed that his career began broadening out with the *Scribner's* acceptance. M. J. Bruccoli contends that "Alone" does not "represent any departure from O'Hara's other work at that time," and even though O'Hara inundated Crichton with additional stories, *Scribner's* bought just one O'Hara story ("Early Afternoon," July 1932) in the early Thirties and only one more during the rest of the decade. O'Hara had to continue to rely on *The New Yorker* as the principal outlet for his short stories.

As a matter of fact, "Alone" is one of very few O'Hara stories to employ a modified stream-of-consciousness narrative technique, or what Grebstein has called "the classic interior monologue." Normally, O'Hara's stories feature a distinctive combination of editorial omniscient narrative combined with "inside" portrayals of some of the character's thoughts, thus welding the objectivity of realism with the subjectivity of modernism. In "Alone," however, despite O'Hara's use of the third-person singular throughout (Hague, the protagonist, never refers to himself as "I," not even in his thoughts), the action takes place almost entirely within the consciousness of the central character. Consequently, "Alone," is technically different from "O'Hara's other work at that time"; the point of view is more personal, the flow of thoughts more inchoate, and the sense of reader identification more immediate.

For all that, "Alone" is still one of O'Hara's classic "sensibility" stories, its action psychological and its chief purpose to generate empathetic understanding. Such "plot" as the story has is rudimentary: in his

From "John O'Hara's 'Alone': Preview of Coming Attractions," *John O'Hara Journal* 5, no. 1–2 (Winter 1982–1983). Reprinted by permission of Charles W. Bassett.

boyhood bedroom, the widowed Hague awaits burial services for Nora, his recently drowned wife. Nothing really "happens" in the story, if by "nothing" the reader means immediate, material, and physical circumstances effecting a significant change in the protagonist's life. Yet in the 1500 words of "Alone," we join Hague (we never learn his given name) in confronting the terribly empty facts of death, loneliness, and despair. Plotless though the story might be in a traditional sense, it is almost Joycean in its evocation of an "epiphany"—our realization of the meaning of "Alone."

At the same time, O'Hara remains the realist throughout this short story, as he does in all his published work. Hague is a demonstrably "ordinary" person, the kind of character—abounding in O'Hara's fiction—who is both intellectually and morally unequipped to cope with disaster. Because Hague seems so ineluctably shallow and his thoughts so quotidian, the unwary reader could dismiss him and his plight as simply pathetic. However, lurking just beneath the unremarkable surface of "Alone" are the themes that O'Hara made it his job to explore in story, novel, and play for forty years: family relationships, guilt, sex, and death.

Moreover, O'Hara's unerring sensitivity to the social locus of his character, to the paraphernalia of Hague's bourgeois existence ground these thematic abstractions in a solidly explicit milieu. The limits of the short story form itself force O'Hara to suggest rather than enumerate the components of social place—a concision that critics find wanting in his novels—but Hague is certifiably of this time, of that place.

We know Hague's middle-class background (and therefore some of his characteristic modes of reaction) because O'Hara includes just enough significant detail to allow us to infer it. Hague has always had his own bedroom in a suburban house (he remembers a backyard tent and a stable-garage). He has won a tennis trophy (now tarnished by age) at camp. Hague is a college man (he handles a tobacco pipe with an inlaid silver "C"—Cornell? Colgate?) and has married Vassar-graduate Nora. Hague's family is traditionally Protestant (his sister had been kept from marrying a Catholic), and we expect his wife's funeral services to be held in Hague's family's church (her parents are dead, hence the ceremonies become Hague's responsibility). His job in a city office is important enough that he can expect a two-month leave of absence because of his bereavement. Finally, Hague seems to earn an adequate though not munificent salary (a trip to Bermuda to forget "wouldn't cost much"), and Nora had had the twenty thousand dollars (now, guiltily, Hague's) which her father had left her.

All in all, then, in "Alone" O'Hara focuses on a thoroughly conventional young man whose life has been unalterably affected by the accidental drowning of his wife. Most of John O'Hara's fiction is consistently haunted by at least a soupçon of cosmic irony—the inexplicable and unfair disastrousness of fate. At the same time, O'Hara is less interested in the operations of a cosmic nemesis than in the emotional ramifications of catastrophe, both in its effects on the ill-equipped human psyche and in the possible implications of character with fate. O'Hara's Hague is a victim of calamity—though obviously poor, drowned Nora is unluckier even than he—but "Alone" is best understood as a study in deep-seated anxiety, in sexual guilt, and in dependency.

Nora's death has forced Hague out of the routines of his "adult" life and transmitted him back to his childhood—his mother, his family house, his past. O'Hara's recreation of Hague's patterns of thought shows us that Hague has never really broken free from his mother, indeed, that despite several abortive attempts to revolt against his mother, Hague's marriage itself is a repetition of the guilty dependency of his earlier maternal relationship. Archetypically, Hague has feared abandonment by the maternal figure, and with Nora's drowning, that fear has come true.

Consciously, Hague has attempted to establish himself as an independent individual: in the face of maternal disapproval, Hague has married Nora, thus "breaking" the Oedipal pattern. However, the seat of Hague's mother's objection to the marriage—that Nora is older than Hague—only accentuates the Freudian conflict here: Hague's mother fears her displacement by Nora, a mother-surrogate, and Nora gets both child and lover in the younger Hague. Either way, the "revolt" of Hague is doomed from the onset, if indeed his conduct can be considered a revolt at all. More probable is the hypothesis that Hague simply craves maternal security.

Nevertheless, Hague cannot admit his dependence, least of all to himself, and he uses sexual activity to demonstrate his autonomy. In defiance of his mother's restrictiveness, he had lived with Nora before their marriage, and, ultimately, legitimized his defiance: "He knew now that that was as close as his mother dared come to telling him not to marry Nora. Well, he had married her, God damn it, and he had been happy." On the other hand, Hague is not content with "maternal" domination by Nora either; he carries on semiserious flirtations with other women after his marriage: "He remembered a night when he had kissed a girl Phil had brought to their apartment." Consequently, Hague at once cherishes the safety of maternal oversight, but he also establishes a habit of sexual assertion in his effort to "be a man."

O'Hara uses Hague's boyhood tennis trophy to suggest the ambivalence of these contradictory impulses. Hague has won the trophy, a now-tarnished cup, in "manly" competition with his peers, hence establishing his prowess. But this cup, age-old symbol of the female, is absolute, tarnished, soiled, empty. "Winning" the prize, in sexual as well as athletic competition, has proven to be hollow for Hague, the insubstantiality of his victories ultimately as meaningless as his putative revolts.

Despite the despair implicit in this insight, Hague is too committed to ingrained patterns of experience to understand the origins of his ambivalence. Not a particularly insightful or introspective man, Hague has simply lived with his women, expecting them to indulge his expectations, nurturative or carnal, as need be. He has not understood the contradictions inherent in this mother-mate combination; consequently, he feels, but does not comprehend, the guilt that the contradiction generates. O'Hara introduces more than a trace of the incest taboo in Hague's musings over his mother's "predatory" struggles to maintain control of her son and over his sister's virginity. However, Hague needs conventional authority figures, helpmates without sexual allure, so that he can be punished for his unnatural desires.

Hague's guilt is exacerbated by his knowledge that Nora was pregnant when she drowned. He has a vision of himself as "the father of two children and the husband of a healthy girl," but he does little to convince us of his mature understanding of the paternal role. Given his generally childish egocentricity, we are led to believe that Hague might well have considered his offspring more a rival than a charge. Accordingly, that the unborn child dies with Nora can be considered another victory, but one achieved with even more enormous costs in guilt.

Hague's competitive nature and his consequent suspicion of potential rivals becomes even clearer in his thoughts about Phil Casey, his and Nora's closest friend. Hague would prefer to believe that Casey "liked Nora so much because he was so fond of Hague," but he cannot be sure. The only other person save the physician to know of Nora's pregnancy, Casey has been too close to the Hagues' sexual life to be entirely trustworthy. So Casey's consolation after Nora's death must also be rejected as "unbearable, unbearable."

Ultimately Hague emerges as a paradigm of self-pity. Although he may be more sinned against than sinning, he hugs his grief solipsistically and indulges his tears. (Hague weeps three times in "Alone," but more for himself than for Nora.) Doubtless he "loved" Nora in his own way, but inescapably he loves himself more. After all, Nora left him alone, and Hague cannot entirely forgive her for that.

When his mother finally appears to call him to the services, Hague is characteristically driven by assertiveness and guilt. He is brutal to his timid mother, reducing her to tears in which he is only too eager to join. "He put his arms around her, and he knew that in all the world there was nothing he wanted but to hold her like that. He didn't care what she said as long as she wept for him."

Thus O'Hara ends this very effective and affecting story with our understanding of the protagonist's genuinely doleful situation tempered by our insight into his neurotic failings. O'Hara's approach to Hague's loss and grief is compassionate, but the story also graphically demonstrates that true compassion involves forgiveness for the unworthy, for the weakling, for the self-pitying. Irony, therefore, leavens compassion in "Alone," and the result is a truly outstanding early example of John O'Hara's mastery of the short story. If he did as well in other stories, he rarely surpassed "Alone." We can only lament the fact that most modern readers will never be able to appreciate his achievement.

Joseph McElroy

In the story's main scene a prep school master conducts an interrogation in his dorm office adjoining, significantly, his living quarters. (He was a student here, of course, and O'Hara's laying it on thick.) The title, "Do You Like It Here?" is a question addressed to the new boy who's been called in without being told what it's all about, and the question proves as ironic as the interrogation itself which betrays the interrogator, not the boy. The issue is whether a watch suddenly produced by the master in the middle of the interview was in fact stolen and clandestinely returned to Van Ness's office by the boy Roberts. But the real issue is Van Ness and the small world whose good name he self-importantly claims to guard.

The story is over almost before it has begun; yet a parallel duration measured by Van Ness's laborious, mean tactics gives the story its true weight. Brief encounter narrows toward nasty anti-climax: Van Ness insinuates that the boy is the thief without ever saying so; the boy makes the charge explicit by denying it, but the master won't listen, interrupting him on the phrase "word of honor"; back in his room sitting on his bed, the boy says over and over, "The bastard, the dirty bastard"—and here the story not too abruptly ends. The boy speaks, O'Hara has told us, "first violently, then weakly," but if the venom of his elder has taken effect, the boy has come through undefeated—he's answered the devious, sarcastic requests for autobiography openly, without guile or irony; meanwhile, the master, busy rooting out evil in the cherished old school, has betrayed his resentment of the boy: envy of the boy for travels on which, by contrast, the boy with his unsettled family life sets little value, and more specific envy of the boy for having, among his many schools, attended one in Switzerland; but Van Ness's is also the deep, murky resentment felt by one who is in a static place of power through which he watches others come and go.

From "Reflections on at Least One Story of John O'Hara's," *John O'Hara Journal* 3, no.1–2 (Fall/Winter 1980). Copyright ©1980 by Joseph McElroy. Reprinted by permission of Melanie Jackson Agency, LLC.

Part 3

Every detail in O'Hara's economy "works," right down to the seated pedagogue's pedantic, sarcastic word "peripatetic" for the boy's recent history which O'Hara indicates has given the boy if not an education in life a real introduction to it. The boy doesn't slip once, not even into cleverness; the man, petty and cruel but more pompous than sadistic, prepared for the kill as if he were ambushing a belligerent equal, but he looks steadily bad, a tyrant here, doubtless a sycophant elsewhere, and instead of setting an example of clarity and frankness, he is so overcome by the mysterious mess (as I read the story) inside him that he upholds alma mater's honor by the vainest attempt to demoralize an adolescent.

But more important, that other duration I mentioned emerges like a lengthening shadow cast upon the stuffy life of Van Ness and cast *by* it upon its *chooser* who is, as I read the story, haunted by what's outside his world. That other, parallel duration opens out as the story ends, like a shadow of some past that was once the future, or like a future which for this prep school hack might be a static present if he were to think about it. He'll go on instructing his boys, and he'll make his inspections and give out his punishments, and he'll sit in his rooms and, by the condition of the life he's in, he will always be irked by an outside that's beyond him. This is the cruel shadow lengthening beyond any crime he might hope to pin on this new boy.

And yet how am I to feel Van Ness's plight? The story's point of view is that of the boy, and whatever Roberts may later recall about Van Ness, John O'Hara need show (and may show) only what can be shown from the boy's point of view. No question, we're with him all the way; in the face of danger, his behavior is more than attentive and correct—it is exemplary.

But the center of the story is the teacher Van Ness and we might seem to be free to follow his predatory pettiness into its puerile twilights. Still, O'Hara hasn't quite risked showing me some fullness of the passion in this villain's spirit. Van Ness has tried to avoid speaking openly to the boy, has tried to avoid losing his unfair edge on the unknown outsider. But like a parody of Thoreau's man who "sits more risks than he runs," Van Ness has compounded his losses by spilling and squandering the force of his anger against his new boy, Roberts. Unlike O'Hara, Van Ness has not "cut his losses."

Roberts's point of view lets us leave that master's office, and though Roberts will remember, will always remember, Van Ness, the neatness which that point of view gives O'Hara for his ending retracts that shadow without the disturbing human passion and threat in Van Ness's

154

psyche being once and for all given to us. Hawthorne, Babel, Lawrence, even Katherine Anne Porter would not have let the story get away like that into compact decorum. O'Hara would say that it's the boy's story. But the agony is the man's, and O'Hara has arranged not to have to earn for us some further, raw knowledge of that contemptible antagonist. An opportunity missed, I think. Yet a fascinating one.

Morris Freedman

What is so appealing about an O'Hara story or novel? He spins a good yarn smoothly. His style is unobtrusive, even flat—what is sometimes called transparent. He rarely uses metaphors and commonly uses monosyllabic words. The writing is as comfortable, as inviting, as the intimate, fluent talk of articulate and attentive old friends, involved and at ease with one another. It is free of affectation, of quotable bits. His dialogue has the fidelity and quirkiness of tape recording. O'Hara prided himself on his perceptive ear to the point of vanity. He was a master of vignettes. Consider how much we glean about the man and woman in the following fragment:

> ". . . I also notice you're wearing your Phi Beta Kappa key. I never knew you were one."
> "I was wearing the key the first night I danced with you," I said.
> "Maybe you were, but I didn't know what it was. I never knew what it was till my brother made it. But you must have stopped wearing it."
> "Vests are coming back," I said.
> "That's not why you're wearing it. You're running for judge. Don't try to fool me, Phil."

As a sometime reporter and editor, O'Hara knew the kinds of events and their details that command the attention of daily readers, that make headlines and feature stories. O'Hara's raw material has the coarseness and universal appeal of gossip, efficiently processed to be free of irrelevancies, pointless ugliness and repetition, penetrating characterization, specious sentimentality. Matter that turns melodramatic and nonsensical in the hand of, say, Judith Krantz or Sidney Sheldon remains convincingly tragic and moving in O'Hara through the truthfulness and precision of his writing.

Reprinted from "By O'Hara Besotted," *The American Scholar* 66, no. 4 (Autumn 1997). Copyright ©1997 by Morris Freedman.

O'Hara's fiction seamlessly interweaves documentary care with fictional virtuosity. We learn as much about the specific operations of an automobile franchise in a small town as about the owner's qualities as a man and husband, and about the place of the business in the social and political structure of the community. When we meet a rising lawyer, we learn about the intricacies of his practice and his private life. . . .

One problem with liking O'Hara, certainly for many serious readers, is that it takes so little work to get him. We were taught to find literature hard. O'Hara speaks to us at once. He is immediately accessible. This is one ground for the charge that he was finally trivial and superficial, that he didn't sufficiently weigh—or weight—his material. Yet he was never just an uninvolved, unartful recorder, which he has been described as being, like a video camera, a disciple of the Goncourts. He exercised an exquisite selectivity in moving through his terrain. Gore Vidal, in the opening of a *New York Review of Books* essay, charged O'Hara with not making enough of the "details" he meticulously amassed. Yet he went on to say how much he was affected exactly by the bareness of one narrative. Less can become more in many ways.

"More than anyone now writing," Trilling wrote of O'Hara's short stories in an early tribute,

> O'Hara understands the complex, contradictory, asymmetrical society in which we live. He has the most precise knowledge of the content of our subtlest snobberies, of our points of social honor and idiosyncrasies of personal prestige. He knows, and persuades us to believe, that life's deepest emotions may be expressed by the angle at which a hat is worn, the pattern of a neck-tie, the size of a monogram, the pitch of a voice, the turn of a phrase of slang, a gesture of courtesy and the way it is received. . . . For him customs and manners are morals.

O'Hara was more than an alchemist who turned customs and manners into morals as end product. He was a moralist from the start in his selection of customs and manners to anatomize. He was virtually a puritan in taking life seriously and in requiring us to take seriously his seriousness. Through his maneuvering of character and event, and his accompanying commentary, he made us share his values. We champion his characters who survive adversity through strength and decency, reject those who fall through self-indulgence or plain nastiness, and feel a wrenching sympathy with those felled by forces utterly outside their awareness or control.

Reading O'Hara can be discomfiting. He holds persons responsible for their deeds while never judging anyone simplistically or without compassion. Good and evil have infinite and elusive coloration in O'Hara. Arrogant, selfish actresses turn out to be genuinely civilized, generous, hardworking, in need of common sympathy and friendship; cocky teenagers can be ultimately justified for us in their abrasive toughness. We recognize as fellows his most irritating creations. In the tight course of a single work, as in "Imagine Kissing Pete," O'Hara has us repeatedly adjust our feelings about Pete as he metamorphoses stolidly from detestable to sympathetic. O'Hara knew that it may take a lifetime to shape up.

We get caught up in O'Hara because of his scrupulous dissection of motives and rationalizations we ourselves incline to slight or blur. Sanity, hard work, decency, superlative competence are not always pure and do not triumph without difficulty or compromise over pathology, selfishness, nastiness, stupidity, thoughtlessness, klutziness. O'Hara makes us alert to lapses and recoveries, to hues of black and white. His confident and delicate sorting of life's trickiest variables obliges us to concentrate, and to glory with him, at least, when goodness is recognized. Like all good writing, O'Hara's leaves us satisfied. . . .

In spite of finding themselves over and over again in challenging and extravagant situations, O'Hara's people are in substance unspectacular. They are often of working-class origin. That iconic universality which marks so many of Hemingway's and Shakespeare's characters, O'Hara's lack. O'Hara wrote mainly of types who swell a scene, who live at their finest and most definitively at moments only in commonplace settings, who rise to valor, or plunge to destruction, in little worlds. In this respect, he is like Cheever, though Cheever concentrated on middle-class persons and their middle-class troubles. John Updike, who respects O'Hara and has followed his manner of cataloguing the worldly possessions of characters to define them, reaches for mythical import.

Like other great localists, O'Hara remained one of the natives whose activities he examined. O'Hara's Gibbsville, Pennsylvania, his name for Pottsville, his birthplace, where much of his fiction is set and where many of his characters come from, belongs in the atlas with Balzac's Paris, Dickens's London, Joyce's Dublin, Anderson's Winesburg, Faulkner's Yoknapatawpha, Edgar Lee Masters's cemetery, Cheever's Westchester, Singer's *shtetlach*. . . .

O'Hara had as determined a command of his craft as, say, did Joyce, whose *Dubliners* he knew. He read Lord Byron, Saki, and other masters of comic and satiric forms. His altogether solemn dedication to his writing repeatedly comes up in his letters and in the introductions to his collections. He spoke about his "business" in life being to leave a full and accurate record of the time in which he lived. He had a high estimate of his place in world literature, believing that he should properly have been in contention for a Nobel Prize. He decided his chances were finally dissipated when Steinbeck, "another" American, got the prize. He harbored no bitterness toward those he regarded as fair competitors. But he resented authors and their publishers who he felt engaged in immoderate self-promotion and literary politicking, more eager to garner prizes than to produce results. He cherished the honors that did come to him, not least those bestowed by Yale.

He thought of himself with the same amiable affection he displayed toward his readers, whom he considered as partners in his enterprise as writer. "I had a wonderful experience at Trenton," he wrote one time to his daughter. "I waited on the platform, in case you did not take that train. Right in front of me there was a Pullman car, and I happened to notice that an austere woman was reading *Sermons and Sodawater* (the three-volume edition). I knocked on the window, and she was understandably confused until I pantomimed 'book' with my hands and pointed to myself. She got it, got all excited, and spoke to her husband in the chair adjoining hers. He was delighted, recognizing me right away, and so did a woman who was in the other neighboring chair. Then the people in the other chairs, overhearing the excitement, all laughed and waved at me. So I clasped my hands like a prizefighter and took off my hat and bowed. I'm sure I'll get a letter from my reader on the other side of the Pullman windows. It was fun."

Kathryn Riley

Critics of John O'Hara traditionally have classified the settings of his works according to three social and geographical divisions: New York, Hollywood, and the small Pennsylvania city of Gibbsville, modeled after his home town of Pottsville.[1] While most of O'Hara's fiction does indeed fall into these divisions, critics have overlooked a series of stories from his later collections that cannot be placed in the New York/ Hollywood/Gibbsville categories. Where O'Hara had tended to write, in earlier stories, about characters in relatively specialized and removed worlds—Hollywood actors and actresses, smalltime hoods moving in their own moral framework, aristocrats imprisoned in the protected shell of the past—the stories discussed here, those set in post–World War II suburbs, reflect O'Hara's movement beyond the concerns associated with the major settings of his earlier fiction.

All of O'Hara's suburban stories deal, to some extent, with the tension between day-to-day "normality" and the intrusion of emotions and events that conflict with the *status quo*. The setting of these stories reinforces that conflict for O'Hara's depiction of suburbia ties in with his protagonists' attempt to maintain a façade that belies a deeper unrest. Within this general area of concern, the stories fall into several groupings that show O'Hara gradually adapting his earlier approaches to more modern material and themes. Additionally, they reveal his ability to universalize the suburban experience without falling into the easy trap of stereotyping it.

Most of O'Hara's suburban fiction appeared in the 1960's, for several probable reasons. In addition to the fact that the suburbs were themselves coming into prominence during the decades following World War II, O'Hara had moved to a suburban residence near Princeton in 1957.

"The Suburban Vision in John O'Hara's Stories," *Critique: Studies in Modern Fiction* 25 (Winter 1984): 101–13. Reprinted with permission of the Helen Dwight Reid Educational Foundation. Published by Heldref Publications, 1319 Eighteenth St. N.W., Washington, D.C. 20036-1802. Copyright ©1984.

Also, according to his preface to *Assembly* (1961), he had written almost no short fiction between 1949, when he broke with *The New Yorker* over Brendan Gill's negative review of *A Rage to Live*, and 1961. Returning to the short story after this hiatus, O'Hara approached the form with new vigor.[2]

This new period, in turn, brought with it several shifts in the author's approach to the short story. Changes in both technique and, to a greater extent, tone between O'Hara's earlier and later work have been noted. The later stories gain in length and complexity while still retaining the economy that characterizes O'Hara's short fiction. Overshadowing the irony and satire of his earlier work is a more compassionate tone, one that remains realistic rather than sentimental but that reflects O'Hara's greater empathy with the mature characters who populate his later work.[3]

The first group of stories to be discussed recalls O'Hara's earlier, more naturalistic work and reflects fairly strongly the popular image of suburbia at the time he was writing, in the early 1960's.[4] In "The Twinkle in His Eye," "Justice," "The Jet Set," and "The Madeline Wherry Case,"[5] O'Hara brings to the suburban setting his career-long concern with secrets that build up over time toward irreversible, and often fatal, emotional and physical violence. The length and complexity of these pieces also lend them a "case history" flavor, as does the omniscient narrative point of view that probes the characters' intricate psychological motivations. These stories reflect a writer in transition, taking a traditional approach to contemporary material.

The melodramatic quality of these stories about suburban violence also derives from their overwhelming atmosphere of seemingly preordained corruption. O'Hara gives credence to the power of social codes, both internally and externally imposed, yet invests the neatly structured suburban world with an undercurrent of more turbulent, less easily codified passions. In "Justice," for example, the protagonist Norman Daniels is exiled by the community after his lover is murdered by her jealous husband. The complex issue of Daniels' guilt is sustained by the first-person narrative viewpoint. He tries to explain and justify his role in the scandal, and it quickly becomes clear that Daniels "doth protest too much": he both deceives himself about the extent of his involvement and fails to convince the reader of his moral superiority. Having confused *de jure* innocence with *de facto* innocence and unable to comprehend why his public image cannot exculpate him, he sinks into moral limbo.

Part 3

In a similar act of self-deception, Gordon Whittier, of "The Twinkle in His Eye" harbors a passionate hatred of his wife, a hatred founded on small incidents that, unknown to her, have built up his resentment over the years. His hatred comes into conflict, however, with his equal passion for maintaining a respectable façade. Hence, he remains imprisoned in a state of permanent mediocrity, unable to act upon the emotions that obsess him. Characters like Daniels and Whittier, who rationalize their own weaknesses by pleading the need to protect a public image, quickly reveal themselves as hypocrites—not only in our eyes but in the eyes of their communities as well.

"The Jet Set" and "The Madeline Wherry Case" also use violent death to dramatize the question of moral responsibility. In the first story, a man's knowledge of a dark secret in a woman's past eventually drives her to suicide. Lawrence Graybill's culpability, O'Hara suggests, is shared by the community at large; these suburbanites, banded together by their "passion for competitiveness," choose toughness over compassion. The story points toward one inescapable clause in the moral contract, that of accepting responsibility for one's actions and of refraining from the disabuse of powers over others.

The question of victimization by the community also arises in the second story, which recounts the events that drive an adulteress, Madeline Wherry, to murder her husband. By tracing Madeline's actions before the murder, O'Hara builds up the contrast between her vital relationship with her lover and her stifling marriage to a husband who has himself been unfaithful. Here again the protagonist is caught between two worlds, that of an external social code and a more powerful one of private emotions. As in the other stories of destruction, O'Hara hints at no reprieve for Madeline Wherry: just as surely as she will be punished for her crime of passion, her life with Bud Wherry would have constituted a more subtle but equally dehumanizing punishment. While Lawrence Graybill and Madeline Wherry arrive at greater self-knowledge than do Whittier and Daniels, they attain it too late to act positively on it.

This first group of stories, then, contains O'Hara's most disparaging view of suburban life, one in which emotional and physical violence are as much a part of the landscape as are the country club and the commuter train. In one sense, he seems merely to filter stereotypes of suburban corruption through the lens of melodrama. Despite their violent and somewhat sensationalist nature, however, these stories do not limit themselves entirely to expose tactics or a fatalistic condemnation of suburban life. Although both adultery and violent death are consummate within the pages of "Justice," "The Jet Set," and "The Madeline Wherry Case," O'Hara handles the baser details of such acts off-stage, so to speak, leading us to look for the story's focus beyond the obvious sources of drama in its plot.

If we follow this lead, we discover a more complex vision than might be immediately apparent. In several cases, it is not the victim of the violence who gains our interest but, instead, a protagonist who has had a relationship with that victim. O'Hara draws a direct correlation between the protagonist's self-knowledge and his freedom to act, and this theme is intimately related to the suburban setting. In all of the stories, we encounter characters whose self-knowledge has been clouded and distorted by their acquiescence to the suburban social structure.

O'Hara's point is that while suburbia may seem to be the villain in these stories, that is not entirely so. The suburbs in these stories, like their inhabitants, exhibit varying degrees of morality. The protagonists within them all fail to meet the same challenge: that of recognizing the point where the community can no longer define their moral code and where they must begin defining it themselves. Norman Daniels and Gordon Whittier never achieve the ability to control their own actions; Lawrence Graybill and Madeline Wherry achieve it, but too late.

A pattern that recurs in a second group of suburban stories involves a more subtle kind of disruption, an outsider's intrusion into a protagonist's calm existence. The conflict in this set of stories, like that in the first, lies in the disparity between acceptable morality and behavior and violations of that code. While in the stories just discussed this conflict manifests itself in irreversible consequences, in this second group of tales O'Hara remains more ambivalent about the possibility of balancing the *status quo* and the inner life. The protagonists of these stories begin with the assumption that, by obeying outward signs of social and moral propriety, they are operating under a self-sustaining philosophy of life. An interruption of the external routine, however, forces the central character to the point of greater self-awareness.

The intrusion of such an outsider forms the basis for "Saturday Lunch," in which two suburban housewives suddenly realize that they have both been sexually propositioned by the same man, a seemingly harmless real-estate man named Duncan Ebberly. As the disrupter of their world, Ebberly embodies the ugliness that lies just beneath the calm surface of suburban existence. Carol Ferguson's and Alice Reeves' encounters with him open their eyes to that sordid dimension of life which their society denies simply by ignoring its existence.

Part 3

Although much of this narrative recounts the incident during which Ebberly approaches Carol, the real revelation O'Hara is aiming for has more to do with Carol's and Alice's relationships with their husbands. Even more disturbing than Ebberly's advances is the distance between Jud Ferguson's and Joe Reeves' images of their wives and the private ordeal that these women have sustained. O'Hara implies that even apparently "normal" suburbanites have secrets that are belied by the appearances they maintain, just as Ebberly appears to be no more than a harmless, stammering, middle-aged bachelor. The author makes this point subtly, through interchanges such as this one between Jud and Joe, remarking on their wives' sensitivity to the weather:

> "Is anybody cold here?" said Carol Ferguson. "Jud, will you go back and see if that kitchen door blew open?"
> "I wasn't going to say anything," said Alice Reeves. "But I think there must be a door open somewhere."
> "So delicate," said her husband.
> "Christ, aren't they?" said Jud Ferguson. (295–96)

Both husbands display a protective, slightly patronizing attitude toward their spouses, absurd in light of what the reader has learned about the women. In suburbia, the same reliance on appearances that allows Ebberly to prey on women also prevents his victims from retaliating.

A similar lack of communication—a problem that lies at the heart of many marriages in O'Hara's suburbs—is revealed in "The Clear Track." Although composed of eight pages of almost straight dialogue, this story really concerns the Loxley's inability to talk to one another about the problems at the crux of their marriage. Their respective affairs with others are discussed only by accident, in the course of conversations about other things, and neither partner has the courage or the energy to follow through on them. As a result, each gives the other the "clear track" to pursue infidelity, even though both immediately realize that it is not the direction they want to take.

O'Hara's method in this story reinforces his message: by focusing on "the numerous small transactions that are the formalities of a marriage during trying times" (13), he shows the Loxleys relegating their marital problems to the same level of small talk with which they discuss interior decorators and other instances of "how things will look." By the end of the story the reader feels the same sense of frustration that informs the couple's relationship, for the barrier of triviality surrounding their marriage prevents either confrontation or resolution. Just as the dialogue in "Saturday Lunch" and "The Clear Track" leaves the most important things unsaid, so their characters' hesitancy to ruffle the smooth surface of their existence prevents them from getting to deeper issues.

Chance encounters with outsiders also figure in "The Time Element" and "Sunday Morning." The irony of the first story derives from the reversal in the circumstances of Rob Wilson and Kit Dunbar, two former lovers who meet after nearly a decade. Their conversation reveals, subtly, that her life has steadily improved in an almost inverse pattern to his inward demise. Despite their superficial similarities—both have several children and are in the same social class (Wilson has learned about Kit's life in Chicago because his wife "gets the Junior League magazine")—telling changes have upset the balance of power between them. Kit, Wilson notices immediately, is more beautiful at thirty-five than when he jilted and deceived her nine years before; she vetoes sitting in a bar because, she says, "I don't want a drink and I'd rather you didn't too"; she has given up smoking ("I suppose I ought to," he replies) and is clearly in control of the interview: "I can ask questions, and you can't. I didn't ask to see you, you know" (125–26). Although their conversation is short and mainly factual, it is filled with the undertones of Kit's disgust toward Wilson and her anxiousness to end the meeting.

By the end of their interview, Wilson understands the nature of the "simple mysterious thing," the indefinable malaise that has been bothering him: reminded of how he betrayed Kit, he realizes how his dishonesty has affected his own marriage. The narrator suggests that Wilson's former self-deceit will be replaced not by optimism but by the middle ground of realism: "He would be late for dinner, but not very late" (128). O'Hara's understated handling of the story's end, like that of "Saturday Lunch" and "The Clear Track," complements his subject: the sense of a confining existence that, by relying more on form than on content, leaves its inhabitants in a paralyzed, static state that must be resisted.

Similarly, "Sunday Morning" takes its protagonist to the point of revelation but leaves her just short of transcending her ennui. The action consists of Marge Fairbanks' brief trip into town for the Sunday papers. Within this apparently simple story, O'Hara relates a series of small events from Marge's point of view, leaving the reader with a full sense not only of her daily life but also of her frustration with it. Her "independence" is measured by small acts of defiance and attempts to break out of the routine existence she has fallen into.

165

Part 3

Her sojourn into town exposes her, and the reader, to small reminders of the pettiness and hypocrisy of her fellow suburbanites: she sees, on their way to Mass, a couple who were too drunk to drive the night before; she is greeted rudely by the drugstore proprietor; most disturbingly, a neighbor sounds her out on the possibility of having an affair. Her exchange with Ralph Shipstead reveals her own ambivalent feelings and the fortuitous set of values by which she lives. She brushes him off abruptly; but then, driving home, her thoughts go back to their meeting. She finds him a "loathsome man"—ostentatious, unrespectable, overconfident—but still, "he wanted her, and it excited her to think that in her present frame of mind he could almost have her. Almost"(354).

Marge's conflicting emotions range from sarcastic thoughts about her neighbors ("Would anyone be interested to learn that Nannie Martin was thinking of changing to Presbyterian? Would the *Herald Tribune* send a reporter to interview Dixie Green if they knew that Dixie had once had a date with a gentleman who now sat in the White House?") to a dread, all the more disturbing for its vagueness, of returning home to her mundane family life. Her exact problem lies in the mediocrity of her situation, for she is defined only by her position as a wife, a mother, a potential partner in adultery:

> But what was *she*, Marge Fairbanks? A secure wife, yes and a conscientious mother, yes. But what else? But she, she, she? What was she, apart from husband and children, apart from Ralph Shipstead's mechanical lechery for her? And worst of all, what did she want, what could she be, other than what she had and what she was? Was this all? Was it worth it? (355)

Marge Fairbanks' malaise, then, is brought on not by the presence of any definable qualities in her life but rather by the absence of those qualities. From an outsider's perspective, she really has nothing to complain about: her life, like her husband's lovemaking, is "usually all right." The seriousness of her situation is not revealed until the end of the story, when the car, out of gas, stalls on the road to her home, and she sits there in reverie:

> The drizzle on the windshield reminded her of tears, and she waited for the thought to bring the tears, but they did not come. She was not even that unhappy.

166

> She put the keys in her pocket and got out of the car, and as she
> began the homeward walk she kicked the front tire. It hurt her toe,
> and now she could cry, a little. (355–56)

This final scene, which shows her need for an external reason to cry and
to release her emotions, suggests that she is just beginning to attain a
tentative self-knowledge. Although able to ask herself some crucial
questions, she remains nonetheless unable to answer them because the
apparently "all right" nature of her suburban life prevents her from seeing beyond its, and her own, surface.

Although less overtly dramatic than the tales of physical violence discussed above, this second group of stories nevertheless contains disturbing elements. Their lack of catharsis and their overwhelming tone
of anticlimax and stasis are in their own way as pessimistic as the
destructive outcome of a story like "The Madeline Wherry Case." In
these stories we are more likely to perceive the suburbs as a place of
potential psychological entrapment; for while the characters in the first
group do achieve a kind of dismal escape through adultery and violence,
characters like the Loxleys and Marge Fairbanks may be doomed to
repeat the present.

A final group of stories offers O'Hara's strongest suggestion of an
alternative to the violence seen in the first group of stories and the
ennui portrayed in the second. O'Hara never goes so far as to suggest
that life in the suburbs can be idyllic; his characters all, invariably, face
threats to that illusion. What he offers as a means of coping, in its place,
are a willingness to compromise and, more important, a sense of compassion. In keeping with the technique used in the second set of stories, O'Hara uses the pattern of an epiphany effected by an outsider or
an unexpected incident. The characters in this final group of stories,
however, unlike those in the first two, seem able to incorporate their
new knowledge into their suburban existence.

Several of these stories revolve around domestic scenes including not
only a husband and wife but also their children. O'Hara thereby suggests that encounters between parents and children are one way of
investing values and ideals with new vitality. In "The Father," "The
Lesson," "Appearances," and "Family Evening," O'Hara examines the
difficulties and rewards of achieving understanding through such
encounters. For example, Miles Berry in "The Father" undergoes a
change when his sister sends him an old photograph of his wife, a newspaper clipping that shows Vilma as a young, single woman of seventeen

at a Frank Sinatra concert in 1945. His shock of recognition at this evidence of her once-vital spirit comes amidst the banality of their current life, placing the present in sharp relief against the past. The photo is a reminder of Vilma's and, by extension, his own lost youth and romanticism.

Fortunately, the contrast is strong enough to show Berry how precious that romanticism is, and he is able to translate his awareness into a new sensitivity toward his daughter, Ava. The final implication is that Berry will alter his habit of taking his wife's and daughter's emotions, as well as his own, for granted, and of subordinating the sentimental to the pragmatic (O'Hara—not accidentally, it would seem—assigns Berry the occupation of a mechanic). The structure of this story reinforces its theme, the ability of small, seemingly unassociated incidents to evoke strong memories and emotions and to provide everyday reminders of age and mortality. Consistent with O'Hara's overall treatment of suburbia, the protagonist's revelation comes in an almost accidental way. Its effect is no less profound, however, for its understated quality.

In a similar way, the daughter in "The Lesson" must bridge the gap of years and emotions between her divorced parents. Having grown up with her mother, the daughter learns from her father that, prior to the divorce, both parents had been involved in a series of affairs. Unexpectedly, this insight gives both father and daughter new knowledge and respect for one another. Mimi, now married and about to have her own child, must reassess her mother's version of her father—"She's made you sound like such an awful son of a bitch that you couldn't possibly live up to it" (206). But she has also built up an image of him, through pictures, as a football hero in his college days. She learns from their meeting that neither of these black-and-white extremes is accurate.

The father, in turn, is equally surprised by his daughter's mature ability to accept the past without condemning him. While Mimi's insight is accompanied by a slight edge of cynicism, she gains in perception what she loses in idealism. Like Miles Berry, both Mimi and her father must acknowledge shortcomings in their own assumptions before they can connect with other people. Again, the changes in them are more subtle, internal ones, unlikely to change the outward patterns of their lives but certain to transform their private visions.

"Appearances" reverses the roles of parent and child somewhat: in this story the daughter's affair has broken up her marriage. By building the story's structure around three separate conversations—between father and mother, father and daughter, and mother and daughter—

O'Hara delineates the different degrees of communication among these three family members. Once more, he focuses on the need to temper an adherence to the *status quo* with an acceptance of weaknesses in oneself and others, and again he reinforces that theme through a series of understated events that culminate in a subtle but transforming revelation.

The three conversations in "Appearances" lend several levels of meaning to the title. Following a talk with his daughter, Amy, Howard Ambrie believes he has had a breakthrough in communication with her, though actually he has barely scratched the surface of the truth concerning her marriage and divorce. Amy appears to have been "a hell of a nice girl," but the history of her marriage indicates otherwise. Only the mother, Lois, who regards her daughter first as a woman and only then as her child, is able to act as Amy's *confidante*. Like Mimi in "The Lesson," Lois Ambrie transcends the expected behavior associated with her family role and, hence, brings honesty and compassion to her dealings with Amy.

The potential for maturity in a parent-child relationship also forms the subject of "Family Evening." Like "Appearances," this story comments on the bond between mother and daughter; like "The Father," it suggests the positive power of the past. Bob Martin, the guest whom Norman and Libby James invite to dinner, belongs to what their daughter, Rosie, jokingly refers to as the "B. D's"—Better Deads—a categorical term for anyone over thirty. As the evening evolves, it gradually becomes clear that Martin was once Libby's old flame. The subtle humor derives from Rosie's viewpoint as the youthful chaperone of the group and her clear disapproval of her mother's sudden gaiety.

After dinner, alone with Rosie for a few minutes in her room, Libby wants to suggest that they all "step out." During a poignant moment, Libby studies herself in the mirror and asks her daughter how she "really" looks:

> "You look fine," said Rosie.
> "No, I don't," said her mother. She turned away from the mirror. "Do me a favor, Rosie. *You* suggest it."
> "Me! . . . All right, if you stop feeling sorry for yourself all of a sudden. You and the rest of the B. D.'s."
> Her mother smiled. "Dear Rosie. It hurt, but it worked." She got up and followed Rosie down the hall, humming "Do It Again," a danceable number of 1922. (133)

The reversal of roles here, with Rosie assuming the task of being the "sensible" member of the group, demands that she suspend her youthful disapproval of her mother's frivolity. In addition, she foregoes an after-dinner outing with her own friends in order to give her mother a chance to "step out." By doing so, she earns her mother's gratitude and willingness to confide in her as well as a new degree of maturity.

Two final stories in this third group show how compromise tempered with compassion can rescue individuals from seemingly hopeless situations. In both stories, O'Hara returns to the paradox explored in "The Twinkle in His Eye" and "The Time Element": that of a materially successful man who nevertheless feels despair. Unlike the more fatalistically inclined characters in those stories, though, the protagonists of "How Can I Tell You?" and "The Pig" are saved by their ability to connect with other human beings.

In "How Can I Tell You?" O'Hara recounts a day in the life of Mark McGranville and creates a disturbing portrait of alienation and confusion. Each event that should, theoretically, raise McGranville's spirits— a highly profitable afternoon in his job as a car salesman, a leisurely drink after work—leaves him not merely depressed but in an even worse state, that of an undefinable neutrality and emptiness.

When, in their bedroom, his wife Jean tentatively asks him what's wrong, he replies, "How the hell can I tell you when I don't know myself?" (121). After she falls asleep, and after he himself has slept for an hour, he quietly slips back out to the living room and tries to analyze his feelings:

> He was thirty years old, a good father, a good husband. . . . His sister had a good job, and his mother was taken care of. On the sales blackboard at the garage his name was always first or second, in two years had not been down to third. Nevertheless he went to the hall closet and got out his 20-gauge and broke it open and inserted a shell.

As he sits in semi-darkness smoking a cigarette he hears his wife:

> Her voice came softly. "Mark," she said.
> He looked at the carpet. "What?" he said.
> "Don't. Please?"
> "I won't," he said. (122)

These final lines, while hardly optimistic, suggest an affirmative vision. O'Hara emphasizes Jean's intuitive quality as Mark watches her sleeping, "making the musical notes of her regular breathing, but the slight frown revealing that her mind was at work . . . in ways that would always be kept secret from him, possibly even from herself" (122). In contrast, Mark's own sleep is so "busy, busy, busy" with mental activity that he does not even realize he has been asleep until he looks at the clock.

By juxtaposing their two ways of sleeping, O'Hara underscores the contrast between their reactions to Mark's despair. Each of their reactions is, in its own way, extreme. Mark's, of course, because of the irreversibility of the act that he contemplates; Jean's because of its understated quality. Yet the gentleness of her request is precisely what reveals her understanding of her husband. While not the "logical" approach to the situation, Jean's is, intuitively, the right complement to Mark's failure to find rational sources for his ennui. It also allows him to change the course of his actions while saving face: his wife, by recognizing her husband's isolation and expressing her need for him, provides him with the crucial human connection that breaks through his emotional barrier.

Lawrence Chandler, the protagonist of "The Pig," also contemplates suicide, but for a reason more definable than Mark McGranville's: Chandler has just learned that he has terminal cancer. On the way home that evening on the commuter train, he confides in his friend and business associate, Mike Post. Chandler's alternative plan to committing suicide is to postpone telling his wife, Ruth, of his impending death. He fears that Ruth, because of the lingering nature of his disease, will eventually wish that he would stop "hanging on." Post understands but tries to persuade him otherwise.

To make his point, Post relates a parable about Pig Pignelli, a soldier who served under him in World War II. "Before we were shipped overseas he was hopeless. Always out of uniform, buttons undone, hat on crooked, dirty equipment," he tells Chandler. "But once we got overseas . . . he became the most reliable soldier I had" (316). The Pig volunteered for what was essentially a suicide mission, an act that cost him his life. What this proved to Post was that "people you count on want to be counted on. The Pig knew perfectly well that I was going to have to ask him to volunteer, and while I was figuring out how to say it, he saved me the trouble." To give Ruth the same opportunity to help him through this crisis, Post tells Chandler, would be "The highest compliment you could ever pay her. . . . That you need her, and need her so much that you had to tell her right away" (316). Like Mark McGranville, Lawrence Chandler must adjust his own assumptions about the limits

171

of his wife's strength in order to be worthy of her compassion. The end of the story indicates that he will follow this course.

Although O'Hara did not turn to the suburban setting until relatively later in his career, his treatment of it reflects both concerns carried over from his earlier fiction and concerns particular to the suburban setting itself. Thematically, the tension common to these stories involves the disparity between appearance and truth—a theme integral to the suburban way of life, defined as it is in his stories by the sometimes overwhelming control of the *status quo* over his characters. His perceptive portrayal of the dynamics of marriage, particularly the problems of adultery, reflects a commitment to the belief that "ordinary" people harbor ideas and emotions that, if explored, are intrinsically interesting enough to merit a realistic treatment.

In terms of style and tone, his frequent reliance on dialogue, understatement, and reportage are consistent with his preference for indirect rather than explicit moral statements. In turn, his application of these techniques to the stories set in suburbia enhances their artistry. For, while much of his non-suburban fiction concentrates on portraying aristocratic, or, at the opposite end, lower-class characters, in these stories his goal is the evocation of lives that are, like his craft, filled with everyday detail, casual conversation, and apparently insignificant events.

This is not to underestimate his skill at portraying the world of Gibbsville or of pre–World War II Hollywood and New York; O'Hara displayed his intimate knowledge of these times and places as well until the end of his career. What we get in the suburban stories that is missing in much of his earlier work, however, is a sense of form reinforcing content: O'Hara's suburban stories frequently offer us a fragmented view of reality, a momentary inkling of truth, a glance at the inner life of a character—subjects that demand a more understated treatment.

These stories, then, shed additional light on the integrity of his fiction, a body of work which is due for the same careful re-evaluation that his biography has received over the past decade. They reveal that his writing was not as restricted to the traditionally recognized settings in his canon as his critics have assumed and show his ability to distill the essence of a setting that was developing contemporaneous to his writing about it. To paraphrase the title of Don Schanche's interview with him, John O'Hara is alive and well in the *second* half of the twentieth century, too.[6]

Notes

1. Sheldon Grebstein, *John O'Hara* (New Haven: Twayne, 1966), p. 33, divides O'Hara's fiction into two sections, Pennsylvania and New York-Hollywood. Charles C. Walcutt, *John O'Hara* (Minneapolis: Univ. of Minnesota Press, 1969), p. 6, finds three divisions: Eastern Pennsylvania, the movie industry in New York and Hollywood, and a Philadelphia-New York-Washington triangle of business, war, and society.

2. John O'Hara, *Assembly* (New York: Random House, 1961), p. ix.

3. Grebstein, pp. 134–35.

4. Representative articles that reflect the popular image of postwar suburbia include the following: Harry Henderson, "The Mass-Produced Suburbs," *Harper's*, November and December 1953, pp. 25–32 and pp. 80–86; "Spur to Conformity," *Commonweal* 64 (21 September 1956): p. 602; "Suburbia: The New America," *Newsweek*, 3 June 1957, pp. 83–90; Helen Puner, "Is It True What They Say about the Suburbs?" *Parents' Magazine*, July 1958, pp. 42–43, 96–97; "On the 5:19 to Ulcerville," *Newsweek*, 17 August 1959, p. 32; "The Changing Suburbs," *Architectural Forum* 114 (January 1961), pp. 47–104; Peter Blake, "The Suburbs Are a Mess," *Saturday Evening Post*, 5 October 1963, pp. 14–16; "Quit Picking on 'Suburbia,' " *Changing Times*, October 1963, pp. 34–36; Betty Friedan, "Women: The Fourth Dimension," *Ladies Home Journal*, June 1964, pp. 48–55; "Darien's Dolce Vita," *Time*, 2 November 1964, p. 60; and Donald G. Emery, "Memo from Scarsdale: A New Role for Suburban Schools," *Look*, 2 April 1968, p. 18.

5. References to the stories of John O'Hara are to the following collections (publisher, unless otherwise noted, is Random House, New York): *The Cape Cod Lighter* (1962): "Appearances," "The Father," "Justice," "The Lesson," "Sunday Morning"; *The Hat on the Bed* (1964): "How Can I Tell You?" "Saturday Lunch," "The Twinkle in His Eye"; *The Horse Knows the Way* (New York: Popular Library, 1964): "The Clear Track," "The Jet Set," "The Madeline Wherry Case," "The Pig"; *The Time Element and Other Stories* (1972): "The Time Element," "Family Evening."

6. Don Schanche, "John O'Hara Is Alive and Well in the First Half of the 20th Century," *Esquire*, August 1969, pp. 84–86, 142–49.

Chronology

1905	John Henry O'Hara born to Dr. Patrick H. and Katharine Delaney O'Hara, 31 January in Pottsville, Pennsylvania.
1912–1920	Attends Miss Carpenter's School and St. Patrick's School.
1920–1921	Attends Fordham Preparatory School, Bronx, New York.
1921–1922	Attends Keystone State Normal School, Kutztown, Pennsylvania.
1923–1924	Attends Niagara Preparatory School, Niagara, New York; is named class valedictorian.
1924–1926	Reporter for the *Pottsville Journal*.
1925	Dr. Patrick H. O'Hara dies in Pottsville, 18 March.
1927	Reporter for the *Tamaqua (Penn.) Courier*.
1928	Leaves Pottsville, arrives in New York City, early spring. Sells first piece to *The New Yorker*, 15 April.
1928–1930	Reporter for the *New York Herald Tribune*, *Time* magazine, and *Editor & Publisher* magazine. Rewrite man for the *New York Daily Mirror*, and critic and columnist for the *New York Morning Telegraph*, writing as "Franey Delaney."
1931	Marries Helen Ritchie Petit in New York, 28 February. Publicity writer for Warner Brothers, in New York.
1932	Publicity writer for RKO studios, New York.
1933	Managing editor of *Pittsburgh Bulletin-Index*, spring and summer. Divorces Helen Ritchie Petit O'Hara, 15 August.
1934	Writes screenplays for Paramount Pictures in Los Angeles. *Appointment in Samarra* published by Harcourt, Brace, 16 August.
1935	*The Doctor's Son and Other Stories* published by Harcourt, Brace, 21 February. *Butterfield-8* published by Harcourt, Brace, 17 October.

1936–1937   Writes screenplays for Goldwyn and MGM in Los Angeles.

1937   Marries Belle Mulford Wylie in Elkton, Maryland, 3 December.

1938   *Hope of Heaven* published by Harcourt, Brace, 17 March.

1939   Writes screenplays for RKO and Twentieth Century Fox in Los Angeles. *Files on Parade* published by Harcourt, Brace, 21 September.

1940   Writes book for *Pal Joey* musical in New York. Collection of Pal Joey stories published by Duell, Sloan & Pearce, 23 October. *Pal Joey* opens on Broadway.

1940–1942   Writes "Entertainment Week" column for *Newsweek;* writes screenplays for Twentieth Century Fox in Los Angeles through 1941.

1941–1943   Works for the Office of Inter-American Affairs; trains with the OSS.

1944   Writes for *Liberty* magazine as war correspondent in the Pacific.

1945   *Pipe Night* published by Duell, Sloan & Pearce, 24 March. Wylie Delaney O'Hara born on 14 June in New York.

1945–1946   Writes screenplays for MGM and United Artists in Los Angeles.

1947   *Hellbox* published by Random House, 9 August.

1949   *A Rage to Live* published by Random House, 16 August. Stops submitting work to *The New Yorker.* Moves to Princeton, New Jersey.

1951   *The Farmers Hotel* published by Random House, 8 November.

1952   Broadway revival of *Pal Joey,* January.

1953–1954   Writes "Sweet and Sour" column for the *Trenton Sunday Times-Advertiser.*

1954   Death of Belle Wylie O'Hara, Princeton, New Jersey, 9 January.

1954–1956 Writes "Appointment with O'Hara" column for *Collier's* magazine.

1954 *Sweet and Sour* published by Random House, 18 October.

1955 Marries Katharine Barnes Bryan, 31 January. Writes screenplays for Twentieth Century Fox in Los Angeles. *Ten North Frederick* published by Random House, 24 November.

1956 *Ten North Frederick* receives National Book Award, February. *A Family Party* published by Random House, 16 August.

1956–1957 Writes screenplays for Twentieth Century Fox.

1958 *From the Terrace* published by Random House, 27 November.

1960 *Ourselves to Know* published by Random House, 27 February; *Sermons and Soda-Water* published by Random House, 24 November.

1961 *Five Plays* published by Random House, 11 August; *Assembly* published by Random House, 23 November.

1962 *The Big Laugh* published by Random House, 29 May; *The Cape Cod Lighter* published by Random House, 29 November.

1963 *Elizabeth Appleton* published by Random House, 4 June; *The Hat on the Bed* published by Random House, 28 November.

1964 *The Horse Knows the Way* published by Random House, 26 November.

1964–1965 Writes "My Turn" column for *Newsday*.

1965 *The Lockwood Concern* published by Random House, 25 November.

1966 *My Turn* published by Random House, 14 April.

1966–1967 Writes "Whistle Stop" column for *Holiday* magazine.

1966 *Waiting for Winter* published by Random House, 24 November.

1967 *The Instrument* published by Random House, 23 November.

1968 *And Other Stories* published by Random House, 28 November.

1969 *Lovey Childs* published by Random House, 27 November.

1970 Dies in Princeton, New Jersey, 11 April.

1972 *The Ewings* published by Random House, 28 February; *The Time Element and Other Stories* published by Random House, 23 November.

1974 *Good Samaritan and Other Stories* published by Random House, 16 August.

1979 *Two by O'Hara* published by Harcourt Brace Jovanovich/Bruccoli Clark, 22 November.

Selected Bibliography

Primary Works

Short-Story Collections

Listed below are the titles of O'Hara's short-story collections, followed by the names of the stories in each collection. Excluded from this listing are books that reprint previously collected stories.

The *Doctor's Son and Other Stories*. New York: Harcourt, Brace, 1935. Thirty-seven stories: "The Doctor's Son," "Early Afternoon," "Pleasure," "New Day," "The Man Who Had to Talk to Somebody," "Mary," "Ella and the Chinee," "Ten Eyck or Pershing? Pershing or Ten Eyck?" "Alone," "Coffee Pot," "The Girl Who Had Been Presented," "Mort and Mary," "On His Hands," "It Wouldn't Break Your Arm," "I Never Seen Anything Like It," "Lombard's Kick," "Frankie," "Mr. Cass and the Ten Thousand Dollars," "Of Thee I Sing, Baby," "Screen Test," "Mr. Sidney Gainsborough: Quality Pictures," "Mr. Cowley and the Young," "Never a Dull Moment," "Master of Ceremonies," "Mrs. Galt and Edwin," "Hotel Kid," "Dr. Wyeth's Son," "Except in My Memory," "The Public Career of Mr. Seymour Harrisburg," "Straight Pool," "Back in New Haven," "Salute a Thoroughbred," "All the Girls He Wanted," "Sportsmanship," "In the Morning Sun," "It Must Have Been Spring," "Over the River and through the Wood."

Files on Parade. New York: Harcourt, Brace, 1939. Thirty-five stories: "Price's Always Open," "Trouble in 1949," "The Cold House," "Days," "Are We Leaving Tomorrow?" "Portistan on the Portis," "Lunch Tuesday," "Shave," "Sidesaddle," "No Mistakes," "Brother," "Saffercisco," "Ice Cream," "Peggy," "And You Want a Mountain," "Pal Joey," "Ex-Pal," "How I Am Now in Chi," "Bow Wow," "Give and Take," "The Gentleman in the Tan Suit," "Good-by Herman," "I Could Have Had a Yacht," "Richard Wagner: Public Domain?" "Olive," "It Wouldn't Break Your Arm," "My Girls," "No Sooner Said," "Invite," "All the Girls He Wanted," "By Way of

179

Yonkers," "Most Gorgeous Thing," "A Day Like Today," "The Ideal Man," "Do You Like It Here?"

Pal Joey. New York: Duell, Sloan & Pearce, 1940. Fourteen stories: "Pal Joey," "Ex-Pal," "How I Am Now in Chi," "Bow Wow," "Avast and Belay," "Joey on Herta," "Joey on the Cake Line," "The Erloff," "Even the Greeks," "Joey and the Calcutta Club," "Joey and Mavis," "A New Career," "A Bit of a Shock," "Reminiss?"

Pipe Night. New York: Duell, Sloan & Pearce, 1945. Thirty-one stories: "Walter T. Carriman," "Now We Know," "Free," "Can You Carry Me?" "A Purchase of Some Golf Clubs," "Too Young," "Joey and the Calcutta Club," "Summer's Day," "Radio," "Nothing Missing," "The King of the Desert," "Bread Alone," "Reunion Over Lightly," "Memo to a Kind Stranger," "The Erloff," "Patriotism," "A Respectable Place," "The Magical Numbers," "On Time," "Graven Image," "Adventure on the Set," "Platform," "Civilized," "Revenge," "Fire!" "The Lieutenant," "The Next-to-Last Dance of the Season," "Leave," "The Handler," "Where's the Game," "Mrs. Whitman."

Hellbox. New York: Random House, 1947. Twenty-six stories: "Common Sense Should Tell You," "Pardner," "Someone to Trust," "Horizon," "Like Old Times," "Ellie," "Life among These Unforgettable Characters," "War Aims," "Clara," "Secret Meeting," "Drawing Room B," "The Decision," "Somebody Can Help Somebody," "The Pretty Daughters," "Everything Satisfactory," "The Moccasins," "Doctor and Mrs. Parsons," "Wise Guy," "The Three Musketeers," "Other Women's Households," "Transaction," "Miss W.," "Time to Go," "A Phase of Life," "The Chink in the Armor," "Conversation in the Atomic Age."

Sermons and Soda-Water. New York: Random House, 1960. Three volumes: "The Girl on the Baggage Truck," "Imagine Kissing Pete," "We're Friends Again."

Assembly. New York: Random House, 1961. Twenty-six stories: "Mrs. Stratton of Oak Knoll," "The Weakness," "The Man with the Broken Arm," "The Lighter When Needed," "The Pioneer Hep-Cat," "The Sharks," "The Girl from California," "A Cold Calculating Thing," "You Can Always Tell Newark," "The High Point," "Call Me, Call Me," "It's Mental Work," "In the Silence," "First Day in Town," "Exactly Eight Thousand Dollars Exactly," "Mary and Norma," "The Cellar Domain," "The Properties of Love," "Reassurance," "The Free," "The Compliment," "Sterling Silver," "The Trip," "In a Grove," "The Old Folks," "A Case History."

The Cape Cod Lighter. New York: Random House, 1962. Twenty-three stories: "Appearances," "The Bucket of Blood," "The Butterfly," "Claude Emerson, Reporter," "The Engineer," "The Father," "The First Day," "Jurge Dulrumple," "Justice," "The Lesson," "Money," "The Nothing Machine," "Pat Collins," "The Professors," "A Short Walk from the Station," "Sunday Morning," "The Sun-Dodgers," "Things You Really Want," "Two Turtledoves," "Winter Dance," "The Women of Madison Avenue," "You Don't Remember Me," "Your Fah Nee Fah Nee Face."

The Hat on the Bed. New York: Random House, 1963. Twenty-four stories: "Agatha," "Aunt Anna," "Eminent Domain," "Exterior: With Figure," "The Flatted Saxophone," "The Friends of Miss Julia," "The Glendale People," "The Golden," "How Can I Tell You?" "I Know That, Roy," "John Barton Rosedale, Actor's Actor," "The Locomobile," "The Manager," "The Man on the Tractor," "The Mayor," Ninety Minutes Away," "Our Friend the Sea," "The Public Dorothy," "The Ride from Mauch Chunk," "Saturday Lunch," "Teddy and the Special Friends," "The Twinkle in His Eye," "The Windowpane Check," "Yucca Knolls."

The Horse Knows the Way. New York: Random House, 1964. Twenty-eight stories: "All Tied Up," "The Answer Depends," "Arnold Stone," "At the Window," "Aunt Fran," "The Bonfire," "The Brain," "Can I Stay Here?" "Clayton Bunter," "The Clear Track," "The Gun," "The Hardware Man," "His Excellency," "The House on the Corner," "I Can't Thank You Enough," "In the Mist," "I Spend My Days in Longing," "The Jet Set," "The Lawbreaker," "The Madeline Wherry Case," "Mrs. Allanson," "The Pig," "School," "The Staring Game," "The Victim," "What's the Good of Knowing?" "The Whole Cherry Pie," "Zero."

Waiting for Winter. New York: Random House, 1966. Twenty-one stories: "Afternoon Waltz," "Andrea," "The Assistant," "Fatimas and Kisses," "Flight," "The Gambler," "The General," "A Good Location," "The Jama," "James Francis and the Star," "Late, Late Show," "Leonard," "Natica Jackson," "The Neighborhood," "The Pomeranian," "The Portly Gentleman," "The Skeletons," "The Tackle," "The Way to Majorca," "The Weakling," "Yostie."

And Other Stories. New York: Random House, 1968. Twelve stories: "Barred," "The Broken Giraffe," "The Farmer," "A Few Trips and Some Poetry," "The Gangster," "The Gunboat and Madge," "How Old, How Young," "A Man on a Porch," "Papa Gibraltar," "The Private People," "The Strong Man," "We'll Have Fun."

The Time Element and Other Stories. Edited by Albert Erskine. New York: Random House, 1972. Thirty-four stories: "Encounter: 1943," "Conversation at Lunch," "Pilgrimage," "One for the Road," "The Skipper," "Not Always," "No Justice," "The Lady Takes an Interest," "Interior with Figures," "At the Cothurnos Club," "The Last of Haley," "Memorial Fund," "The Heart of Lee W. Lee," "The Brothers," "He Thinks He Owns Me," "The Dry Murders," "Eileen," "The War," "Nil Nisi," "The Time Element," "Family Evening," "Requiescat," "The Frozen Face," "Last Respects," "The Industry and the Professor," "The Busybody," "This Time," "Grief," "The Kids," "The Big Gleaming Coach," "For Help and Pity,"

Selected Bibliography

"All I've Tried to Be," "The Favor," "That First Husband."
Good Samaritan and Other Stories. Edited by Albert Erskine. New York: Random House, 1974. Fourteen stories: "The Gentry," "The Sun Room," "Sound View," "Good Samaritan," "A Man to be Trusted," "Malibu from the Sky," "Harrington and Whitehill," "Noblesse Oblige," "Heather Hill," "Tuesday's as Good as Any," "George Munson," "The Journey to Mount Clements," "The Mechanical Man," "Christmas Poem."

Other

The following are collections of other works by O'Hara referred to in the text of this book.

Sweet and Sour. New York: Random House, 1954.
A Family Party. New York: Random House, 1956.
"An Artist Is His Own Fault": John O'Hara on Writers and Writing. Edited by Matthew J. Bruccoli. Carbondale: Southern Illinois University Press, 1977.
Selected Letters of John O'Hara. Edited by Matthew J. Bruccoli. New York: Random House, 1978.
Five Plays. New York: Random House, 1981.

Secondary Works: Biographical

Books

Bruccoli, Matthew J. *The O'Hara Concern: A Biography of John O'Hara.* New York: Random House, 1975.
Farr, Finis. *O'Hara.* Boston: Little, Brown, 1973.
MacShane, Frank. *The Life of John O'Hara.* New York: Dutton, 1980.

Articles

Bassett, Charles W. "O'Hara's Roots." *Pottsville Republican,* 20 March 1971–8 (January 1972).
———. "John O'Hara—Irishman and American." *John O'Hara Journal* 1, no. 2 (Summer 1979): 1–81.
Gary, Beverly. "A Post Portrait: John O'Hara." *New York Post,* 24 May 1959, 18–22.
McCormick, Bernard. "A John O'Hara Geography." *Journal of Modern Literature* 1, no. 2 (1970–1971): 151–58.
Schanche, Don A. "John O'Hara Is Alice and Well in the First Half of the Twentieth Century." *Esquire,* August 1969, 84–86, 142, 144–49.

Secondary Works: Critical and Bibliographical

Books

Bruccoli, Matthew J. *John O'Hara: A Checklist.* New York: Random House, 1972.
———. *John O'Hara: A Descriptive Bibliography.* Pittsburgh: University of Pittsburgh Press, 1978.
Carson, Russell E. *The Fiction of John O'Hara.* Pittsburgh: University of Pittsburgh Press, 1961.
Eppard, Philip B., ed. *Critical Essays on John O'Hara.* New York: G. K. Hall, 1994.
Grebstein, Sheldon Norman. *John O'Hara.* New York: Twayne, 1966.
Long, Robert Emmet. *John O'Hara.* New York: Ungar, 1983.
Walcutt, Charles C. *John O'Hara.* Minneapolis: University of Minnesota Press, 1969.

Articles

Critical Essays on John O'Hara, edited by Philip Eppard, which is listed above, contains 47 reviews and 10 critical essays of O'Hara's work. Most of the criticism of O'Hara's work since his death has appeared in the *John O'Hara Journal,* which published eight issues between 1979 and 1983. Since the *John O'Hara Journal* is hard to locate, the most perceptive critical writing on the short fiction in it has been excerpted in Part 3 of this work, and other critical pieces in it are included in the selected list below, which also includes reviews alluded to in the text of this book.

Auchincloss, Louis. "The Novel of Manners Today: Marquand and O'Hara." In *Reflections of a Jacobite.* Boston: Houghton Mifflin, 1961.
Bassett, Charles W. "John O'Hara and History." *John O'Hara Journal* 2, no. 4 (Winter 1981): 8–12.
———. "John O'Hara's 'Alone' ": Preview of Coming Attractions." *John O'Hara Journal* 5, no. 1–2 (Winter 1982–1983): 18–24.
Becker, Marshall Joseph. "John O'Hara as an Ethnographer of Complex Society: Social Class and Ethnic Tradition in Southeastern Pennsylvania." *Colby Quarterly* 32, no. 3 (September 1996): 169–89.
Bishop, John Peale. "The Missing All." *Virginia Quarterly Review* 13 (February 1937): 120–21.
Browne, Joseph. "From Gibbsville to Glibsville." *John O'Hara Journal* 5, no. 1–2 (Winter 1982–1983): 1–10.
Davenport, Guy. "And Other Stories." *New York Times Book Review,* 24 November 1968, 5.

Selected Bibliography

———. "(On O'Hara)." *John O'Hara Journal* 3, no. 1–2 (Fall/Winter 1980): 75–77.

Dawson, Fielding. "Pal Joey John O'Hara." *John O'Hara Journal* 3, no. 1–2 (Fall/Winter 1980): 116–20.

Eppard, Philip B. "Bibliographical Supplement: Addenda to Bruccoli." *John O'Hara Journal* 2, no. 1 (Winter 1979–1980): 41–45.

———. "Bibliographical Supplement: Addenda to Bruccoli." *John O'Hara Journal* 4, no. 2 (Winter 1981): 59–61.

———. "Julian English outside of *Samarra.*" *Colby Quarterly* 32, no. 3 (September 1996): 190–95.

Freedman, Morris. "By O'Hara Besotted." *American Scholar* 66, no. 4 (Autumn 1997): 585-90.

Goldleaf, Steven. " 'Degrees of Superiority': Automobiles and Social Mobility in John O'Hara." *Kansas Quarterly* 21, no. 4 (Fall 1989): 55–65.

———. " 'When I Couldn't Write': John O'Hara's Lack of Productivity during World War II." *Colby Quarterly* 32, no. 3 (September 1996): 196–206.

Grebstein, Sheldon. "John O'Hara: The Mystery of Character." *John O'Hara Journal* 2, no. 2 (Summer 1980): 14-21.

Higgins, George V. "John O'Hara and His Hounds." *Harper's,* September 1984, 73–75.

Howe, Irving. "The Flaw in John O'Hara." *New Republic,* 27 November 1961, 16–17.

McElroy, Joseph. "Reflections on at Least One Story of John O'Hara's." *John O'Hara Journal* 3, no. 1–2 (Fall/Winter 1980): 143–47.

Monteiro, George. "All in the Family: John O'Hara's Story of a Doctor's Life." *Studies in Short Fiction* 24 (Summer 1987): 305–08.

Riley, Kathryn. "The Suburban Vision in John O'Hara's Short Stories." *Critique: Studies in Modern Fiction* 25 (Winter 1984): 101–13.

Shawen, Edgar M. "The Unity of John O'Hara's *Waiting for Winter.*" *John O'Hara Journal* 5, no. 1–2 (Winter 1982-1983): 25–32.

Trilling, Lionel. Introduction to *Selected Short Stories of John O'Hara.* New York: Random House, 1956.

Updike, John. "The Doctor's Son." In *Hugging the Shore.* New York: Knopf, 1983.

Vidal, Gore. "John O'Hara." In *United States: Essays 1952–1992.* New York: Random House, 1993.

Walker, Nancy. " 'All That You Need to Know': John O'Hara's Achievement in the Novella." *John O'Hara Journal* 4, no. 1 (Spring/Summer 1981): 61–80.

Walton, Edith H. "Mr. O'Hara's Stories." *New York Times Book Review,* 24 February 1935, 7.

Wilson, Edmund. "The Boys in the Back Room." *New Republic,* 11 November 1940, 665–66.

Wright, John. " 'Natica Jackson' and *The Medea.*" *John O'Hara Journal* 2, no. 2 (Summer 1980): 64–8.

Index

Index

Index

Index

The Author

Steven Goldleaf is associate professor of English at Pace University, where he teaches writing. He is the author of *Richard Yates* (with David Castronovo) and has published essays on American literature in *Partisan Review, Kansas Quarterly,* and the *Colby Quarterly.* His short stories have been anthologized in Signet's *Contemporary American Stories* and *The Best of Bad Hemingway.*

The Editors

Gary Scharnhorst is professor of English at the University of New Mexico, coeditor of *American Literary Realism*, and editor in alternating years of *American Literary Scholarship: An Annual*. He is the author or editor of books about Horatio Alger Jr., Charlotte Perkins Gilman, Bret Harte, Nathaniel Hawthorne, Henry David Thoreau, and Mark Twain, and he has taught in Germany on Fulbright fellowships three times (1978–1979, 1985–1986, 1993). He is also the current president of the Western Literature Association and the Pacific Northwest American Studies Association.

Eric Haralson is assistant professor of English at the State University of New York at Stony Brook. He has published articles on American and English literature—in *American Literature*, *Nineteenth-Century Literature*, the *Arizona Quarterly*, *American Literary Realism*, and the *Henry James Review*, as well as in several essay collections. He is also the editor of *The Garland Encyclopedia of American Nineteenth-Century Poetry*.